There's a Fortune in
Your Attic

There's a Fortune in Your Attic

Anthony Curtis

A PERIGEE BOOK

Perigee Books
are published by
The Berkley Publishing Group
200 Madison Avenue
New York, New York 10016

Library of Congress Cataloging-in-Publication Data

Curtis, Tony, date
     Lyle, there's a fortune in your attic / compiled by Anthony Curtis.
         p.   cm.
     ISBN 0-399-51677-8 (alk. paper)
     1. Antiques—Collectors and collecting.   2. Collectibles.
     I. Title.
     NK1125.C8874   1991   91-4525 CIP
     745.1´075—dc20

Printed in the United States of America
     7   8   9   10   11   12   13   14   15

This book is printed on acid-free paper.

Acknowledgements

Abridge Antique & Auction Rooms, Market Place, Abridge, Essex
Allen & Harris (Osmond Tricks), Regent Auction Rooms, Clifton, Bristol
Anderson & Garland, Marlborough House, Marlborough Crescent, Newcastle upon Tyne NE1 4EE
Auction Team Köln, Postfach 501168, D-5000 Köln, Germany
Barbers Fine Art Auctioneers (Chobham) Ltd, The Mayford Centre, Smarts Heath Road, Mayford Green, Woking, Surrey
Bearne's, Rainbow Avenue, Torquay TQ2 5TG
Boardman Fine Art Auctioneers, Station Road Corner, Haverhill, Suffolk
Bonhams, Montpelier Street, London SW7 1HH
Bonhams, 65-69 Lots Road, London SW10 0RN
William H. Brown Fine Art, The Warner Auction Rooms, 16-18 Halford Street, Leicester LE1 1JB
Christie's (International) SA, 8 place de la Taconnerie, 1204 Geneva, Switzerland
Christie's (Monaco) S A M, Park Place, 98000 Monte Carlo, Monaco
Christie's Scotland, 164-166 Bath Street, Glasgow
Christie's South Kensington, 85 Old Brompton Road, London SW7 3LD
Christie's, 8 King Street, St James's, London SW1Y 6QT
Christie's East, 219 East 67th Street, New York NY 10021, USA
Christie's, 502 Park Avenue, New York 10022, USA
Christie's, Cornelis Schuystraat 57, 1071 JG Amsterdam, Netherlands
Christie's SA Roma, 114 Piazza Navona, 00186 Rome
Christie's SWIRE, 1202 Alexandra House, 16-20 Charter Road, Hong Kong
Collector's Mart, The Old Railway Station, Horringford, Arreton, Isle of Wight
Alan Cunningham, 10 Forth Street, Edinburgh EH1 3LD
William Doyle Galleries, 175 East 87th Street, New York 10128
Hy Duke & Son, 40 South Street, Dorchester, Dorset
Du Mouchelles Art Galleries, 409 E. Jefferson Avenue, Detroit, Mich. 48226, USA
Duncan Vincent, Fine Art & Chattel Auctioneers, 105 London Street, Reading RG1 4LF
Finarte, 20121 Milano, Via Manzoni 38, Italy
GA Canterbury Auction Galleries, Canterbury, Kent
Michael C. German, 38b Kensington Church Street, London W8
Goss & Crested China, 62 Murray Road, Horndean, Hants
Graves Son & Pilcher, 71 Church Road, Hove, East Sussex BN3 2GL
W.R.J. Greenslade & Co, 13 Hammet Street, Taunton, Somerset TA1 1RN
Habsburg Feldman, SA 202 rue du Grand-Lancy, 1213 Onex, Geneva, Switzerland
Andrew Hartley Fine Arts, The Victoria Salerooms, Little Lane, Ilkely
Heathcote Ball & Co, 47 New Walk, Leicester
Hobbs & Chambers, 'At the Sign of the Bell', Market Place, Cirencester, Glos.
Lawrence Fine Art, South Street, Crewkerne, Somerset
David Lay, The Penzance Auction House, Alverton, Penzance, Cornwall.
Brian Loomes, Calf Haugh Farm, Pateley Bridge, N. Yorks
Lots Road Galleries, 71 Lots Road, Chelsea, London SW10 0RN
Michael G. Matthews, The Devon Fine Art Auction House, Dowel Street, Honiton, Devon
Michael Newman, The Central Auction Rooms, St Andrews Cross, Plymouth PL1 3DG
Onslows, Metrostore, Townmead Road, London SW6 2RZ
Phillips Manchester, Trinity House, 114 Northenden Road, Sale, Manchester
Phillips Son & Neale, SA, 10 rue des Chaudronniers, 1204 Geneva
Phillips West Two, 10 Salem Road, London W2
Phillips, 11 Bayle Parade, Folkestone, Kent
Phillips, 49 London Road, Sevenoaks, Kent
Phillips, 65 George Street, Edinburgh EH2 2JL
Phillips, 101 New Bond Street, London W1Y 0AS
Phillips, Blenstock House, 7 Blenheim Street, New Bond Street, London W1Y 0AS
Phillips Marylebone, Hayes Place, Lisson Grove, London NW1 6UA
Phillips, New House, Christleton Road, Chester CH3 5TD
Prudential Fine Art Auctioneers, Trinity House, 114 Northenden Road, Sale, Manchester
Prudential Fine Art Auctioneers, 71 Oakfield Road, Bristol
Prudential Fine Art Auctioneers, 13 Lime Tree Walk, Sevenoaks, Kent
Riddetts, Richmond Hill, Bournemouth
Russell Baldwin & Bright, The Fine Art Saleroom, Ryeland Road, Leominster HR6 8JG
Skinner Inc., Bolton Gallery, Route 117, Bolton, MA, USA
Sotheby's, 34-35 New Bond Street, London W1A 2AA
Sotheby's, 1334 York Avenue, 10021 New York, USA
Sotheby's, Summers Place, Billingshurst, Kent
Henry Spencer, 40 The Square, Retford, Notts
Street Jewellery, 16 Eastcliffe Avenue, Newcastle upon Tyne
G.E. Sworder & Son, Northgate End Salerooms, 15 Northgate End, Bishop Stortford, Herts
Tennants of Yorkshire, Old Chapel Saleroom, Market Place, Richmond, N. Yorks
Brian Thatcher, London
Wallis & Wallis, West Street Auction Galleries, West Street, Lewes, East Sussex

Introduction

Antiques are now being hailed as the top alternative investment. Add to that the lure of the treasure hunt, where you just might pick up something for next to nothing which could turn out to be immensely valuable, and it's hardly surprising that more people are taking an interest in such things than ever before.

Not only that, but the range of items being collected has also expanded enormously. Gone are the days when 'antiques' meant Georgian furniture, Sevres china, Byzantine bronzes and classical items which were easy to identify as being potentially valuable. Nowadays, perhaps as a reaction against our modern 'throwaway' society, there is a thriving collectors' market in everything from baseball cards to birdcages, from milk bottles to menus, all of which are things that you just might find in your own attic or garage, the junk shop round the corner or the next local car boot sale.

The trouble is, now that your new treasure trove no longer has to be carefully carved in mahogany or studded with sapphires to be worth big money, how do you go about recognising it when you see it?

Some people who failed initially to recognise just what they had in their possession have been lucky. Take, for example, the carved stick which was picked up in an antique shop in 1989 for $10. It turned out to be an extremely rare Hawaiian god stick, and the owner was stunned when it sold at Phillips for $82,250 in December of the same year. Or the statue of Hercules which came to light when a lake was dredged in the grounds of an agricultural laboratory because a stream was overflowing. For two years after that the statue stood as a mascot in the laboratory, and the people there were amazed when someone told them that they had an important Roman figure on the premises dating from the second century AD. It went on to sell at Phillips in London for £30,800. Or even the Ming vase which was brought in for sale with some odds and ends of porcelain in a cardboard box, the vendor expecting between $1–200 for the lot. The vase in question had been in the family for 70 years, and had sometimes been used for flowers. Alone, it fetched $265,000.

This book will help the layman to sift with a knowing eye through the objects which may come his way, and which otherwise might be thrown away for lack of basic information.

The value of a piece is, of course, often determined by its rarity value. That's why a Goss vase will fetch $10,000 while your average piece of Goss china will be worth only a hundredth of that. Supply and demand, however, also plays an important role, for the more people are interested in that particular field, the greater is the chance of a rare item being fully appreciated – and that of course means an increase in value.

The purpose of this book is to provide the layman with precisely the information he needs to enable him to recognise the item which could make him seriously rich. It is essentially a book of surprises – the weathervane worth $185,000, a teddy bear worth $96,000, or a golf ball which will sell for $27,500. There is something on every page to make the jaw drop in amazement. Moreover, none of the items featured in the book are one-offs – there are more of all of them, and others like them sitting out there just waiting to be discovered.

'There's a Fortune in Your Attic' doesn't just tell you what items are worth pursuing; it also tells you why, and in addition provides fascinating insights into their background and details of their discovery which will stick in your mind waiting to ring that bell whenever your eyes light on a similar treasure that could be waiting for you.

Collecting is a compulsive hobby which can easily become a way of life, for there is always the teasing possibility that round the next corner could be the item which could make your fortune. And with the knowledge gained from this book, you stand a better chance of knowing it when you see it. Happy hunting!

Contents

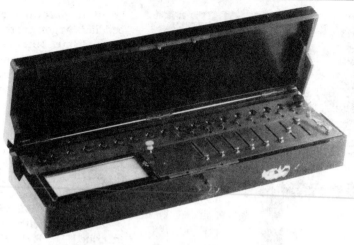

From ancient times man has felt the need for a calculating aid, so it was perhaps inevitable that it should be one of the first machines produced by modern technology. Less to be expected, however, is the fact that early examples of office calculators have now become eminently collectible, and fetch prices that would not disgrace other more conventional antiques.

It is claimed that the first mass produced calculating machine was Thomas de Colmar's 'Arithometer', dating from 1850. One recently sold at Auction Team Koeln's sale in Cologne for $4,726.

Rarity, condition and ingenuity of design can mean as much or more than age however. At the same sale an early German 'Monopol' spoke wheel 4 function calculating machine of 1894, of which only two models are known to exist in the world, realized $5,750.

'Monopol' 1894, early German spoke wheel calculating machine for the four basic calculations, only two known worldwide, a special technical highlight and a pioneer of the German business machine industry.
(Auction Team Koeln)
$5,750

Painted patent medicine peddler's wagon doors, Rhode Island, late 19th century, painted in polychrome with gilt highlights, the exterior of doors bearing likenesses of a child and old man and inscribed *I use Dr. R.R. Whipple's Vegetable Pills*, and *I don't use them*, respectively. The interior of the doors decorated with a farm scene inscribed *Where fireweed and pills are made, Natick, R.I.* and a landscape with Indians, inscribed *Dr. R.R. Whipple's Indian Agent Gathering Fireweed in Texas*, 26^1/$_2$" x 45".
(Skinner Inc)   **$3,000**

A decorative cartridge display board, arranged geometrically in stylized floral motif, 43" square.   **$4,323**

A Beswick china study of the old English sheepdog advertizing Dulux (ICI) paints, specially commissioned by Dulux about 1964 and withdrawn from sale in about 1970, modeled by a Mr. Mortimer, about 13" tall.
(Riddetts)   **$280**

Painted and decorated trade sign, signed *T.M. Woodward*, Worcester, Massachusetts, circa 1873, the rectangular bowed metal panel painted dark green and decorated in polychrome and gold with shaped reserve enclosing a vignette with an Indian maiden seated amid tobacco boxes, smoking a pipe and lifting tobacco leaves from a pile at her feet and the inscription *Rawson Bros & Co. Wholesale and Retail Dealers in Cigars and Tobacco*, attached to wood framework, 48" high. Rawson Bros. & Co. was established in 1873 on Main Street in Worcester, Massachusetts. The company is listed in the Worcester city directory for a period of only five years. Upon the company's closing, the pair of signs were removed and placed in storage on the top floor of the building. The signs were recently discovered by a carpenter working on the present restoration of the building. T.M. Woodward's commercial sign painting shop was located directly across the street from Rawson Bros. & Co.
(Skinner Inc) **$40,000**

Enamel sign, Wincarnis, 'The World's Greatest Wine Tonic and Nerve Restorative, 72" x 40".
(Street Jewellery) **$875**

Important Union porcelain Liberty cup and saucer, Greenpoint, New York, circa 1880, raised and shaped footed bases, white molded body with paneled relief of Justice on the one side and Hermes on the other, the handle modelled to form a figure of Liberty standing on an eagle, 4" high.
(Skinner Inc)   **$2,600**

Fulper pottery urn, Flemington, New Jersey, circa 1915, no. 490, cucumber green crystalline glaze, vertical ink mark, 13" high.
(Skinner Inc)   **$1,700**

Important Union porcelain Heathen-Chinee pitcher, Greenpoint, New York, 1876, molded body, the handle formed to represent a bear-like animal while the spout is of a sea lion mask, the relief on one side of King Gambrinus offering lager to Brother Jonathan, the other side figures of Bill Nye, knife in hand, attacking Ah Sin for cheating at cards, $9^5/8$" high.
(Skinner Inc)   **$3,700**

A slip decorated pierced and incised Redware tobacco jar, Pennsylvania, first half 19th century, with flaring scalloped rim and applied strap handles, decorated with incised scalloped lines at the neck above a band of pierced triangles, 6" high, with lid. Pierced hollowware was among the most ambitious projects a redware potter could undertake. This jar included almost every decorative option available to the craftsman: slip decoration, incised lines and piercing. (Christie's N. York)

$4,950

Early 20th century Dedham pottery plate with Fairbanks house, 8½" diameter.

(Skinner Inc) **$2,200**

Flint enamel lion mantel ornament, Lyman Fenton and Co., Bennington, Vermont, circa 1849-1858, with molded mane, left front paw raised on a ball, the whole raised on a stepped base, brown, green, and blue glaze, 9½" high.

(Skinner Inc) **$10,000**

Rookwood pottery iris glaze vase, Cincinnati, Ohio, 1906, executed by Charles Schmidt (1896-1927), the bulbous top on cylindrical form with decoration of two dragonflies in gray, brown, white and blue on shaded blue to brown ground, impressed with RP logo *909BB* and artist's monogram *CS* incised *W*, 9⅝" high.
(Skinner Inc)   **$4,400**

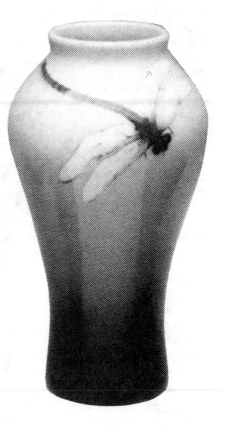

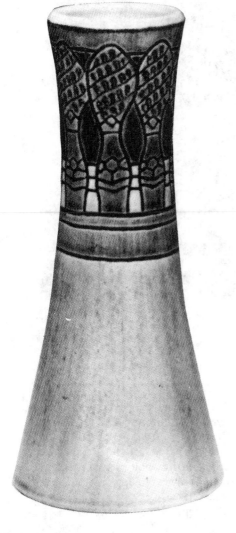

Newcomb College pottery vase, New Orleans, Louisiana, circa 1905, the flaring cylindrical form with incised and painted decoration in blues, green, and white on light blue ground, glossy glaze, painted and impressed marks *NC* and *W*, painted artist's monogram *CR* and *ZZ20*, 9¾" high.
(Skinner Inc)   **$2,600**

Fulper pottery centerpiece on pedestal base, Flemington, New Jersey, circa 1915, squat urn shape centered by three applied scroll feet on platform base, hammered texture in olive green on paler green glaze, vertical mark, 10½" high.
(Skinner Inc) **$1,600**

Paul Revere Pottery decorated vase, Boston, Massachusetts, early 20th century, the swollen cylindrical form with incised and painted band of tree design in green, blue, brown and tan on brown ground, paper label *The Paul Revere Pottery/Boston Mass* and indistinct painted marks, 8½" high.
(Skinner Inc) **$2,300**

Saturday Evening Girls Pottery decorated motto pitcher, Boston, Massachusetts, early 20th century, with incised and painted band of rooster decoration above the words *Oh Up In The Morning Early That Is The Way Quite Clearly*, black and white on turquoise ground, painted marks *103...S.E.G.* and indistinct artist's initials, 9¾" high.
(Skinner Inc) **$2,200**

Saturday Evening Girls Pottery decorated bowl, Boston, Massachusetts, 1913, executed by Sara Galner, exterior with incised and painted band of daffodils in shades of yellow, green, brown, and blue on green ground, interior glazed white with band of yellow at rim, painted marks, *S.E.G./7-13* and artist's initials *S.G.*
(Skinner Inc)   **$9,250**

Arts and Crafts Pottery lamp base, early 20th century, similar to Teco no. 167, in matte green glaze, remnants of paper label, base 15" high.
(Skinner Inc)   **$2,100**

Anna Pottery castle, gray with blue highlights, impressed on base *Anna, Ill, 1882*, 10³/₈" high, Anna Pottery, Anna, Illinois, circa 1882.
(Skinner Inc)   **$3,500**

A classic Navajo chief's blanket, woven in single strand homespun and ravelled yarn, 82" x 62".
(Skinner Inc)   **$35,000**

North-west Coast wooden raven rattle, early 19th century, 14³/₄" long.
(Christie's)   **$35,200**

Quilled tanned skin shirt, circa 1840.
(Christie's)   **$52,700**

Handled burl bowl. North American
Indian, Plains, 19th century, oval form
with shaped ends and carved handles,
14¼" long.
(Skinner Inc)   **$2,600**

An unusual Naskape moose skin
pouch, decorated with imprinted
geometric designs in red paint, a broad
panel of woven polychrome beads
attached to the bottom edge, and
fringed with beaded tassels, 50cm. x
28cm., 19th century.
(Phillips)   **$10,468**

Miniature decorated covered storage
basket, Northeast American Indian,
late 19th century, swabbed with green,
blue, yellow, salmon and red, lined
with newspaper, 5" wide.
(Skinner Inc)   **$2,800**

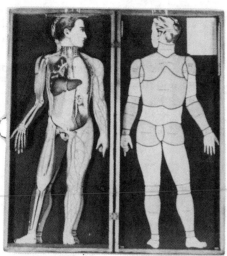

Anatomical teaching device, 'Smith's New Outline Map of the Human System, Anatomical Regions, No. 2', manufactured by American Manikan Co., Peoria, Illinois, 1888, wooden case fitted with two cut-out wooden male figures with applied chromolithographs of the muscular and skeletal systems, with metal hooks for attaching 20 chromolithographed tin organs and muscles, 44" high. *(Skinner Inc)* **$900**

A fine late 19th century composition anatomical figure, of the human male, the front of the body arranged so as to be removed revealing the internal organs for instructional purposes, 23½" high. *(Christie's)* **$1,036**

A superb dog otter, the snarling animal holding a perch with front paw, on rockwork with naturalistic sedges, ferns and grasses, mounted in an ebonized glazed case with gilt inner surround, by Edwards, Aberystwyth, 29½" x 32".
(Spencers)   **$1,225**

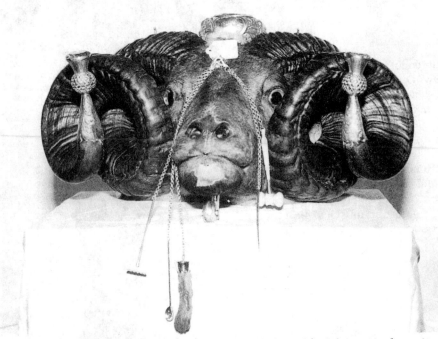

A Victorian Scottish silver mounted ram's head snuff mull compendium, the natural head inset with a gilt beaker and hinged domed cover chased with thistles and with an inscription, surmounted by a faceted crystal, the curling horns with cast thistle terminals and five chain attachments, comprising: an ivory hammer, a rabbit's paw, a rake, a strainer and pointer, approximately 42cm. wide, Edinburgh, 1854.
(Phillips)   **$2,100**

An ostrich egg finely decorated in hiramakie, shell and ivory inlay with a Chinese sage holding a fan accompanied by a young attendant watching pheasants and other birds among bamboo and other plants, unsigned, Meiji period, 15cm. long.
(Christie's) **$6,604**

A Chinese rhinoceros horn libation cup carved in relief with a figure teaching children, another painting a scroll, others beside ladies playing musical instruments, the handle formed as pine boughs coming over the rim of the cup, 17/18th century, 5" high.
(Christie's) **$9,861**

A Harlequin set of four leather blackjacks of graduating size, one painted
with an interlaced monogram and crown, 17th century, the largest 24" high.
(Christie's) **$8,365**

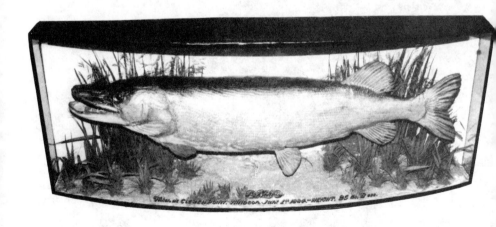

Large cased Pike in reed surrounding, glass cased inscribed *Taken at Clewer
Point, Windsor, Jan. 1st 1884, weight 25lbs 8ozs, 47$^{1}/_{2}$" long.*
(Barber's Auctions) **$1,100**

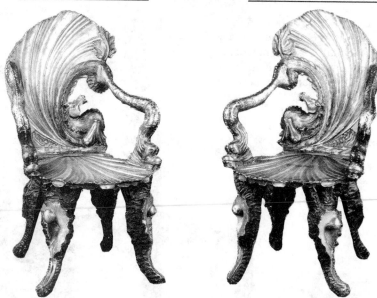

A pair of gilt, silver, black and green-painted grotto open armchairs, each with asymmetric shell-shaped back with scrolling dolphin arms, scallop shell seat on shell-encrusted cabriole legs.
(Christie's) **$10,587**

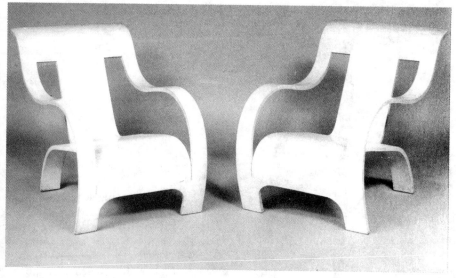

A pair of laminated birchwood open armchairs designed by Gerald Summers, each cut and shaped to form a curved top rail with central splat and curvilinear armrests, on four curved legs.
(Christie's) **$24,167**

An important oak lath armchair designed by Marcel Breuer for the Bauhaus, Weimar, 1924, constructed from vertical and horizontal strips of stained oak, with black linen strung seat and back supports, 94.8cm. high.
(Christie's)   **$48,620**

A fine and rare black-painted high chair, Delaware River Valley, 1730–1760, with four graduated and arched slats flanked by cylindrical stiles with mushroom finials continuing to shaped arm rests above baluster-turned arm supports over a trapezoidal rush seat, on turned front feet, 38" high.
(Christie's N. York)   **$6,050**

A George III painted elbow chair, the oval openwork back rest carved with entwined honeysuckle motif, and painted overall with bellflower. *(Greenslades)* **$1,672**

One of a pair of George II black and gold japanned open armchairs by William and John Linnell, each with stepped rectangular back filled with black and gold Chinese paling, the uprights decorated in raised gilt with buildings and landscape vignettes surmounted by pagoda-shaped crestings, 40¾" high.

These chairs are part of a set of eight armchairs which formed part of the famous suite of japanned furniture supplied by William and John Linnell to the 4th Duke of Beaufort (1709–1759) for the Chinese Bedroom at Badminton House, Gloucestershire.

John Linnell's design for the chair was one of his first major responsibilities as a designer for his father's firm. *(Christie's)* **$346,500**

The Red-Blue chair, designed by Gerrit Thomas Rietveld and made by G.A. van de Groenekan, 1919, 34" high. *(Christie's)* **$83,600**

A Venetian parcel-gilt, silvered and painted grotto chair with scalloped shell back and seat with addorsed dolphin arms on naturalistic rockwork legs.

Grotto furniture was keenly sought after in the 1920s and 1930s by members of the Magnesco Society, founded in 1924 to restore interest in baroque art.

(Christie's) **$6,604**

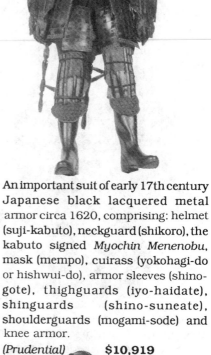

A German codpiece probably from a black and white armor, of bright steel, with central recessed band with strong, lightly roped medial ridge, attachment holes at top and bottom, and traces of tinning inside, mid 16th century, 6" high.
(Christie's S. Ken) **$2,032**

An important suit of early 17th century Japanese black lacquered metal armor circa 1620, comprising: helmet (suji-kabuto), neckguard (shikoro), the kabuto signed *Myochin Menenobu*, mask (mempo), cuirass (yokohagi-do or hishwui-do), armor sleeves (shino-gote), thighguards (iyo-haidate), shinguards (shino-suneate), shoulderguards (mogami-sode) and knee armor.
(Prudential) **$10,919**

A pair of German gauntlets, of bright steel, each comprising a flared boxed cuff made in two pieces, roped turned borders with narrow recessed band and central cusp, five downward-lapping metacarpal plates with cusped edges bordered by pairs of engraved lines, prominent double roped knuckle-plate over the bases of the fingers, all articulated on rivets, late 16th century, 11" long. *(Christie's)* **$4,171**

A rare leather-laced armor, kozakura-kawa-odoshi-no-yoroi, the kabuto with a black lacquered hachi with simulated suji, nihojiro with silvered plates engraved with clouds and overlaid with three gilt shinodare at the front and two at the back, with copper-gilt six-stage tehen no kanamono in 15th century style, the fukigaeshi with gilt tsutamon, circa 1860.

(Christie's)   **$26,000**

Two important reinforcing-pieces for the tilt from the Rosenblatt (Rose-leaf) garniture of the Emperor Maximilian II by Franz Grobschedel of Landshut, of bright steel, comprising grandguard and pasguard, each made of a single piece, the former shaped to fit the left pauldron and upper left of the breast-plate, made in 1571, grandguard 12", pasguard 14¾".

These pieces belong to one of the most famous 16th century armor garnitures, the major portions of which are preserved in the old Imperial Armory now in the Kunsthistorisches Museum, Vienna.

(Christie's)   **$125,000**

A very rare cased set of two single-trigger over-and-under flintlock pistols, comprising a pocket pistol and traveling pistol, the former with reblued octagonal sighted barrels signed in gold on the top flat and with gold lines at the breech, in original fitted mahogany case lined in green baize with trade label and accessories by Joseph Egg, No. 1 Piccadilly, London silver hallmarks for 1815, maker's mark of Moses Brent, 12½" and 6¾". (Christie's)   **$27,000**

A Saxon left-handed dagger, the stout blade of flattened hexagonal section, changing to diamond section at the point, with central fuller on each face and fluted ricasso, the hilt of blackened iron, circa 1570, 15¾" long. (Christie's S. Ken)   **$14,000**

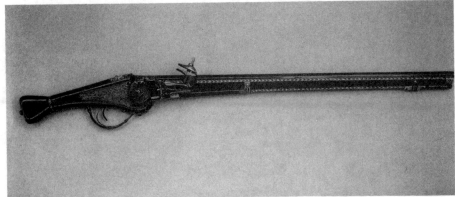

A fine and rare Nuremberg wheel-lock holster pistol with very long blued octagonal barrel engraved and gilt with hatched foliated scrollwork on the muzzle, breech and center the latter involving a winged term, engraved and gilt tang, blued flat beveled lock engraved and gilt with foliated scrollwork involving a bird with a snake in its beak, circa 1600, 31¹/₈" long. *(Christie's)* **$30,800**

Engraved Siege of Boston 'Rhyme' Powderhorn, Charles Town Camp, (Massachusetts), dated 1775, curving cow horn engraved on one side *Lieu:t Simeon Smith / his horn Charles Town / Camp No 3 Dec:r y 12th AD 1775*, 14" long.

This horn belonged to 1st Lieutenant Simeon Smith. The son of Josiah and Abigail (Stoddard) Smith, he was born in Litchfield, Connecticut on August 6, 1741. He moved with his wife and two children to Lenox, Massachusetts in 1767. Records indicate that he was a 1st Lieutenant in Colonel John Paterson's Regiment, part of the 1st Massachusetts Regiment, from April to December of 1775. This regiment was called to respond to the Lexington alarm in April of that year and from May to December in 1775 was engaged in the Siege of Boston. It was during this period in Charlestown that the powder horn was engraved. Simeon Smith died in Lenox, Massachusetts at the age of forty-five in August of 1786.
(Skinner Inc) **$5,500**

ARTIST'S PALETTE

A wooden artist's palette, belonging to Pierre Matisse, circa 1907, a label on reverse bears the inscription *Matisse* *Palette of 1907, (Blue Still Life)*, 9¹/₂" x 13⁷/₈".
(Christie's) **$13,200**

AUTOGRAPHS

Autographs can be a truly fascinating subject, especially if, as in the case of William Shakespeare, there is continuing speculation as to whether in fact the man ever existed. Fewer than ten examples of his signature have so far been discovered, and their value now stands at $1,500,000. No examples of Christ's signature are known to exist, but if you can find one from his near contemporary, Julius Caesar, this might well top the Shakespeare figure by 50% or more.

Automata came into fashion in the 18th century as expensive toys and conversation pieces for the amusement of adults. They were even the subject of public exhibitions staged by makers such as James Cox and Henri Maillardet. One of the greatest names associated with the genre, however, is the family of Jaquet-Droz of Switzerland, who made elaborate models such as writers, piano players and singing birds in cages. By the 19th century they were becoming more and more complex. Acrobats and dancing dolls were introduced around 1810, monkey orchestras and shoecleaners from 1860, while in America walking dolls (autoperipatetikus) with forward, reverse and sideways motion became popular.

They were powered in various ingenious ways, such as compressed air, water, sand, mercury or steam. It was however the coiled spring which was to prove the most popular and efficient means of power.

Early automata by such famous names as Vaucanson, Robertson, Rechsteiner, or, of course, Jaquet-Droz are worth thousands of dollars today, but it was the Victorian period which saw the heyday of the sophisticated automaton. One late 19th century maker was Gustave Vichy whose work is often characterized by its height, many of his models standing over 30 ins high. His Negro figures with musical instruments have particularly fine leather faces with expressive facial movements even to the lips. Both the mechanism and musical movement are contained in the body of the figure or in the background props, so that movement of a foot is possible.

A rare and exquisite Vichy automaton of a pumpkin eater dates from 1870. The head is of papier mâché with a smiling open mouth and fixed brown glass eyes, while the rigid body with papier mâché forearms stands against a wooden cupboard. On a stool by his side is a green painted papier mâché pumpkin, a section of which opens to reveal a mouse. The circular wooden base contains a stop-start keywind musical movement which causes the man's hat to rise, his head to nod and his left arm waves while the right strikes the knife into the pumpkin as it opens to reveal the mouse. He is finely dressed in a brocaded cream satin waistcoat with mother of pearl buttons and figured black silk back, and satin breeches. He stands 20.5 ins high, and though his head and hat movements are inoperative, he still sold at Sotheby's for $38,940.

By the end of the 19th century, toymakers, particularly in Germany had recognised the possibilities of mass-producing automatic toys, and the tinplate toy industry began to boom. The machine-produced results, were cheap and rudimentary, and thereafter mechanical toys came to be associated mainly with children.

A papier **mâché** ginger jar musical automaton, French late 19th century, painted with bamboo and fans, the hinged cover opening to reveal a chinaman in brocade robes drinking tea, 12" high.
(Christie's) **$3,080**

A singing bird automaton with clock, Swiss, probably by Jacquet Droz, circa 1785, 20" high.
(Christie's)   **$44,000**

Clown Equilibriste, a composition headed musical automaton, modeled standing on a ladder, with brown glass eyes, smiling face with clown's make-up including a scarab beetle painted on forehead, as the music plays he rises up on one hand on top of ladder, 35" high, by Vichy.
(Christie's)   **$38,600**

The most popular car club badges are those issued by the A.A. and the R.A.C. which motorists used to display proudly on their mudguards. Patrolmen were ordered to salute members of their organisation. The earliest A.A. badges were made of brass or nickel and fifteen different styles have been produced to the present time. Early ones change hands today at around $200 each. R.A.C. badges are more varied because they were made in several different metals and in a large number of designs. They were first issued in 1907 and it is the early ones that demand the highest prices which can go up to $600.

A Brooklands Automobile Racing Club badge of the 1930s with a 120 m.p.h. badge is worth at least $1,500 while an ordinary club badge is worth about $500. If it has a 130 m.p.h. badge the price goes up to $1,700 however. A 1930s Brooklands Aero Club badge can also cost $1,500 and a Flying Club one about $1,700.

Ferrari Yearbook, 1950, Italian text. *(Christie's)* **$8,699**

A chromium-plated and enameled Aero-Club Brooklands badge, stamped 164, 3³/4" high. *(Onslows)* **$1,710**

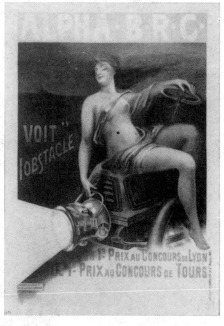

P. Chapellier poster, 'Alpha BRC', on linen, 120cm. x 80cm. *(Onslows)* **$4,440**

E. Ruprecht poster, Grand Prix d'Europe Autos Bern 3–4 Juli 1948, published by Kummerly and Frey, 128cm. x 90cm.
(Onslows) **$3,500**

'Monaco, 19 mai 1957' by B. Minne, lithograph in colors, printed by Imp ADIA Nice, fold marks, small tear to top margin, 47" x 31".
(Christie's) **$3,480**

'How to buy oil – cheaper – cleaner – quicker' by Tom Purvis, published by Shell No. 117, 75cm. x 114cm., 1925.
(Onslows)

$2,450

SA Scuderia Ferrari yearbook 1930/31/32/33, Italian text, 1933.
(Christie's)   **$3,850**

WAGNER, PITTSBURG

Baseball cards were issued by manufacturers of cigarettes, bubble gum, sweets and even sausages, and featured the great players of the day.

The record price for such a card was paid for the Sweet Caporal card of 1910 showing Honus Wagner (1874-1955) one of the greatest all-round baseball players in history. The card was published without Wagner's permission, and, as a non-smoker, he took exception to his image gracing a cigarette card. He complained, the cards were withdrawn, and of the 96 which did get into circulation 30 are believed to be still in existence. It was one of these which achieved the world record price at Phillips of $18,000

Other rare baseball cards include another from Sweet Caporal of the pitcher Eddie Planck. Issued in 1910, 30 are known still to exist and could fetch up to $10,000. Of the Goudey Gum Co's Nap Lajoie card of 1933, 50 are believed still to be circulating and they could be worth $8,000.

BASKETS

Nantucket pocketbook basket, Massachusetts, circa 1949, deep sided oval form of woven splint on an oval base, conforming shallow cover and plaque with applied carved ebony whale, ebony peg fastener and ebony buttons on handle pins, inscribed on base *made in Nantucket Jose Formoso Reyes*, 7 1/2" long. The earliest Nantucket pocketbook baskets were made by Jose Formoso Reyes, circa 1948. The whale on the plaque top was probably carved by Charlie Sayle. *(Skinner Inc)* **$1,400**

Painted two-pocket splint wall basket, Northeast Woodland Indians, mid 19th century, the high back with hanging bracket, painted green, 26" high. *(Skinner Inc)* **$2,000**

Three-pocket wall basket, Northeast American Indian, 19th century, wooden hanging loop above four graduated pockets, traces of red stain, 30" high.
(Skinner Inc) **$2,100**

Nantucket basket, Nantucket Island, Massachusetts, late 19th/early 20th century, bound oak rim above a deep sided circular woven rattan body on a turned wooden base, shaped wooden swing handle, inscribed in pencil *L.H. Macy*, 6" high.
(Skinner Inc) **$2,100**

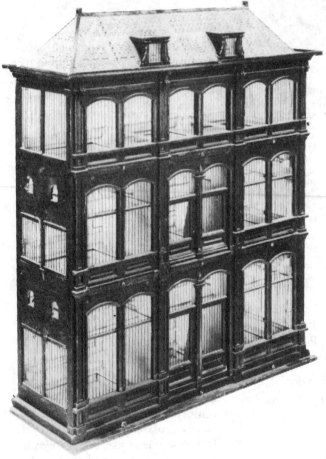

A Dutch mahogany birdcage, the stepped front with four compartments, late 18th century, 41" wide.
(Christie's) **$30,525**

A Dutch oak birdcage of architectural design, the seven compartments with black-painted metal bars and refuse-trays, basically 18th century, 44¹/₂" wide.
(Christie's) **$10,120**

An Anglo-Dutch mahogany and wire birdcage with a central dome surmounted by a finial and flanked by two arches, the front fitted with three doors on a box base, early 19th century, 38" high.
(Christie's) **$5,676**

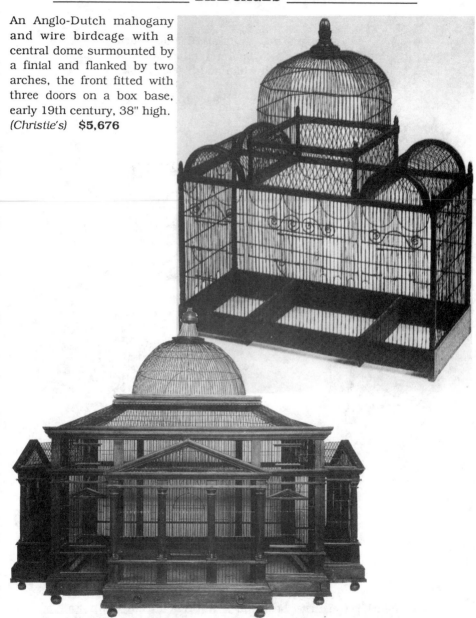

A 19th century mahogany birdcage of architectural form, modeled on Mereworth Castle, the front and side elevations each with a projecting Palladian portico supported by four columns and flanked by simulated windows, the whole surmounted by a cupola, 89cm. square. Mereworth Castle was designed by Colin Campbell and inspired by Palladio's Villa Rotunda.
(Phillips) **$7,956**

A large mid-Victorian Blue-John urn with turned finial and square pedestal edged with white and black marble, 22¼" high.
(Christie's)   **$10,208**

A Blue-John bowl on turned stem and domed base, 8" high.
(Christie's)   **$6,395**

A French Blue-John and ormolu mantel clock, the case in the form of an urn flanked by rams' head masks, on a rectangular base, the time recorded on annular chapters and indicated by a serpent, 55cm. high.
(Phillips)   **$22,950**

Gould (John): The Birds of Great Britain, 5 vols., 367 hand-col. plates approx. 18 with a few light spots on outer margins, 1873.
(Phillips) **$47,320**

'L'Exposition Internationale des Arts Decoratifs Modernes a Turin 1902' (Exhibition Catalogue), director Alexander Koch, text by George Fuchs and F.H. Newbury, vellum bound with gilt decoration, 400 illustrations in color and monochrome.
(Christie's) **$4,303**

Roberts, D., The Holy Land, Syria, Idumea, Arabia, Egypt and Nubia. From drawings made on the spot by David Roberts, R.A., with historical descriptions by the Revd. George Croly, lithographed by Louis Haghe. 2 volumes, folio, 1842–1849. Uncolored lithographic portrait, two lithographed title pages, sixty full page and sixty smaller lithographic plates, all hand colored and mounted on card.
(Woolley & Wallis)
$58,625

Samuel Langhorne Clemens (Mark Twain), autograph manuscript of Chapter 15 (Down the River) from *A Tramp Abroad*, 33 pages, octavo, 1879-80.
(Christie's) **$33,000**

Victor Hugo, *Notre-Dame de Paris*, three volumes in one, octavo, in a cathedral binding of Parisian purple morocco by Kleinhans, Paris, 1836, 8½" x 5½".
(Christie's) **$10,450**

Alberto Sangorski (calligrapher and illuminator) Abraham Lincoln and Walt Whitman *The Gettysburg Speech and The Second Inaugural Address*, London, 1928. Illuminated manuscript on vellum, quarto measure, in a binding of vari-colored morocco by Riviere & Son, 12¼" x 10¼".
(Christie's) **$35,200**

Paul Valery, *Variété*, five volumes, quarto, uniformly bound in purple morocco by Pierre-Lucien Martin, limited editions 1924-44, 8¾" x 6¾".
(Christie's) **$25,300**

Charles White, 'Martingale' *Sporting Scenes and Country Characters*, London 1860, octavo measure, in a jeweled binding of vari-colored morocco with 28 stones by Sangorski & Sutcliffe, 8" x 5¼".
(Christie's) **$22,000**

Ceramic pig whiskey bottle, inscribed *Whiskey 1875* and *put your mouth to my* on the opposite side, 9" long, America, 1860-80.

(Skinner Inc) **$1,600**

Because of the danger of dosing oneself from a poison bottle by mistake, manufacturers made their bottles as recognisable as possible and did this by turning them out in eye catching colors–cobalt blue, viridian green or glowing amber. They also manufactured them in various distinctive shapes.

The first English poison bottle was patented in 1859 and was made of cobalt glass which was the most popular color for the thousands of bottles that followed until the 1950s when cobalt glass was replaced by plastic. It is the shapes of poison bottles that make them interesting to collectors for they turn up with wasp waists, shaped as binoculars and submarines, with U-bends in their necks or with the glass indented, embossed and ridged all over. Some were even coffin shaped – which must have been a pretty dreadful warning – and other had skulls embossed on their sides. A few stoneware poison bottles turn up printed with the names of hospitals and they cost considerably less than the exotic glass varieties.

O'Reilly's Patent, known as Binoculars Poison, embossed on the base *O'Reilly's Patent 1905*, only two of these bottles are known.

(Brian Thatcher) **$1,400**

48

Very rare Stiegel-type bottle, the flattened globular chunky body, with 12 diamond ogival pattern, holds, approximately 12 oz. measured, probably made at the Henry William Stiegel's American Flint Glass Manufactory, Manheim, Pennsylvania, 1770-1774.
(Skinner Inc) **$3,900**

'Harrison's Columbia Ink' master ink bottle, gallon size, whittled, C763, deep sapphire, blue, flanged lip-iron pontil, 11³/₈" high, probably Whitney Glassworks, Glassboro, New Jersey, 1855-65.
(Skinner Inc) **$11,000**

A deep cobalt blue 'Wadsworth Mineral Waters, Cambridge' Dobson-type Codds bottle made by E. Breffit & Co. Ltd., Castleford.
(Collector's Mart) **$1,750**

An early sealed 'shaft and globe' wine-bottle of green tint, the depressed and tapering oviform body applied with a seal inscribed with the initials *IAL* flanked by flowerheads and with calligraphic scrolls below, the tapering neck with string-ring and with kick-in base, circa 1670, 20cm. high.
(Christie's) **$11,220**

An amethyst glass pattern-molded Stiegel-type perfume bottle, probably Pennsylvania, third quarter 18th century, globular with cylindrical neck, the body with enlarged diamond-daisy motif above fluting, 5" high.
(Christie's) **$4,400**

A green calligraphic serving bottle engraved in diamond-point by Willem van Heemskerk, of dark emerald-green tint, the globular body decorated in a calligraphic script with the inscription *Sterken drank maekt wild.* (Strong drink is enraging), the kick-in base inscribed *Omsichtig nutt de geesten van de wijn, Als levend Sap; en doodelijk fenijn* (Be careful imbibing the spirits of wine, They may be elixir of life or deadly venom), signed and dated on the underside *Willem van Heemskerk AE*[S]*. 70¹/₂ A⁰. 1683*, Leiden, 1683, 17.2cm. high.
(Christie's) **$134,574**

Milk was originally sold 'loose'; you took your jug or churn to the dairy or dispensing point and it was filled there for you. Milk bottles did not come into common use until after the First World War, although they were in existence from the late 19th century. Early examples, therefore, are becoming quite valuable.

The earliest known version was 'The Thatcher Milk Protector' devised by an American, Dr. Harvey P. Thatcher in 1885, and examples will now fetch around $550. Worth over $850, however, is the 'Pure Milk' tin screw-top jar with handle. It is colorless, with the Adlam patent on the base, and is very rare indeed.

Anna Pottery 'Railroad' pig, heavily embossed with railroad lines and cities, *Anna Pottery 1882* on side, grayish beige, 7" high, Anna, Illinois, circa 1882. *(Skinner Inc)* **$5,750**

Early 19th century Anglo-Indian ivory sewing box shaped as a cottage, 6" wide.
(Christie's) **$4,384**

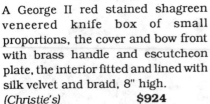

A George II red stained shagreen veneered knife box of small proportions, the cover and bow front with brass handle and escutcheon plate, the interior fitted and lined with silk velvet and braid, 8" high.
(Christie's) **$924**

Crawfords Biscuit Bus OK 3852, with original box, 25.5cm.
(Phillips) **$4,488**

Large presentation tin and wood foot warmer, America, early 19th century, heavy wooden frame with turned corner posts encloses compass-like inscription, tin firebox with punchwork designs, front panel with cut-out legend *Presented by James Price to the Rev. J.H. Jones*, 16" long.
(Skinner Inc) **$1,700**

A painted and decorated document box attributed to Heinrich Bucher, Reading, Bucks County, Pennsylvania, 1770–1780. The hinged domed lid lifting to an open compartment above a conforming case, the whole painted with red, yellow and green churches and houses enclosed by enlarged tulips on black ground, 7" high, 13" wide. *(Christie's)*   **$6,600**

A Georgian Stilton box.
(Hobbs Parker)   **$3,192**

An Anglo French silver mounted dressing table set contained in a brass inlaid rosewood case by G. Rawlings 1821 and P. Blazuiere, Paris 1819–38.
(Christie's)   **$25,740**

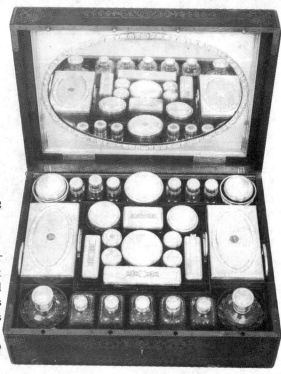

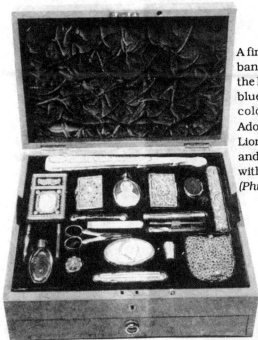

A fine George III satinwood, kingwood banded and boxwood strung casket, the lid applied with four contemporary blue 'jasperware' roundels in gold-colored metal mounts, depicting Adonis, Hercules and the Nemean Lion, Apollo and Hebe and Jupiter; and enclosing a velvet lined interior with a tray of fitments, 33cm. wide.
(Phillips) **$17,595**

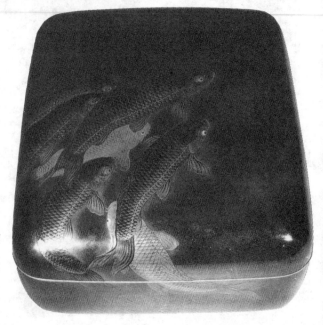

A large rectangular document box and convex cover richly decorated with seven carp swimming in hiramakie, hirame, aka-fun and aogai on a maki-bokashi and roiro-nuri ground, the interior with pine trees in gold takamakie and hiramakie, unsigned, silver rim, with label of H. Nishimura of Kyoto, Meiji period (1868-1912), 45 x 37.5cm.
(Christie's) **$50,000**

Wallpaper covered wooden hat box, America, circa 1840, of oblong form, the fitted lid covered with 'Castles in Spain' pattern, the box covered with a coach scene pattern in pink, white and green on a blue-green ground, 11½" high.
(Skinner Inc) **$3,500**

A James I fruitwood box and cover of oval form carved with a skeleton, incised flowers and leafage and an inscription to one side, the reverse with an inscribed square tablet, surrounded by castellated border, surmounted by a winged angel, with skull and crossbones to base, dated 1616, 4".
(Hy Duke & Son) **$7,000**

Wallpaper covered hat box, labeled 'Joseph S. Tillinghast, Band Box Manufacturer and dealer in French and American Paper Hangings, one door west of the Post-Office, Union Street, New Bedford', Massachusetts, circa 1832, 12⅛" high.
(Skinner Inc) **$950**

Maori treasure box, circa 1830, 6¼" long.
(Christie's) **$154,800**

A Victorian oak miniature pillar box, with a hexagonal top, the cylindrical body with a hinged brass aperture for letters, the panel door with a postal rate card, the interior leather lined and stamped *H. Rodrigles, Maker, 42 Piccadilly, London*, 15¾" high.
(Christie's) **$5,390**

A pair of cutlery urns, each with a slightly domed circular lid with stop-fluted border and ball **molding**, the central pinnacle carved with acanthus and surmounted by a flaming urn carved with rams' heads, on a stepped circular base carved with lotus leaves, 29" high.
(Christie's) **$5,775**

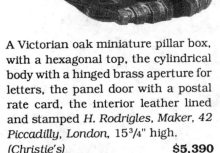

A Louis Wain porcelain pig vase, the stylized figure with shaped aperture on its back, decorated in green, yellow, russet and black enamels, 12.4cm. high.
(Christie's) **$2,602**

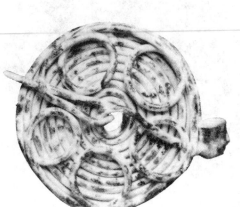

Staffordshire pottery coiled and twisted pipe, England, early 19th century, underglazed enamel sponge decorated in green, blue and raspberry, bowl molded as a bust head, 8½" long.
(Skinner Inc) **$1,100**

A Wade Heath novelty teapot as Donald Duck in blue sailor's outfit, printed marks, circa 1935, 8" wide.
(Christie's S. Ken) **$1,490**

An old-fashioned water bottle depicting an unrecorded picture of The Spinning Wheel, fruit and foliate decoration, the blue and red reversed on each side.
(Phillips) **$2,800**

A Bow white bust of a Mongolian with a moustache and pointed beard, wearing a scroll-molded cap applied with small balls and a jacket with frill collar and molded frogging, on a fluted socle and octafoil base molded with balls at each corner, circa 1750, 25.5cm. high.
(Christie's) **$16,362**

A Royal Doulton boxed set of napkin rings, comprising the Dickens figures, Mr. Pickwick, Mr. Micawber, Fat Boy, Tony Weller, Sam Weller and Sairey Gamp, *printed marks.*
(Christie's)   **$2,310**

A pair of rare First Period Belleek ice pails and covers, in matt and glazed parian, from the service ordered by the Prince of Wales, designed by Robert Williams Armstrong, mark for 1868, 46cm. high.
(Allen & Harris)   **$7,084**

A Derby yellow-ground cylindrical cup and cover painted with two hounds in a wooded landscape within a gilt octagonal cartouche flanked by two oval gilt cartouches of a parrot and a goldfinch, the cover with four panels of birds, a horse and a cow between gilt line rims, Duesbury & Kean, circa 1795, 4" high.

(Christie's)   **$11,375**

A rare Burleighware wall plaque with a design of a galleon in full sail by Charlotte Rhead.

(Michael Newman)   **$1,550**

A very rare Bow egg cup of plain ovoid shape on a spreading circular foot, glazed in white and molded with three flowering prunus sprigs, 7.7cm. *(Phillips)* **$1,925**

A Copeland Parian bust 'The Veiled Bride' after Rafaelle Monti, raised upon a waisted cylindrical socle impressed *Crystal Palace Art Union.* Impressed mark and date code for 1879, 38cm. high.
(Spencers) **$3,150**

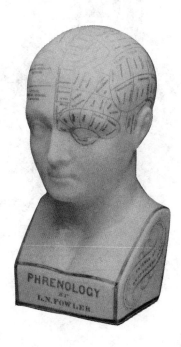

A ceramic Phrenology head, signed *L.N. Fowler, 337 Strand, London,* 19th century, labeled with the various characteristics of the skull, 11½" high.
(Christie's) **$1,045**

A pair of Derby Mansion House dwarfs, wearing brightly colored striped and flowered clothes, their hats inscribed *Lectures on Chemistry*, and *Auction of Elegant Household Furniture*, Robt. Bloor & Co., circa 1830, 16cm. high and 17.5cm. high.
(Christie's) **$3,365**

It's everyone's dream – taking an old vase on the mantlepiece along to the Antiques Roadshow and being told it's worth thousands. That's exactly what happened in the case of 'Ozzy' an owl-shaped jug with detachable head, which had been used occasionally by its owners as a flowerpot. It turned out to be a rare Staffordshire slipware drinking vessel, dating from the 1770s. It is thought that the design originated in Germany, and was copied by English potters such as the Thomas Toft family at the end of the 18th century, when they produced high quality owl vessels as novelties.

Very few examples survive and this one finally went home to roost at the Stoke on Trent City Museum and Art Gallery, England, having been auctioned at Phillips London for $37,000

Two Chelsea eel-tureens and covers naturally modeled with their bodies curled, their tails forming the handles, painted in brown, cream, purple and green, circa 1755, 18.5cm. wide. *(Christie's)* **$35,420**

A Bow documentary cylindrical ink-pot with a central circular well surrounded by five holes to the shoulder, painted by James Welsh in a pale palette with a loose bouquet, scattered flowers and a dragonfly, the shoulder with quills, dividers, rulers, a mathematical manuscript and a geometrical equation, circa 1758, 9cm. diameter. The painter James Welch (sic.) together with his wife, was recorded at Chelsea in October 1750; by the summer of 1754 they had removed to Bow. The burial register of St. Mary's Church, Hornsey records 1762. 27th. April. James Welch, from Tile Kiln in Edmonton Parish. *(Christie's)* **$21,252**

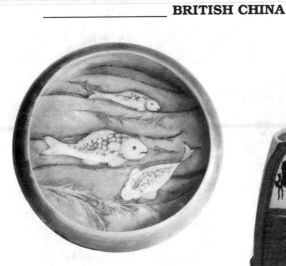

Moorcroft shallow bowl with inverted rim, the interior decorated with three carp on an overall blue and green ground with matt glaze, signed and impressed on the base, 12½"diameter. *(William H. Brown)* **$1,750**

A Louis Wain porcelain cat vase, the stylized figure with a shaped aperture on its back, decorated in white, green, russet and black enamels, 15.5cm. high.
(Christie's) **$2,602**

A Pennington Liverpool ship bowl painted in blue with a ship in full sail, with five matchstick figures on the deck, inscribed *Success to the Perseus, Capt. Gibson, 1790*, the exterior with flower sprays, a scroll border inside, 25cm. diameter.

Ship bowls were usually made for privateers or merchantmen, but in this example a naval vessel has been depicted. The 'Perseus' was a 6th rate of 20 guns, built by Randall of Rotherhithe in March 1776, she was first commissioned in 1783.

Recommissioned in May 1787 under the command of Captain John Gibson, she was stationed in the Irish Sea and consequently would have regularly visited Liverpool. In March 1792 she sailed for Jamaica and was paid off December 1794. In May 1798,

commissioned as a 'bomb' with ten guns and in 1799 joined operations at Alexandria and in Naples Bay. The 'Perseus' was finally broken up at Sheerness in 1805.
(Phillips) **$5,474**

A rare Chelsea Kakiemon-style leaf dish delicately incised with veining and enameled and gilt with an exotic bird in display and another perched on a prunus branch by a banded hedge, the molded underside with stem feet, 8½" long, raised anchor period.

(Tennants) **$6,552**

'Girl in a Swing' gold-mounted owl's head bonbonnière inscribed *La nuit donne conseil*, 1749–54, 2" wide.
(Christie's) **$28,611**

A Wrotham slipware dated tyg by Thomas Ifield, the tapering redware body with four double loop handles applied with cream slip studs and edged with ropetwist-pattern and terminating in cream slip terminals, flanking rectangular medallions, including the initials *T.I.* above a plant, the date *1643* above a stylized roundel, 14cm. high.

Only five other examples by this potter would seem to be recorded. Thomas Ifield married Marie Richardson at Ightham in 1628, thus uniting two great Wrotham pottery families.

(Christie's) **$17,556**

Chang Ware was named after a Chinese master potter of the Sung Dynasty and it was an effort by Doulton to produce glazes which old Chinese potters had also tried to create. The first Chang pottery appeared in 1925 and was characterized by thick textured layers of flowing glaze in lustrous colors which give a lava like appearance. It was used on vases, some of them festooned with dragons or lizards.

Dragon vase in Chang glazes, earthenware, 7½" high, circa 1920.

(Abridge)   **$4,480**

A large Carter, Stabler & Adams Ltd. ceramic vase, with polychrome painted, stylized floral decoration with impressed mark *Poole England*, painted monogram *HY*, 40.8cm. high

(Christie's)   **$5,600**

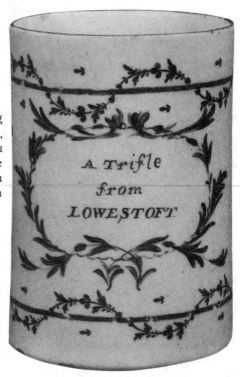

A Lowestoft inscribed cylindrical mug with shaped scroll-molded handle, inscribed in black *A Trifle from Lowestoft* within a puce foliage cartouche between turquoise ribbon and garlands of black flowers, circa 1790, 12cm. high.
(Christie's) **$4,250**

The Six Swans, a Maw and Co. two-handled lustre vase designed by Walter Crane, the swollen form rising to a narrow neck with bell-shaped rim, with two scrolling handles each of which is modeled with swan's head terminals. The buff ground decorated in shades of red lustre with swans and human figures between foliate borders, the base with enameled monogram and dated 1890, 26.7cm. high.
(Christie's) **$6,853**

The Clifton Dish, a highly important slipware dish made at Clifton in Cumbria, press-molded and trailed in two tones of brown slip on a cream ground, the design based on the British Royal Arms with a shield including a lion, harp and **checker** pattern.

The townships of Great and Little Clifton are situated near Workington and from 1755 belonged to Sir James Lowther. The Lowther Papers housed at Cumberland Record Office show a number of potters worked around Clifton but early records are mostly lacking. The Crossborrow pottery at Clifton was active in the 18th century and there was a further pottery at Gins House.

(Phillips) **$33,810**

BRONZE

A pair of archaic bronze and silver-inlaid chariot axle fittings of cylindrical form, with two raised bands above a flaring socket, each decorated overall with a geometric design in silver inlay, Warring States, 8cm. high.
(Christie's) **$8,662**

The bronze was sent for sale with a group of 19th and 20th century garden statuary to Sotheby's in Billingshurst, having been bought by the present owner in the early 1950s. Elizabeth Wilson saw the photograph in the Billinghurst catalog and immediately recognized it as being an important work and it was withdrawn from the sale and sent on to London for research.

A highly important Prague bronze statue of the 'Dancing Faun' by the leading Mannerist sculptor Adrien de Vries (circa 1545-1626), which had been standing in an English garden for nearly forty years was identified by Elizabeth Wilson, head of Sotheby's European Works of Art Department, and sold by Sotheby's in London for £6,820,000.

It has been dated on stylistic grounds to circa 1610-1615 when the sculptor was working in Prague. The extremely fine finish of details such as the fingers, toes and veins, and the brilliant modeling of the musculature are characteristic of his work at this date. A sample of the terracotta core that remained intact inside the bronze was tested by thermoluminescence analysis at the Oxford Research Laboratory and found to date from between 1450 and 1630. The original wax model, formed on the terracotta core was lost in the casting process and the bronze is therefore unique.

The bronze dancing faun was inspired by the ancient marble, now in the Uffizi Gallery in Florence, excavated in the 16th century and traditionally said to have been restored by Michelangelo. The ancient marble faun, much admired by Bernini, was reproduced many times in bronze at the end of the 17th century, but this newly discovered figure appears to be the earliest existing example of an adaptation of it.

A fine pair of French 19th century bronze busts of a Nubian man and woman also known as 'Venus Africaine', both wearing traditional dress, he signed on the right shoulder *Ch. Cordier 1848*, she on the truncation of the left arm *Cordier* and on the truncation on the right *simonet peret fils fondeurs*, the bronze silvered and apparently covered in a dark lacquer, 83cm. and 79cm. high.

Charles-Henri-Joseph Cordier (1827–1905) was celebrated since his debut in the Paris Salon in 1848 for his Romantic bronzes portraying ethnographic types and for his taste for polychromy and unusual treatment of bronze and other materials.

There are several other pairs of these busts known, one in the Musee de l'Homme in Paris, one in the Art Institute of Chicago, and one in the Royal Residence of Queen Victoria at Osborne House on the Isle of Wight.
(Christie's) **$166,980**

Benin bronze head for an altar of an Oba, early period, pre 1550, 8¼" high.
(Christie's) **$2,085,600**

A magnificent 19th century French bronze parcel gilt and enameled bust with amethyst eyes and onyx drapery of 'La Juive D'Alger', by Charles-Henri-Joseph Cordier, signed and dated *Cordier 1863*, on rouge marble socle and rouge marble plinth with ormolu mounts, 71cm. height of bust.

This celebrated composition first appeared in the exhibition of 1862 in London, for which it was presumably specially produced. The present bust is probably the one shown in the Paris Salon of 1863 and the Paris Exposition Universelle of 1867. In 1869 yet another was presented by the French government to the museum in Troyes.
(Christie's) **$301,070**

A rare late 19th century English new sculpture bronze statuette of Perseus, cast from a model by F.W. Pomeroy, triumphantly holding aloft the Gorgon's head, 51cm. high.
(Christie's) **$22,308**

One of a pair of inlaid bronze mask and ring handles, Warring States/ Western Han Dynasty, the masks 9.5cm. wide, the rings 9cm. diameter. *(Christie's)* **$86,515**

A magnificent French parcel-gilt and silvered bronze bust of an Egyptian harem girl entitled 'Jeune femme fellah en costume de harem', cast from a model by Charles-Henri-Joseph Cordier, the alluring maiden wearing a harem decolleté dress with elaborate jeweled headdress and necklaces, long plaits falling down her back, inscribed on the truncation of the right arm *Le Caire C Cordier* and bearing the date *1806* instead of 1866, 76cm. high.

This sensuous harem girl is characteristic of Cordier's skilful blending of beauty and ethnographic detail. He was fascinated by ethnographic accuracy and was commissioned by the Paris Museum of Natural History to produce busts for a specifically ethnographic gallery. In this pursuit Cordier traveled extensively, and in 1866 went to Egypt on an ethnographic mission sponsored by the French government. He returned with seven plaster studies, of which one was the present model. A version of the present model in bronze, gold, silver, turquoise and porphyry was exhibited in the Exposition Universelle of 1867. *(Christie's)* **$187,000**

'Coming Through the Rye', an important bronze equestrian group inscribed *Frederic Remington copyrighted 1902* and *Cire Perdue Cast. Roman Bronze Works N.Y. 1902* and *1*, 30³/₄" high.

Frederic Remington used earlier painted works as the direct source for this complex bronze. Both his 1888 illustration 'Dissolute Cow Punchers' for Century and his oil of the following year 'Cowboys Coming to Town for Christmas' depict four cowboys riding at full gallop.

(Christie's)   **$4,400,000**

An amusing German bronze group, cast from a model by Gustav Adolf Daumiller, as two naked children, the girl with her hair dressed with flowers and carrying a bouquet, her shy male companion preserving his modesty behind a small satchel with a hunting horn motif, 54.5cm. high, founder's mark *Guss, Priessmann, Bauer Co., Munchen.*

(Phillips) **$4,401**

A mid 19th century French silvered bronze figure of Sappho, cast by Victor Paillard from a model by Jean-Jacques Pradier, standing pensively beside a column, on a base signed and dated *J Pradier 1848* and with foundry mark *V Paillard 1848*, 86cm. high.

A bronze 'Standing Sappho' was first exhibited at the Paris Salon of 1848; it was Pradier's first portrayal of the poetess. The sculpture incited an enthusiastic appraisal from Theophile Gautier.

(Christie's) **$106,260**

A Regency/Empire bronze and ormolu inkstand in the manner of Thomas Hope, the tall cylindrical pots supported by kneeling figures of Egyptian maidens, centered by a rhyton-type vase terminating in a bull's head with applied bands of anthemion and acanthus leaves, 13" wide.
(Christie's) **$58,344**

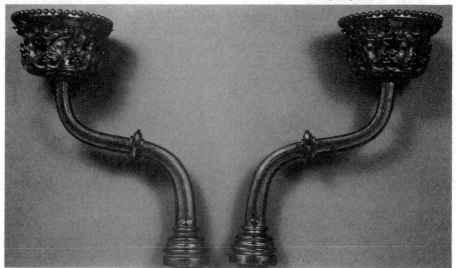

A pair of Magdelen College, Oxford, gilt-bronze candlesticks by L.N. Cottingham, the fluted curved columns with octagonal ribs, the cup-shaped drip pans applied with cast foliage and beaded rim, detachable nozzles, 1832, 38.5cm. high. *(Christie's)* **$7,315**

Frederic Remington, original bronze sculpture, 'The Cheyenne', 20¹/₄" high, 1901, on verso *Copyrighted by Frederic Remington 1901* and *Cire Perdue Cast Roman Bronze Works.* Sculpture is numbered *2* above and on the left side of the foundry mark. This was the second casting ever made for Remington by Roman Bronze Works using the lost wax process. *(Du Mouchelles)*   **$550,000**

BUCKETS

A George III brass-bound mahogany bucket of navette shape with brass liner and swing-handle, 14¹/₂" wide. *(Christie's)*   **$3,765**

One of a pair of George III brass-bound mahogany buckets of navette shape, each with swing-handle and liner, 12½" wide.
(Christie's) **$3,432**

A Lehnware painted wooden bucket, Joseph Long Lehn (1798–1892), Lancaster County, Pennsylvannia, second half 19th century, with three metal bands painted with stylized trailing floral vines, sponged red surface overall, the swing wire handle with turned wooden grip, 9½" high.
(Christie's East)   **$5,280**

Born in Liverpool in the latter part of the 18th century, George Bullock exhibited as a sculptor at the Royal Academy and the Liverpool Academy from 1804–16, and was President of the Liverpool Academy in 1810 and 1811. In 1805, Bullock was in partnership as a cabinet maker, general furnisher and marble worker in Liverpool, firstly with a man named Stoakes, and then from 1809–11 with Joseph Gandy.

In 1813 Bullock was established in London, where he continued to work as a sculptor and furniture maker. He was also proprietor of the Mona Marble Works, which worked quarries in Anglesey. From 1814–19 Ackerman's 'Repository' contained six plates of Bullock's designs for furniture and chimneypieces, and a seventh plate appeared in 1824. Bullock supplied furniture to Blair Castle, the seat of the Dukes of Atholl, and from 1816–18 he worked in cooperation with the architect William Atkinson to supply pieces for his friend Walter Scott at Abbotsford. With his death in 1818 his workshops ceased production, though the Times announced in the following year that 'British Oak Furniture ... to the late Mr Bullock's designs' was being made by cabinet-maker E.T. Cox.

Bullock worked in a heavy, neo-Classical style, described by one of his contemporaries, Richard Brown, as 'massy and ponderous'. He did, however, also pioneer the use of native plants for ornament and the revival of Gothic and Elizabethan forms, and revived the brass inlay technique associated with Boulle.

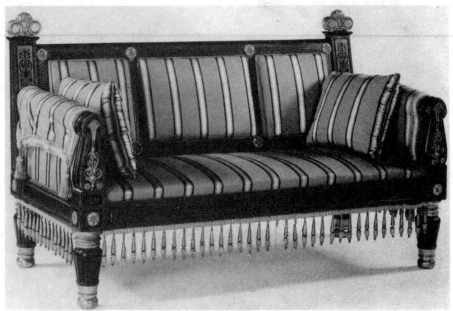

A Regency oak and parcel-gilt sofa attributed to George Bullock. *(Christie's)* **$106,920**

A Regency ormolu-mounted rosewood footstool supplied by George Bullock for Napoleon's use at New Longwood, the padded seat upholstered in green velvet, 13³/4" wide. The design for this stool, with an additional floral clasp on the frieze, appears in the Wilkinson Tracings Book of Bullock/Bridgens designs. *(Christie's)* **$21,252**

One of a pair of Regency pollard oak side cabinets attributed to George Bullock, 39" high x 53¹/2" wide. *(Christie's)* **$387,200**

A fine 17th century Florentine ebonized and parcel gilt ripple molded scagliola table cabinet, containing a central deep drawer decorated with a vase of flowers between projecting columns with architectural pediment drawer above and another below. 3ft. 7½" wide.

For centuries the art of scagliola was forgotten, the technique is believed to have been originally invented by the ancient Romans and was revived during the Renaissance in Florence in the 16th century by artists working in the Grand Ducal Workshops of the Medici family. A composition was made from a mixture of finely ground colored marbles, selenite mixed with plaster of Paris and glue. This was ground into a paste and then inlaid and 'painted' into a fine wet plaster which, on drying, would then be polished.

(Phillips) **$140,000**

A large Japanese free-standing Meiji period brass mounted lacquered cabinet with 2 doors enclosing 11 drawers, the cabinet well decorated with junks, exotic birds, Mount Fuji and feathers, 41.5".

(Graves Son & Pilcher) **$23,625**

A fine Ernest Gimson walnut bureau cabinet on stand, the two cupboard doors with cross banding enclosing fitted interior with two small cupboard doors above fall flap enclosing fifteen pigeon holes, on black painted stand with trellis work on three sides joined by platform stretcher, circa 1906, 191.2cm. high.

(Christie's) **$16,830**

A fine Georgian mahogany coin cabinet in the manner of Thomas Chippendale, the top with baluster gallery, the sides paneled, one with applied carved scrollwork in the rococo style, the door opening to reveal twenty sliding trays for coins, supported upon slender baluster legs carved with scrollwork and foliage and ending in knurled feet, 41cm. wide.

(Spencers) **$288,750**

Thompson's revolver camera was patented in France on 20 January 1862, no. 52,713. Although designed by Englishman John Thompson the camera was manufactured by A. Briois of Paris. It was demonstrated to the Société Française de Photographie on 4 July, 1862.

The camera had a number of new features including the taking of four circular exposures on a single circular plate. The exposure was made via a rotary shutter. The front lens had a combined use as a viewing lens which dropped into position as the taking lens. The process of releasing the lens and dropping it into position activated the shutter. This procedure allowed four exposures to be made in rapid succession.

A very rare Thompson revolver camera no. 48 with a polished mahogany handle, lacquered brass body with upper rear mounted viewing tube with sprung sliding front section, front lens element signed in pencil *AF*, opening back section with rotating wheel and rotating internal section with four 23mm. diameter windows.

Only three other Thompson revolver cameras have been traced.
(Christie's) **$30,481**

An extremely rare, important and unusual half-frame Leica camera with an internally mounted Compur-type leaf shutter with a top plate mounted tension-setting knob with inset 79-exposure counter dial, the body covered in red-painted vulcanite and with a Leitz Elmar 3.5cm. f. 3.5 lens. This camera was designed by Helmut Schäfer who had originally worked as a draughtsman on the 'O' series Leicas. The camera is largely assembled from normal chrome Leica Standard parts and dates from circa 1945-1946. The camera is likely to have been made in very limited numbers ie. under three examples within the Leitz factory.
(Christie's) **$19,635**

Marion and Co. Ltd., London. A 140 x 90mm. tropical stereoscopic reflex camera with inset brass binding, red bellows, red leather viewing hood and a pair of Ross compound homocentric 5 inch f 6.8 lenses.
(Christie's)   **$8,811**

A very good, rare and unusual 6½ x 7½ inch mahogany collapsible camera with brass fittings, lens panel with rising and horizontal movement and a brass bound Horne and Thornthwaite lens No. 3722 with rack and pinion focusing, three washer stops and cap and rear focusing screen with inset plaque *outside*, camera top with plaque *Horne & Thornthwaite, Manufacturers, 121, 122 & 123 Newgate, London.*
(Christie's)   **$12,727**

A very rare 8 x 38cm. 'Periphote' panoramic camera no. 114 with polished nickel and aluminium body with a 'Jarret, Paris' anastigmat 55mm. f. 5.6 lens and clockwork shutter mechanism (defective) contained in maker's original case.

The Lumiere Periphote camera was the subject of Swiss patent no. 23746 of 1901. The camera was worked by clockwork which moved the camera lens while the film stayed stationary, panoramas could be 180 or 360 degrees.

(Christie's) **$17,930**

A 35mm. high polish platinum and karung leather covered Leica R6 camera no. 1750000 with a platinum and skin barreled Leica Summilux f. 1.4 50mm. lens no. 3500075, camera back with platinum plate engraved *150 Jahre Photographie, 1989*. This unique high polish Leica R6 camera has been specially handmade by Leica GmbH in Solms, West Germany for the 150th anniversary of photography and 75 years of Leica photography both being celebrated during 1989.

(Christie's) **$43,032**

The 'Ben Akiba' camera cane invented by E. Kronke, Berlin 1903, and manufactured by A. Leh, with 24 exposures and ten spare rolls of film, carried in the shaft, 35" long.

(Michael C. German) **$7,000**

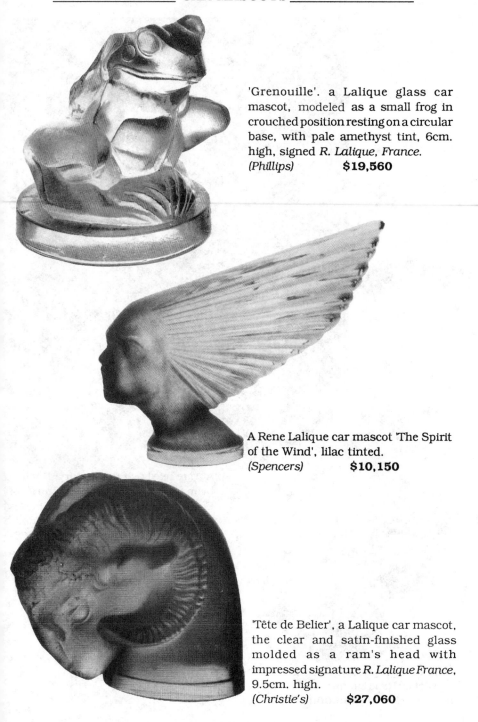

'Grenouille'. a Lalique glass car mascot, modeled as a small frog in crouched position resting on a circular base, with pale amethyst tint, 6cm. high, signed *R. Lalique, France.*
(Phillips) **$19,560**

A Rene Lalique car mascot 'The Spirit of the Wind', lilac tinted.
(Spencers) **$10,150**

'Tête de Belier', a Lalique car mascot, the clear and satin-finished glass molded as a ram's head with impressed signature *R. Lalique France*, 9.5cm. high.
(Christie's) **$27,060**

A rare early 20th century English bronze statuette of the Spirit of Ecstasy, cast from a model by Charles Sykes, 60cm. high. This fluent composition by Charles Sykes (1875-1950) has been used since 1911 on a reduced scale as a mascot for Rolls-Royce motor cars.
(Christie's)   **$9,295**

'Tête de Paon' frosted blue glass car mascot by René Lalique, 17.5cm high.
(Christie's)   **$66,000**

A carved wood horse, Prancer, the figure in skygazer pose with deeply carved flowing mane, jeweled trappings, tasseled blanket and saddle with a gladiator holding a shield at cantle, 53" long.
(Christie's)   **$20,900**

A carved wood stork, the figure in a striding pose with deeply carved feathers, saddle with a baby at cantle and blanket, 67" high.
(Christie's) **$25,300**

Camel carousel figure, possibly New York State, 19th century. The stylized carved and painted figure of a camel with hemp tail and fringed leather and canvas saddle, mounted on a rectangular base, painted in polychrome, 48" wide. *(Skinner Inc)* **$10,000**

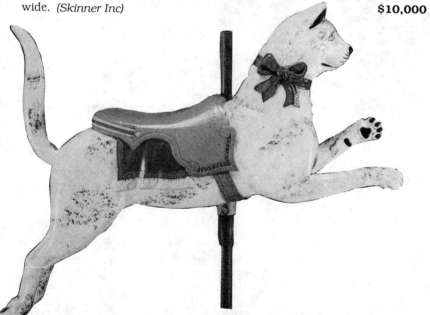

A carved wood cat, the figure in a leaping pose, with a sweet expressive face and deeply carved bow at the neck, with saddle and blanket, 49" long. *(Christie's)* **$19,800**

A Hawaii god stick, akua ka'ai image, carved from a hard wood of reddish hue, either Alphitonia sp. or Colubrina sp., the figure surmounting the tapering double notched stake, stands with legs flexed and arms held from the side of the narrow chest with prominent pectorals, the heel of the palms resting on the thighs, the disproportionately large head has a crest which represents a warrior's feather helmet, carved with a metal implement, probably mid 18th century. *(Phillips)* **$82,250**

Carved and painted figure of Father Time, Kentucky, circa 1870, in the full-round, the standing draped, winged figure casually leaning on a globe supported by a grain-painted pedestal and holding a scythe. Raised on a rectangular platform bearing the signature *B.W. Smith*, painted in polychrome, 39" high. *(Skinner Inc)* **$69,000**

Victorian painted wood figure of a large salmon, 48" long.
(Woolley & Wallis) **$3,062**

Fine and unusual coromandel wood crab with central locking compartment.
(Michael G Matthews) **$752**

A fine early Victorian Scottish carved walnut standing jardiniere, circa 1850, attributed to John Taylor & Son, Edinburgh, the bowl boldly carved with fruit and with a scrollwork collar, on carved baluster stem and tall triangular base supported by winged caryatides and satyr masks at the corners, the sides with convex bosses above Janus masks, 69" high.
(Sothebys) **$10,000**

A pair of late 19th century painted and gilded wooden Venetian blackamoor torcheres, each holding an oar and standing on a gondola, on painted and decorated tapering cylindrical stands with square bases, 84" high.
(Andrew Hartley) **$12,250**

A Bavarian carved bear revolving piano stool.
(Spencers) **$3,500**

German boxwood cup and cover, early 18th century, 14⅝" high.
(Christie's) **$41,923**

Flemish boxwood group of the Virgin and Child, late 17th century, 11" high.
(Christie's) **$19,541**

Swabian (Ulm) limewood altar wing carved with the Adoration of the Magi by Niclaus Weckmann the Elder, early 16th century, 65¼" x 47⅝".
(Christie's) **$462,000**

CARVED WOOD

Snuffing Highlander 84" high, from the contents of Bacon's the Tobacconist, Cambridge, England. *(Christie's)* **$15,831**

Carved and painted figure of an Indian squaw, America, circa 1870, the boldly carved full-bodied polychromed figure carrying a box quiver, decorated with applied carved and polychromed arrows, circular bosses and tomahawk, mounted on a metal stand, overall height 45½". *(Skinner Inc)* **$26,000**

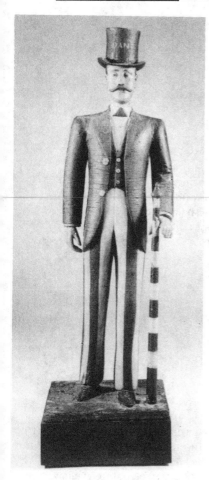

A painted wood 'Dapper Dan' trade sign, Philadelphia or Washington DC, circa 1880, overall height 77¼".
(Sotheby's) **$258,500**

A carved and painted soldier whirligig, American, 19th century, carved as a soldier, with blue-painted hat and tunic, the white trousers painted with red stripes, one arm with tin axe, 20" high.
(Christie's) **$30,800**

A Congo female fetish figure standing with legs flexed astride, the arms pressed to the side of the body, the hands placed on either side of the scarified navel, the abdomen with attached block of fetish material pierced with three iron shards and the up-tilted heart shaped face with white enamel inlay at the eyes, 35cm. high. *(Phillips)* **$10,320**

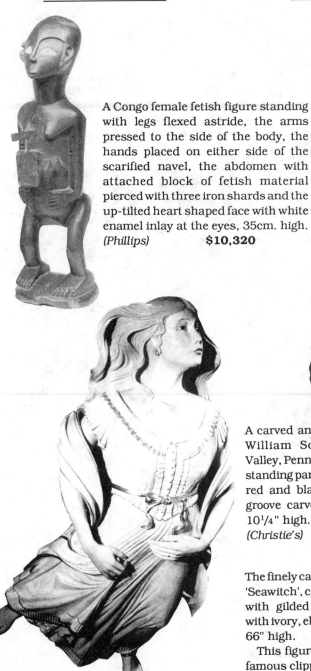

A carved and painted pine parrot by William Schimmel, Cumberland Valley, Pennsylvania, 1865-1890. The standing parrot, painted yellow, green, red and black with carved tail and groove carved feet grasping a base, 10¹/₄" high.
(Christie's) **$7,700**

The finely carved limewood figurehead 'Seawitch', carved by Greg Powlesland, with gilded details, the eyes inlaid with ivory, ebony and mother-of-pearl, 66" high.

This figurehead is named after the famous clipper ship that did not have a figurehead.
(Sothebys) **$25,000**

Carved and painted watch hutch, New England, early 19th century, painted brown and heightened with brick red, the case inset with inscriptions *JST 1808* and *Time*, 9⁷/₈" high.
(Skinner Inc) **$3,250**

Carved spoon rack, America, 18th century, the tombstone-shaped crest above a chip-carved back mounted with two racks for spoons, 18" high.
(Skinner Inc) **$7,500**

19th century German, carved bear plant stand.
(Michael G Matthews) **$2,275**

A 19th century tobacconist's carved wood and polychrome shop sign in the form of a soldier in full Highland dress, wearing a plumed bonnet, a gorget to the breast of his tunic, holding an open snuff mull, 69" high.
(Christie's)   **$16,360**

A South German carved and grained pine brown bear hallstand with a bear cub amid the branches of a tree held aloft by a standing growling bear upon a naturalistic base, third quarter 19th century, 79" high.
(Christie's)   **$4,800**

CARVED WOOD

Carved and painted eagle and shield, attributed to John H. Bellamy, Kittery Point, Maine, late 19th century, the shield painted red, white and blue and a green sprig to the side, weathered surface, 55" wide. *(Skinner Inc)* **$5,000**

A magnificent pair of Japanese wood sculptures depicting two koma inu boldly carved in yosegi-zukuru technique, one with a horn and closed mouth, the other with mouth open, each with crystal eyes with black and gilt pupils, their bodies with traces of black and green paint, Kamakura period (1185–1393), 50cm. high.

The crystal eyes (gyokugan), are segments of rock crystal lined with silk cloth or some other material on which the pupils of the eyes are painted in gold and color, imparting a lifelike effect and very fashionable in the Kamakura period. *(Christie's)* **$92,400**

99

A Casteldurante squat drug jar painted in colors with the naked Fortune arising from the waves on the back of a dolphin within a roundel above a scroll inscribed with the name of the contents *Avolane*, circa 1580, 23.5cm. wide.
(Christie's) **$27,280**

A pair of Casteldurante Albarelli for 'V. Lava' and 'Dia Catolicon', painted with Fortune riding a dolphin, on a blue ground, a trofei in brown, circa 1580, 18.5cm. high.
(Christie's) **$26,895**

An early Victorian papier-mache center table, the molded circular tip-up top painted with a romantic lakeside scene with a lady in a shell drawn by swans, the foreground with a fountain, flowers, fruit, a parakeet, and a peacock, 48" diameter. *(Christie's)* **$7,807**

An Irish Regency giltwood center table by Joshua Kearney, the circular white marble top inset with five rectangular pietra dura panels, the central panel with a vase of flowers, the other panels with buildings and people by a river and a gondola, flanked and divided by micro-mosaic medallions depicting Roman ruins, 41" wide.

Joshua Kearney had premises at 186 Great Britain Street, Dublin, from 1797-1804. Between 1805 and 1844 he was working from 49 Henry Street. From 1831 he described himself as 'Carver & Gilder & Looking Glass & Patent Lamp Warehouse'.
(Christie's) **$84,480**

An Anglo-Indian carved ebony library table, circa 1850, the hinged circular top with a carved border and inlaid with a radiating plume design in a large variety of indigenous woods within chevron bandings and surrounded by inlaid ivory teardrops, on lobed stem with square section base with scrolled corners, 47" diameter.
(Sothebys)   **$32,725**

An early Victorian oak center table, with circular Roman micro-mosaic table top, inlaid with a circular vista of St. Peter's Square flanked by vignettes depicting the Pantheon, Castel St Angelo, tomb of Metellus, the Forum, Trojan's Arch, Temple of Vesta, Capitoline Hill and the Colosseum. 19th century, 39$\frac{1}{2}$" wide.
(Christie's)   **$78,760**

It was the great Doulton designer Charles Noke who first saw the possibilities for a 20th century revival of the old Staffordshire Toby jug tradition and developed it with a completely new approach to the old 'face jug' concept.

He had in mind the creation of a series of characters from English legend, history and literature, which would be much more colorful than their prototypes but would, like them, have an immediate appeal for his own and future generations.

Though Noke joined Doulton in 1889, it was not until the early 1930's that he had the time and opportunity to put his concept into production. The first such jug to appear was John Barleycorn, which was an instant success. It was soon followed by Old Charley, the Night Watchman, Dickens' Sairey Gamp, Parson Brown and Dick Turpin.

Other leading Doulton designers joined Noke in the production of these jugs, such as Leslie Harradine and Harry Fenton. Harradine was responsible for many Dickens' characters, while Fenton contributed in addition such figures as John Peel, Old King Cole and the Vicar of Bray. Later names associated with the genre are Max Henk (Long John Silver, Lord Nelson etc) and David Briggs (Town Crier, Veteran Motorist, and many others.)

The range has also been extended to include modern personalities from all walks of life from politicians to stars of stage and screen, pop stars, as well as contemporary types such as Golfer and Fireman.

Given the basic high quality of design and production, the value of each jug is often determined by its rarity, for many have a colorful history attached to their launch. Small variations in color and design can also make an enormous difference.

The two faces of Mephistopheles D5757 designed by H. Fenton, issued 1937–1948. *(Abridge)* **$1,440**

The Clark Gable character jug was conceived as the first in a series of six celebrity jugs in 1983 (the others are Louis Armstrong, Mae West, Groucho Marx, W C Fields and Jimmy Durante). They were commissioned for the American market by American Express. About 150–200 were sent to the US as a trial, and immediately fell foul of the Clark Gable Association who informed the Retailers Association of America that they were issuing a writ against Doulton for copyright reasons. Doulton didn't argue, but immediately withdrew the jugs. Most were pulled back, leaving about 50 in circulation. For this reason, while others in the series fetch only $70–$80, Clark Gable will fetch a cool $4,000.

The first Doulton clown jug was the red-haired version with a multi-colored handle which was produced in the late 1930's. There is a visible difference in coloration between early examples and those produced during the war years when the supply of materials was restricted, so much so that the later ones have become known more or less unofficially as Brown haired clowns. The Red/Brown haired versions were in any case superseded after the second World War by the White haired clown which was manufactured between 1951–55. The Red and Brown haired versions will fetch $2,125 while the White haired clown will fetch around $850. Only one Black haired clown has turned up at auction so far, where it fetched $20,000. This dates from the Red haired period of the late 1930's and seems to have been a one-off commission to Doulton by a family in memory of their grandfather, who had in fact been himself a black-haired clown.

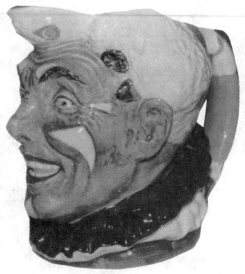

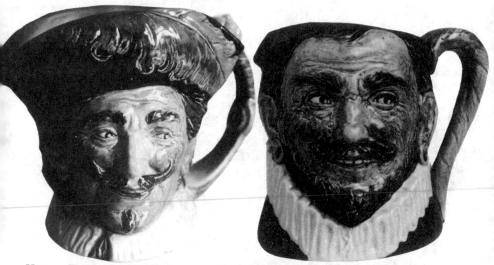

Harry Fenton's 'Drake' jug was introduced in 1940. In the first version the rim is the character's hair, but in later versions it became his hat. The earlier jug, known as 'The Hatless Drake' carries the inscription 'Drake he was a Devon Man' and was produced only in limited numbers. Today, a 'hatless' Drake will sell for around $3,000, while the hatted version will fetch only about $100.

The normal Old King Cole character jug, D6036, designed by H. Fenton and issued 1939–1960 has a reddish brown crown and handle and as such is worth $200. With a yellow crown and a greenish colored handle, issued 1939–40, it is worth $1,500 and if it comes complete with a musical movement, D6014, issued in 1939 it is worth over $3,000.

The basic version of 'Arriet, D6208, issued 1947–1960 with brown coat, green hat and handle, worth $200.

'Arry and 'Arriet are favorite Doulton jugs designed by Harry Fenton, with somewhat complicated variations. These figures of a Cockney costermonger and his wife were introduced in the mid 1940's and withdrawn by 1960. 'Arry is predominantly brown in color. In some variations however he is embellished by having brown or white buttons on his hat (a reference to the costermongers' custom of dressing up on high days and holidays as Pearly Kings and Queens) when he becomes Brown Pearly Boy, and can be worth $1,300. Even more rare is the version with pinkish white buttons on a brown hat with blue peak, when he becomes Blue Pearly Boy and fetches $4,000!

'Arriet is subject to slightly less complicated versions. Her basic form is a brown coat with green hat and handle. Her festive wear consists of a

blue collar, and green boa on her mauve hat and she then becomes Blue Pearly Girl and will be worth $7,500.

The Churchill character jug, made during the Battle of Britain, was one of the first jugs to be withdrawn. The first version was cream colored with two black handles and bears the inscription *Winston Spencer Churchill Prime Minister of Britain 1940*. It was withdrawn after only eighteen months however because, it is said, Churchill himself was not pleased with the likeness. Because so few were produced this jug is an extremely rare and desirable item, coveted by collectors throughout the world. The second version has natural coloring and bears the number D6170. The cream version, which was rather longer on the market before withdrawal, has fetched over $9,000, while one with natural coloring, which is even rarer, recently sold at Sotheby's for a staggering $30,000.

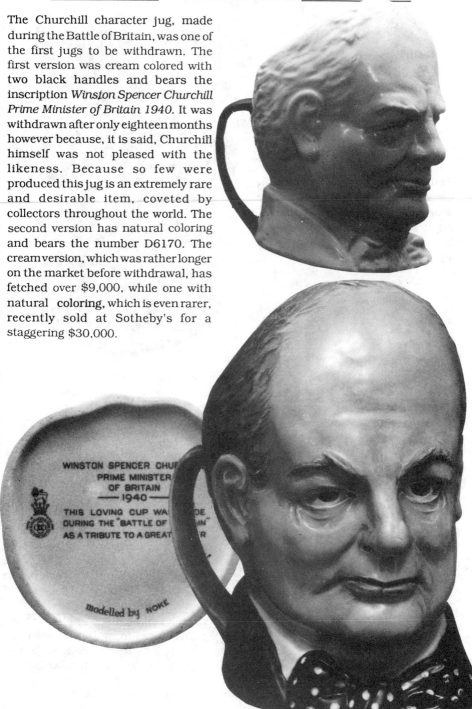

The Maori was a pilot jug which never went into production. It was made circa 1939 in two forms, one of which was more of a caricature than the other. Some examples did escape however and either version will fetch up to $18,000.

Doultons were involved with the beer and spirit trade from the beginning of the 19th century and they produced all manner of promotional items for these industries ranging from public house tiled or terracotta frontages and ceramic beer pump handles to ashtrays and spittoons for public bars.

This large Kingsware character jug, 'The McCallum', was made for D. & J. McCallum Whisky Distillers, circa 1930.

(Abridge)   **$2,320**

Grain painted pine blanket chest, New England, 18th century, the molded top overhangs a dovetailed case with a well and open till over two thumb-molded drawers on a molded bracket base, turned wooden pulls, all-over fanciful gray and blue graining, 43¼" wide.

(Skinner Inc)   **$27,000**

Roycroft oak bridal chest, East Aurora, New York, circa 1912, with extended serpentine sides with keyed tenons centering lift top with copper strapware, box incised with *Roycroft* across the front, 36½" wide.
(Skinner Inc)   **$6,750**

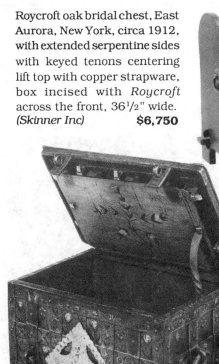

A 17th century decorated iron strong box of Armada type, the hinged top opening to reveal a complex locking device concealed by a similar painted panel cover, the front with dummy cartouche key plate with carrying handles to the sides, 74cm. wide.
(Christie's) **$5,250**

Fine painted and decorated poplar blanket chest, Western Pennsylvania or Ohio, circa 1820, with decoration of painted ochre ground with bold black designs, the top painted light ochre with central incised compass work pinwheels flanked by freehand designs with stipple and stripe border, 40$^{1}/_{2}$" wide.
(Skinner Inc)   **$27,000**

A rare and important carved painted oak and pine Hadley chest, Hampshire County, Massachusetts, 1670–1710, the molded rectangular top flanked by shaped cleats lifting above a deep compartment, the case with three carved panels, the center panel with carved heart, scrolls and initials *L.M.* flanked by two panels with stylized tulips and scrolls over two long drawers, 46" wide. This chest is one of the group so called Hadley chests which were made in the upper Connecticut Valley between 1670-1710.
(Christie's)   **$132,000**

A George III mahogany commode in the manner of Thomas Chippendale with eared molded serpentine top, fitted with two short and three long drawers mounted with ormolu rococo handles, the chamfered scrolled angles carved with acanthus and edged with rockwork, on bracket feet, 46" wide.

The gilt-bronze handles are a model favored by Chippendale and appear on the pair of commodes supplied circa 1770 to Daniel Lascelles at Goldsborough Hall. One of the drawers is fitted with an S-pattern lock, also favored by Chippendale.
(Christie's) **$56,760**

A William and Mary blue, black and red-painted chest with a rectangular top naively painted with a black speckled panel on a cream ground within a blue border above two short drawers decorated with wavy red lines on a cream ground above three long-fielded paneled doors each simulated as two drawers with conforming decoration, the drawers lined with pages from the Classics, 41" wide.
(Christie's) **$40,898**

A William and Mary marquetry chest of drawers with oyster walnut veneers, crossbanded and inlaid with oval panels, with birds and flowers and the top with floral spandrels incorporating some stained ivory, with later handles and bracket feet, 38" wide.
(Lawrence Fine Art) **$21,750**

A fine Chippendale mahogany serpentine chest of drawers, North Shore, Massachusetts, 1770–1790, with a serpentine molded top above a conforming case with four cockbeaded and graduated long drawers, on short cabriole legs with ball-and-claw feet, 40" wide.
(Christie's) **$82,500**

A Queen Anne maple high chest of drawers, New England, 1740-1760, in two sections, the upper case with molded swan's-neck pediment centering three ball and spire finials above three short thumb-molded drawers over three graduated long drawers, 80" high x 38³/₄" wide.
(Christie's)   **$26,900**

Painted two-part apothecary chest, brown paint, 68³/₄" high.
(Skinner Inc)   **$1,900**

Painted chest on frame, New Hampshire, circa 1830, the flaring cornice molding above a case of six graduated thumb-molded drawers, on cabriole legs with arris pad feet, all over salmon paint, 36" wide.
(Skinner Inc)   **$151,000**

A George I walnut bachelor's chest, with rounded rectangular top inlaid with feather-banding above two short and three graduated long drawers on bracket feet, 30" wide.
(Christie's)   **$30,294**

'The Butterfly Dancer', an unusual painted bronze and ivory figure cast and carved from a model by **Demêtre** Chiparus, 43cm. high.
(Phillips) **$33,300**

'Les Amis de Toujours', a bronze and ivory figure cast and carved from a model by Demêtre Chiparus, of a standing lady, flanked by two borzois, wearing a long dress with decorated bodice and jeweled belt and collar, 63cm. high.
(Christie's) **$22,440**

'Semiramis', cold-painted parcel-silvered gilt-bronze and ivory figure of a dancer, cast and carved from a model by Demêtre Chiparus, early 20th century. *(Christie's)* **$176,000**

As early as the 18th century the concept of the Christmas card existed in the rudimentary form of a 'Christmas piece', samples of writing and artistic prowess which children presented to their parents at the end of the year. From about 1820 these became a little more formalized and often had engraved borders.

In 1843, however, Sir Henry Cole, who had a large circle of friends, commissioned from John Calcott Horsley RA a card with the scene of a family drinking and the message 'A Merry Christmas and a Happy New Year to you' within an ivy frame. Hand colored and litho-printed in sepia tones, 1000 were produced and sold at 10c each. They were not to meet with immediate universal acclaim, and some people complained that they encouraged drunkenness!

It was, however, one of these cards sent by Cole to William Makepeace Thackeray which achieved the record price for such a card of $4,500.

The concept soon caught on, and Victorian cards began to be made in all shapes, depicting children, reindeer, robins, snow scenes, kittens, clowns, but, surprisingly, very rarely religious themes.

CIGARETTE CARDS

Just when the first cigarette card was issued and by whom remains shrouded in mystery. The giving away of advertizing cards by tradesmen to their customers dates from at least the 1860's, and it could well be that cigarettes were among the products thus promoted. There is also a theory that Robert Peacock Gloag may have used cigarette cards as early as the time of the Crimean War. It is generally agreed, however, that they originated in America, and the oldest card known to exist is in the Metropolitan Museum in New York. It was produced for Marquis of Lorne cigarettes in 1878 and features a portrait, presumably of the Marquis himself.

The reverse side of the earliest cards were usually blank or used as advertizing space. An apocryphal tale relates that all this changed due to one Edward Bok, a famous US journalist, who picked up a card on the street one day which bore a picture of a currently popular actress. The reverse was blank, and it occurred to Mr Bok, as a professional relayer of information, that this space could be usefully filled with interesting and informative text. Certainly this became the new style around the turn of the century, which has come to be regarded rather as the Golden Age of the cigarette card. It was also, later on, to save them from proscription in the Germany of Adolf Hitler, since Goebbels pointed out to the Fuehrer that, instead of being a source of distraction for the young, they could provide a useful instrument of propaganda.

Back in the early 1900's, however, cigarette cards became in a way the 'bullets' in the so-called Tobacco Wars of 1900–2 when James B Duke's American Tobacco Co, having cornered the US market, set its sights on Britain as well. Duke's American companies were already producing beautiful cards, and, having snapped up the British firm of Ogden's in Liverpool in 1901, he set about issuing vast quantities of Tabs and Guinea Gold cards. These were photographic cards of politicians, actresses and events of the day, and, perhaps because of the current vogue for photography, proved immensely popular.

Under serious threat, the British tobacco companies launched a counter-attack in November 1901, when WD & HO Wills and twelve other companies formed the Imperial Tobacco Company and in turn started issuing a vast array of cards. In the case of Duke at least, the cards were often of such high quality that they cost more to produce than the cigarettes, and the war was proving extremely costly for both sides. In 1902 therefore, an armistice was called, and the world market was carved up between the two giants.

British cards had first appeared in

the 1880's and by the end of the Tobacco Wars sets depicting just about everything under the sun were being issued by all major brands. This continued until the outbreak of war in 1914 and the resultant paper shortages. After the war, however, the custom reasserted itself, and collecting the cards became recognized and popular hobby for young and old alike, with the production of special albums, relevant books and magazines, and the formation of collecting clubs.

Taddy was a British tobacco company which closed down in 1921. Their 'Clown' set is variously dated as far apart as 1900 and 1921 and was, in fact, a pilot set which never saw the inside of a cigarette packet. This makes surviving sets extremely rare, although there are believed to be about 20 in existence. The set featured achieved the world record price of $30,000 when auctioned by Phillips.

A Ronson 'Touch-Tip' petrol-fuelled table-lighter, shaped as a bar with a negro barman, partially chromium-plated and enamel painted, circa 1935, 15.3cm. long.
(Christie's) **$836**

Dunhill set of lighter and cigarette case, enameled, 1929.
(Habsburg, Feldman) **$6,800**

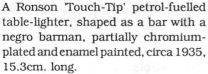

A nine carat gold compact by Dunhill, opening to reveal an ivory aide memoire, cigarette lighter, time piece and pencil.
(Spencers) **$2,450**

The legendary Clarice Cliff was born in 1899 in, perhaps inevitably, Staffordshire, where she started work at 13 in one of the local potteries, painting freehand onto pottery.

Her formal training comprised a year, when she was 16, at the Burslem School of Art, and a later year at the Royal College of Art, where she studied sculpture. At 17, she had gone to work at the firm of A.J. Wilkinson, and she remained with them, and their subsidiary the Newport Pottery, for the next two decades, ending up as Art Director and marrying the boss, Colley Shorter, when she was forty.

During the 1920's she painted Tibetan ware, large jars painted with floral designs in bright colors and gold, and she also transferred on to pottery designs by such distinguished artists as Paul Nash and Laura Knight.

In 1928, however, she painted 60 dozen pieces of her own design to test the market at a trade fair. These proved so popular that by 1929 the whole factory was switched to producing her Bizarre ware.

Cliff's style is characterized by combinations of bright colors, such as orange, blue, purple and green, or black, yellow orange and red. Her pieces are often angular in shape and strongly Art Deco in style. Major ranges, besides Bizarre, include Crocus, Fantasque, Biarritz and Farmhouse.

At the beginning of the Second World War, the factory was commandeered by the Ministry of Supply, and Wilkinson produced only a few white pieces. After the war, the market had changed and production was not resumed.

Clarice Cliff's work was largely ignored then, until it was rediscovered in the 1960s. It was featured at major exhibitions in Brighton in 1972 and the London Gallery in 1973, after which it once again caught the public imagination. Enthusiasm for Clarice Cliff has continued right up to the present time and her best works regularly fetch four figures at auction. One of her most expensive pieces is a plaque depicting one of Diaghilev's costume designs for the Ballet Russe, which sold for $14,000 at Christie's.

A superb wall plaque by Clarice Cliff, painted with a scene inspired by Diaghilev's costume design for the Ballet Russe.
(Christie's) **$14,000**

Clarice Cliff appliqué Palermo pattern wall plate, 13" diameter.
(G.E. Sworder & Sons) **$5,250**

A Clarice Cliff Bizarre circular charger, painted with a central house in yellow with a vivid orange roof, 42cm. diameter.
(Phillips)   **$2,580**

Clarice Cliff Bizarre Fantasque vase in the Farmhouse pattern.
(Michael Newman)   **$2,640**

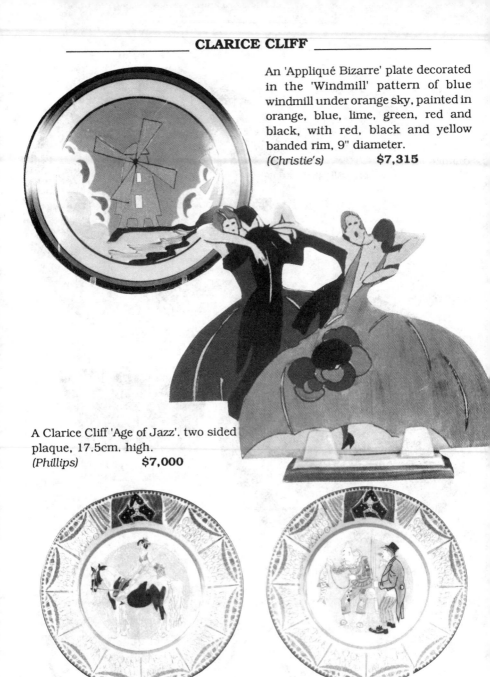

An 'Appliqué Bizarre' plate decorated in the 'Windmill' pattern of blue windmill under orange sky, painted in orange, blue, lime, green, red and black, with red, black and yellow banded rim, 9" diameter.
(Christie's) **$7,315**

A Clarice Cliff 'Age of Jazz'. two sided plaque, 17.5cm. high.
(Phillips) **$7,000**

Two Bizarre circus plates designed for Clarice Cliff by Dame Laura Knight, one depicting two clowns fishing, the other a show girl on a skewbald pony, both with audience and clown printed borders.
(G.E. Sworder & Sons) **$2,275**

Burr walnut, ivrene, enamel, silver-plated, agate and mother-of-pearl mantel clock, designed by Josef Urban for the Paul Hofner Restaurant, Vienna 1906, 22⅝" high.
(Christie's) **$44,000**

Guilloché enamel silver-gilt table-clock, marked *Fabergé*, workmaster Michael Perchin, St. Petersburg, circa 1880, 4⅝" wide.
(Christie's) **$33,000**

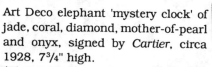

Art Deco elephant 'mystery clock' of jade, coral, diamond, mother-of-pearl and onyx, signed by *Cartier*, circa 1928, 7¾" high.
(Christie's) **$748,000**

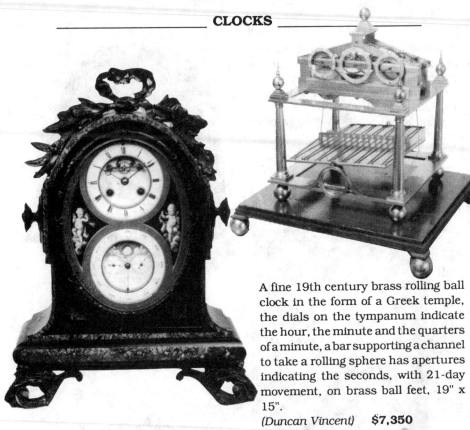

A fine 19th century brass rolling ball clock in the form of a Greek temple, the dials on the tympanum indicate the hour, the minute and the quarters of a minute, a bar supporting a channel to take a rolling sphere has apertures indicating the seconds, with 21-day movement, on brass ball feet, 19" x 15".
(Duncan Vincent)   **$7,350**

A rare and unusual English electrical mantel timepiece by The Reason Manufacturing Company Ltd., Brighton, the circular glass chapter-ring with roman numerals, visible skeletonized movement and bi-metallic balance wheel below.
(Christie's)   **$11,250**

A French ormolu mantel clock in the form of the front facade of Notre Dame Cathedral, with pierced ormolu circular dial with quarter striking, going barrel movement, on stepped base, 22" high.
(Christie's)   **$5,313**

An unusual 19th century French gilt bronze and porcelain mounted carriage clock, bearing the Drocourt trademark on the back-plate, in an ornate rococo case, 23cm. high.
(Phillips) **$7,098**

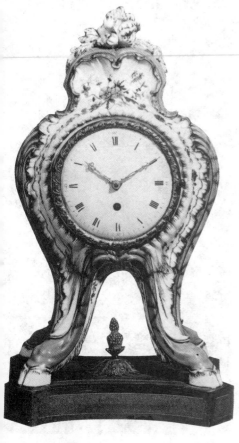

A Louis XV petit vert mantel-clock on four feet, on Louis XVI ormolu base, 1761.
(Christie's) **$71,600**

French novelty clock, late 19th century in brass with silvered parts, in the form of a ship's stern, eight-day striking movement. Helmsman sways to steer as pendulum swings.
(B. Loomes) **$3,060**

A bronze and ormolu mantel clock in the form of Big Ben, each of the four sides with silvered circular dials, the going barrel movement with platform lever escapement striking on bell, on stepped black marble base and bracket feet, 29½" high.

The clock for the new Palace of Westminster, popularly known as Big Ben, was made by Edward John Dent and installed in 1859. The architects were Sir Charles Barry and A.W.N. Pugin.

(Christie's) **$3,542**

Rare Federal gilt gesso painted banjo timepiece, the eight-day weight driven movement stamped *A Willard Boston 1808*, with eglomise rectangular tablet depicting 'Hercules assisting Atlas in supporting the globe', 45" high.
(Skinner Inc) **$210,000**

A French gilt and patinated metal mantel clock in the form of the Eiffel Tower with circular yellow dial, the backplate stamped *R & C* for Ricard & Co., in a drum-shaped case surmounted by an angel blowing a horn, 25" high.

The Eiffel Tower, designed by Gustav Eiffel, was completed in 1889.
(Christie's) **$3,365**

A Scottish Arts and Crafts ebony and silver timepiece with rectangular case in dark wood with flat metal top, the circular face having black enameled Art Nouveau numerals supported on four legs of triangular section with pad feet, 23.80cm. high, signed *J.H. McNair.*

J. Herbert McNair was the brother-in-law of Charles Rennie Macintosh and was himself a talented designer and artist. He was married to Florence MacDonald, the sister of Margaret MacDonald, the group being known collectively as the 'Glasgow-four'.
(Phillips) **$12,800**

A boned corset of brown canvas lined with white linen, with tabbed waist, circa 1770.
(Christie's) $4,620

An open robe of cotton printed with exotic flowering branches in rose madder, brown and blue, circa 1770.
(Christie's) $8,118

A late 17th century lady's waistcoat of undyed linen embroidered with colored silks in chain stitch and designed with flower sprays and birds, having a flat quilted ground and yellow silk binding with front button fastening and laced shoulder ties, circa 1680's.
(Phillips) $6,358

A dress of blue cotton printed with brown leaves, the oversleeves, neckline and trained hem printed *a disposition* with a patterned border, with detachable long sleeves, circa 1800.
(Christie's) **$6,314**

A rare baby's closed robe of salmon pink silk satin woven with white flowers, with green selvage and bound at the neck, shoulders, cuffs and hem with pink silk braid, early 18th century.
(Christie's) **$5,051**

A fine suite of early 18th century vestments, cape, chasuble, maniples, chalice veil, stole and associated items.
(Phillips Manchester) **$7,175**

A gentleman's linen nightcap embroidered in red and green silk, silver-gilt thread and sequins with coiling foliage, the upturned brim trimmed with gold lace and paillettes, English, circa 1600.
(Christie's) **$34,650**

Set of highland dress given by Edward VIII to his ghillie at Balmoral in 1936.
(Phillips) **$4,550**

Two 1920's silk dresses by Mariano Fortuny with Delphos pleating and stenciled belt.
(Phillips) **$5,250 each**

Costume and textiles have long had a devoted, if select, following in the antiques world. It's not often that they really hit the headlines with record prices. At Christie's South Kensington, however, a fine gentleman's doublet dating from circa 1625 came under the hammer. Made of ivory silk, woven in pink, yellow, blue mauve and green with sprays of lilies, tulips and other flowers, it was pinked with small square holes, and the sleeves and bodice were slashed and edged with pink braid. The buttons were of ball shaped braid, and it was lined with raspberry silk, the front with a 'belly' stuffed with buckram and covered in pink satin, had lacing holes at the waist. Thought to be Italian or possibly French, it had, unsurprisingly after all this time, a slight tear and a few buttons missing. Nevertheless, it sold for $109,000, an auction record for an item of costume.

A 1920's dress of brown chiffon embroidered in chain stitch with green and crimson silks, having chiffon ties to either side, bearing the maker's label *Gabrielle Chanel, Paris*. *(Phillips)* **$5,642**

Dress of pale blue and gold striped satin and gold ribbed silk, labeled *Josephine G. Egan*, circa 1876. *(Christie's)* **$4,372**

A mantua of blue silk damask woven with large sprays of exotic flowers and leaves, the cuff weighted, the bodice lined with blue silk and the train carefully pieced to be looped up in the fashion of the time, circa 1730-1740. *(Christie's)* **$9,020**

One of the most valuable comics in the world is Action Comic No 1, in which Superman made his debut in 1938. The creation of Joe Schuster and Jerry Seigal, he had already been rejected by most of the major American publishing houses. A copy of this will now fetch in the region of $40,000.

That other legendary character, Batman, has also celebrated his 50th anniversary, and the recent film and flurry of publicity had made him a major contender for the slot of most valuable comic hero. He first appeared in Detective Comics No 27 in May 1939 and a copy sold recently for $50,000. His sidekick, Robin, made his first appearance in No 38 of the same publication, and copies of that issue change hands at around $16,500. In 1940, Batman and Robin were given their own 'Batman' comic and the No 1 issue will sell for around $25,000.

The first edition of the Beano appeared from the D.C. Thomson publishing group on July 30 1938, with Big Eggo the Ostrich on the front cover and the lure of a free Whoopee mask inside. If you can come up with a copy in good condition and with the mask, you could be richer by $3,500. Without the mask, a first issue will still be worth a few hundred however, depending on condition.

Hans Coper has been described as 'quite simply the most important studio potter of the 20th century'.

Born in 1920, Coper was a German, who after internment and service in the Pioneer Corps joined another refugee, Lucie Rie, in her mews 'button factory' in London. She swiftly recognized his genius, and allowed him scope to develop his own designs.

Using clay to make pottery and sculpture, his works prove that the two mediums could be successfully combined. His breakthrough came in 1962 when he was commissioned by Basil Spence to make two sets of candlesticks for the new Coventry Cathedral. Hans Coper died in 1981.

An early bottle form by Hans Coper, white textured to reveal the brown body, the base and rim black, impressed *HC* seal, circa 1956, 13¼" high.

(Bonhams)   **$24,500**

A rare early stoneware shallow dish by Hans Coper, covered in matt manganese glaze, the interior with carved decoration through to a pitted translucent white glaze of abstract design with stylized fish, impressed *HC* seal, circa 1950, 37cm. diameter.

(Christie's) **$37,202**

A tall stoneware composite bottle vase by Hans Coper, the tapering cup-shaped rim above vertically set disk-shaped body on cylindrical foot, one side of body and the foot incised with spiral, the manganese brown body covered in a buff slip, burnished and textured in areas to reveal matt-manganese body, impressed *HC* seal, circa 1965, 25.8cm. high.
(Christie's) **$24,024**

A bottle vase by Hans Coper, the oviform body with short cylindrical neck, circa 1958, 65,2cm. high.
(Christie's) **$23,760**

A rare large black-glazed stoneware waisted cup form by Hans Coper, on cylindrical stem, with incised spiral decoration, covered in a brownish-black burnish and textured glaze, impressed *HC* seal, circa 1965, 19.4cm. high.
(Christie's) **$14,850**

Gustav Stickley dinner gong, circa 1904, round hammered copper striking plate suspended from dark oak framework by copper straps, the whole raised on five angular feet, signed with red decal, 37" high.
(Skinner Inc) **$1,400**

A rare copper slave badge by John Joseph Lafar, Charleston, South Carolina, 1823. Diamond-shaped, with canted corners and pierced with a hole for suspension, struck with five rectangular dies inscribed *Charleston, No., Servant, 1823* and *I.I. Lafar*, and punched with number 1419, marked, 2³/₄" high.

Slave badges were issued to slaves who worked for wages paid by outside employers. They served to distinguish these part-time workers from runaway slaves. While hired-out slaves were common in the South, the wearing of badges was only required in Charleston, Savannah, New Orleans, Mobile, and Norfolk. In Charleston, the City Treasurer's Office distributed badges and kept records of the hiring agreements between owners and employers.
(Christie's) **$3,300**

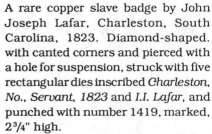

A Georgian brass dishcross, English, 18th century, of typical form, each of the feet cast as a scallop shell sliding to a gadrooned center with drop, 14¹/₄" wide, extended.
(Christie's) **$2,750**

A brass cat, the ring-turned supports and legs around a central urn, early 19th century, 15½" high. Cats were made of metal or wood and were used for keeping food or dishes warm beside a fire.
(Christie's) **$463**

A rare copper tea kettle marked *Hunneman*, Boston, circa 1810, globular, with flat arched swing handle, slightly domed lid with brass urn finial and curved spout, 11" wide.
(Christie's) **$2,420**

A good 17th century brass candlestick with heavy ribbed column, central reeded drip pan, on broad molded circular foot, 7.75" high.
(Phillips) **$6,080**

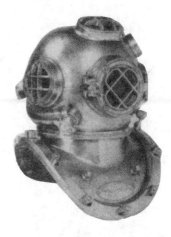

A Nara period copper gilt square plaque decorated in repoussé with Amida, 7th/8th century, 11.3cm. x 11.3cm. *(Christie's)* **$13,992**

A copper and brass diver's helmet, date 8.29.41, with clamp screws, valves, plate glass windows and guards, 20" high. *(Christie's)* **$2,032**

A massive brass and copper one hundred and fifty gallon cheese vat of cylindrical shape with molded brass toprail, the sides with carrying-handles and three taps, inscribed *Pond & Son Limited*, Blandford, 51½" diameter.
(Christie's) **$4,089**

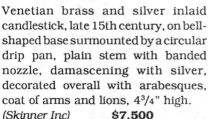

Venetian brass and silver inlaid candlestick, late 15th century, on bell-shaped base surmounted by a circular drip pan, plain stem with banded nozzle, damascening with silver, decorated overall with arabesques, coat of arms and lions, 4¾" high.
(Skinner Inc)   **$7,500**

Set of three late Victorian brass churns, tradesmens or shop fittings, each with engraved inscriptions, *Special Cows Milk kept for Infants and Invalids,* etc., largest 20" high.
(Russell Baldwin & Bright)
          $5,250

An 18th century gilt brass curfew of typical form, repoussé decorated with portraits, animal and figure subjects and pseudo coats of arms, surmounted by a carrying handle, 17" wide.
(Christie's)   **$1,165**

A fine George II silver-gilt cow creamer with textured body, the oval, hinged cover chased with flowers and applied with a fly, by John Schuppe, 1756, 5ozs. *(Phillips)* **$24,310**

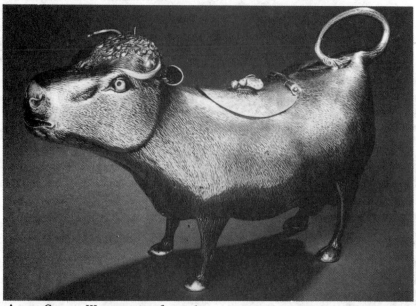

A rare George III cream jug formed as a cow, with realistically chased hide and hinged flap surmounted by a fly, by Peter and William Bateman, 1814, 7³/4" long, 12 ozs. *(Christie's)* **$21,252**

A Staffordshire creamware tortoiseshell-glazed candlestick of Whieldon-type, the cylindrical nozzle supported on a slender knopped stem applied with bearded masks, rosettes and swags, circa 1750, 21.5cm. high.
(Christie's) **$21,175**

A Creamware model of an owl of Whieldon type, naturally modeled with crisply molded plumage and incised eyes, perched on a wedge-shaped rockwork base, covered in streaked manganese-brown glazes, circa 1750, 22.5cm. high.
(Christie's) **$105,875**

A late 18th century creamware 'boxing mug'.
(Spencers) **$960**

A rare Creamware toby jug, late 18th century, the seated toper shown clutching a frothing mug of ale to his ample ·belly, wearing a frock coat, striped in manganese, green and ochre, and a tricorn hat, 10¼" high.
(Sothebys) **$28,875**

A Staffordshire Creamware figure of a leveret of Whieldon type with brown slip eyes, crouching on an oval mound base and streaked all over in brown, the base splashed in green and gray, circa 1760, 8.5cm. long.
(Christie's) **$11,011**

A German papier-mâché, parcel-gilt and black-painted cup and saucer decorated with two romantic vistas, the saucer inscribed *Augustine*, late 18th century, probably Stobwasser, the saucer 5¼" wide.
(Christie's) **$1,540**

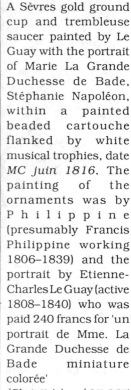

A Sèvres gold ground cup and trembleuse saucer painted by Le Guay with the portrait of Marie La Grande Duchesse de Bade, Stéphanie Napoléon, within a painted beaded cartouche flanked by white musical trophies, date *MC juin 1816*. The painting of the ornaments was by P h i l i p p i n e (presumably Francis Philippine working 1806–1839) and the portrait by Etienne-Charles Le Guay (active 1808–1840) who was paid 240 francs for 'un portrait de Mme. La Grande Duchesse de Bade miniature colorée'
(Christie's) **$27,885**

Meissen armorial Chinoiserie teabowl and saucer from the Clemens August service, painted by C.F. Herold, circa 1735.
(Christie's) **$45,000**

A Derby coffee-can and saucer, the former painted by George Complin with two goldfinches strutting beside and perched upon a cluster of ripened fruit within a gilt rectangular cartouche, the white ground with bands of blue-centered pink spots divided by gilt stars, impressed letters G on can and H on saucer, puce Crown, crossed batons and D marks and numbers 259 on cup, Wm. Duesbury & Co., circa 1790.
(Christie's) **$23,100**

A Vincennes bleu lapis coffee-cup and saucer with loop handle, each side of the cup and the center of the saucer painted with two birds within shaped gilt trellis and trailing flower cartouches, blue interlaced L marks enclosing date letter A for 1753.
(Christie's) **$3,414**

One of a pair of Meissen yellow-ground soup cups and two-handled deep saucers, circa 1735, the saucers 7" wide.
(Christie's) **$75,000**

A Vincennes bleu celeste teacup and saucer with gilt entwined branch handle, painted with trailing flowers from cornucopia-shaped bleu celeste borders edged with gilt flowers beneath gilt dentil rims, blue interlaced L marks enclosing date letter B for 1754.
(Christie's) **$5,122**

One of a pair of Meissen Chinoiserie two-handled beakers and saucers, circa 1728.
(Christie's) **$55,000**

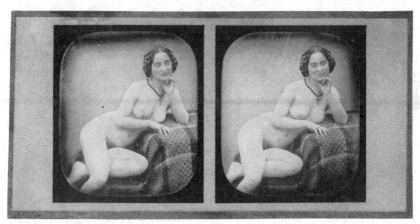

'Reclining female nude', 1850s, stereoscopic daguerreotype, hand-tinted, painted black glass and gilt paper surround.
(Christie's) **$8,662**

Anon, group portrait of girls, 1850s-60s, half-plate daguerreotype, lightly hand-tinted, gilt surround, in thermo-plastic union case with geometric and scroll design.
(Christie's) **$1,540**

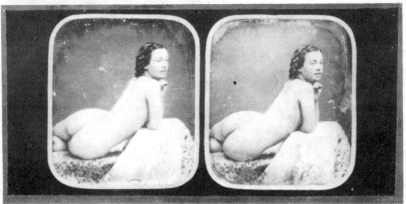

Anon, nude, 1850s, stereoscopic daguerreotype, lightly hand-tinted and with gilt highlights, paper-taped with label numbered *No. 14/209* on verso.
(Christie's) **$8,140**

Stereoscopic daguerreotype 'Two young men with a woman plucking game', 1850s, hand-tinted, printed paper label on reverse *Mr T.R. Williams, 35 West Sq., St George's Rd., Lambeth*, passe-partout. *(Christie's)* **$7,172**

'Three hunters', stereoscopic daguerreotype, hand-tinted, gilt-painted surround, printed paper label *City Stereoscopic Depot...87 Gracechurch Street...*, on reverse, 1850s. *(Christie's S. Ken)* **$2,937**

A rare half-plate cased daguerreotype of the Maharaja of Travancore, showing him seated next to a table on which rests a gold and precious jewel testing kit, the Maharaja is dressed in traditional attire, his head-dress, sash and jewel being tinted. *(Phillips)* **$4,725**

The brothers Auguste(1853-1909)and Antonin (1864–1930) Daum were glass craftsmen, working in a similar style and technique to Gallé. Generally, their designs tend to be less fine and extravagant, with more traditional motifs, such as cameo-cut floral decoration. Their work is often characterized by mottled or streaky backgrounds. They were members of the Ecole de Nancy, a group of French Art Nouveau artists who drew inspiration from Gallé's style and technique, and they founded a factory at Nancy producing Gallé-inspired works and concentrating on enameling. Later they worked in pâte de verre, and in the 1930s they also produced a number of pieces in etched, geometrical glass.

The factory is still flourishing today under the name of Cristallerie Daum. Its mark is Daum Nancy with the Croix de Lorraine motif.

A Daum hanging shade, the shallow bowl shape terminating in a flattened knop, the milky and frosted acid-treated ground overlaid with acid-cut decoration of coral-colored berries and leaves, with triple rope suspension and ceiling cup, engraved *Daum Nancy*, incorporating the Cross of Lorraine.
(*Christie's*)　　$3,718

A large Daum vase, the bun foot and bulbous body spreading to a flaring cylindrical rim, the mottled green, yellow, pale blue and frosted glass ground overlaid with clear glass. With curved and polychrome enamel painted decoration of trumpet flowers, highlighted with gilding, gilt signature *Daum Nancy* incorporating the Cross of Lorraine, 58.9cm. high.
(*Christie's*)　　　　**$4,275**

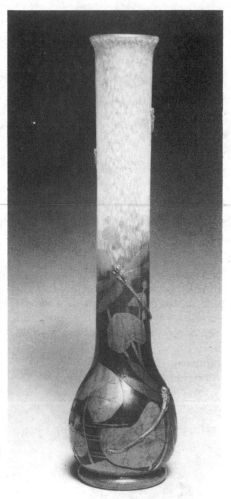

A Daum carved, acid-etched and applied cameo vase of flared and shouldered cylindrical form with everted neck, on bun foot, the mottled clear ground overlaid in shades of green and yellow with marsh marigolds and lilies, and with two applied dragonflies, engraved signature Daum Nancy with the Cross of Lorraine, 20.1cm. high.
(Christie's)   **$37,500**

'Grand Vase Libellules', a Daum carved, acid-etched and applied cameo vase, the bulbous base on bun foot, and rising to a tall cylindrical neck with everted rim, the mottle clear, blue and purple ground overlaid in shades of green and yellow with marsh marigolds and lilies, with four applied and carved dragonflies, 60.2cm. high.
(Christie's)   **$98,615**

A Daum acid-textured and carved double overlay vase of flaring shouldered form with two small handles at the neck, the blue and yellow mottled glass overlaid in white and black with birds in a winter landscape, 24.5cm. high.
(Christie's)   **$24,167**

A Daum cameo glass lampshade of domed form with protruding centre, the body streaked with yellow and orange, overlaid with brown glass acid-etched with Chinese lanterns and foliage, 19.5cm. diameter, signed *Daum Nancy*.
(Phillips)   **$4,401**

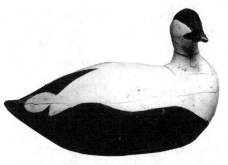

Eider decoy, Monhegan Island, Maine, late 19th century, hollow carved with inletted head, open braced beak with mussel, incised eye, original paint, 11" high, 21" long.
(Skinner Inc)   **$19,000**

A pair of painted wooden American Merganser decoys, a hen and drake, by L.T. Holmes, circa 1855/65.
(Christie's)   **$93,500**

A carved and painted fish decoy, possibly Harold Rickert (1923-present), Lake St. Clair, Michigan, modeled as a rainbow trout in red, green, blue and black with yellow speckles, seven metal fins, and applied eyes, 8" long.
(Christie's)   **$440**

When the first ships of the Dutch East India Company arrived back from the east bringing with them dazzling examples of Chinese porcelain, the drab European world of pewter and stoneware was rocked to its foundations. The West could produce nothing to compete with the brilliance of the colors or the hardness and translucence of these Chinese imports, but the industry nevertheless set itself to fight back. The result was delft.

Delft is essentially tin-glazed earthenware known elsewhere in Europe as faience, from the town of Faenza in Italy where it had its origins. It appeared first in the Netherlands in the early 17th century when attempts were made in Delft and Harlem to produce a finer body. It was hand painted by craftsmen known as plateelschilder, using brushes called trekker. The high temperature kilns in which it was baked allowed a very restricted palette but skilful painters could nevertheless achieve amazing results in terms of tones and shading. Delft was predominantly blue and white in imitation of Chinese porcelain, though some polychrome was made in the first half of the 17th century when techniques were improving, and its production was never abandoned.

Dutch delft copied the patterns and shapes of the Oriental imports, though, later, European motifs mixed happily with these. Thus European Coats of Arms, Royal portraits, etc would coexist with Wan-li type borders. Delft was used for all manner of items, from baluster vases to apothecary jars, and, very importantly, tiles, which were exported throughout Europe and became more and more popular as the supply of Hispano-Moresque tiles dried up.

Delft faience entered it finest period from the mid 17th century until 1730, when taste began to swing towards the lure of enamel colors and porcelain.

A strong tradition existed also in England. English delft was never as sophisticated as its Dutch counterpart, however, although many Dutch potters worked in England.

A London delft dated large candlestick of tapering cylindrical form with wide fluted drip-pan, on a fluted conical foot painted in underglaze blue with the initials *I/I.T* and the date *1653* with three flowerheads within a crowned oval escutcheon, 1653, 25.5cm. high.
(Christie's) **$258,720**

A London Delft blue-dash royal portrait charger painted with a full-length portrait of Charles II in his coronation robes, holding his orb and scepter and flanked by the initials CR and two stark trees, a lion at his feet, circa 1685, 32.5cm. diameter.
(Christie's)   **$29,040**

A Liverpool delft dated cylindrical ink-pot, the sides painted in a Fazackerly palette with trailing flowering branches and the initials *RW* with the date *1756* below, the sloping shoulder pierced with three holes beneath a short flared cylindrical neck, 1756, 7cm. diameter.
(Christie's)   **$27,720**

A London delft inscribed Royal portrait wine-bottle of small size with loop handle, painted in underglaze blue with a three-quarter length portrait of Charles II in armor, flanking an ochre and blue crown above, circa 1660, 16cm. high.
(Christie's)   **$258,720**

A rare English delftware circular butter dish and cover, the exterior with a scene depicting a man running in a wooded landscape interspaced by houses, the cover with blue sponged tree decoration, the glazed interior with a conical spur, 5" high, circa 1740 (probably Bristol).
(Bonhams) **$7,525**

A London Delft heart-shaped pill-tile painted with a man and his dog mounting some steps towards a building on the right with a sponged tree above in an extensive wooded landscape, with a gabled house beside a gate and a further building to the left, birds in flight in a cloudy sky above, circa 1750, 34.5cm. high.
(Christie's) **$24,024**

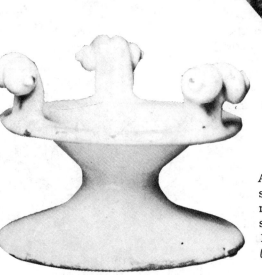

A London delft white salt, the shallow circular bowl with flat rim and three scroll lugs, on a spreading circular foot, circa 1675, 12cm. diameter.
(Christie's) **$12,012**

An important Dutch Delft plate painted in blue by Frederick van Frytom, late 17th century. *(Phillips)*
$10,675

An impressive English Delft wassail bowl and cover, on a domed circular foot, 51cm. high.
(Phillips) **$18,150**

A London Delft dated salt modeled as a youth with pale-brown and manganese hair, wearing a striped blue coat, striped blue socks and manganese shoes, holding a foliate tray with a central depression inscribed with the date 1676 with a flourish below, the corners with insects and spiders, seated on a fluted D-shaped stool, the underside with a blue dragonfly, 1676, 19.5cm. high.
(Christie's) **$295,680**

A London Delft blue and white dated barber's bowl of conventional form, the center painted with a comb, scissors, shaving brush and other implements of the trade, the flared border with a circular depression and inscribed *Quarter Day Pray Gentlemen Pay 1716*, 26cm. diameter.
(Christie's) **$42,592**

A Delft blue and white oval royal portrait plaque of Queen Anne, the crowned monarch depicted quarter length and wearing a necklace of pearls, within a border of scrolling foliage and flowers (some minute glaze flaking to rim), blue E mark to the reverse, probably London, circa 1705, 23cm. high.
(Christie's) **$17,710**

The most expensive piece of furniture ever sold is the magnificent Nicholas Brown desk and bookcase. It belonged to Nicholas Brown, the eldest of four brothers who inherited from their father and uncle the most powerful commercial company in Rhode Island.

They continued to expand and develop the firm's interests in their lifetime, while making equally important cultural, intellectual and financial contributions to their town, colony and state.

It is believed that all four brothers owned a blockfront and shell carved desk, of which three are known to survive, (the fourth having possibly perished in a fire at Moses Brown's farmhouse in the 19th century) while a number of other related examples exist elsewhere.

The Nicholas Brown desk is attributed to John Goddard, who worked out of Newport, R.I. between 1760–70. It is in two sections, the upper with a small molded pediment surmounted by three fluted urn flame finials on fluted plinths. The pediment is divided into two blocked panels, above three blocked cupboard doors, each carved with a shell, opening to the interior with moveable shelves and vertical partitions, the upper case flanked by stop-fluted quarter columns and the lower case with a slant lid blocked and carved with three shells. This encloses a fitted interior centring a blocked and shell-carved prospect door flanked by scalloped valance drawers above pigeon-holes with scalloped dividers over blocked drawers, flanked by banks of blocked and shell-carved short drawers.

The desk was documented in the inventory of Nicholas Brown's personal estate, made shortly after his death in

1791, where it is described as 'a bookcase with books' and valued very highly at £95. This is more than seven times higher than the value of any other furniture listed and higher in value than Brown's entire collection of silver, which shows how highly regarded it was as a piece even at that time. It has passed in unbroken descent through the family to the present Nicholas Brown. It was sold by Christie's, New York for a world record $12,100,000.

DESKS

A 19th century rosewood bonheur du jour with pierced brass gallery.
(Spencers)   **$56,430**

A rare Queen Anne japanned kneehole bureau, probably Boston area, 1730-1750, with a central recessed bank of five graduated drawers, the surface areas japanned with exotic landscape on red and black tortoise shell ground, 34 1/4" wide.
(Christie's N. York)
$264,000

Wells Fargo walnut desk with burr walnut panels, raised gallery back, two arched panel, folding doors, dummy and other letter box inscribed *Manufactured by The Wooton Desk Co, Indianapolis Ind.* and patent number, revealing maple lined interior with incised slope, fall front, pigeon holes and numerous drawers, 40" wide.

(Prudential Fine Art)   **$10,561**

A George III mahogany pedestal partners' desk, the lift-off top with three frieze drawers on each long side, the top 69" x 36³/₄".
(Tennants)   **$26,350**

A William IV burr-yew Davenport with three-quarter spindle gallery and green leather-lined sloping flap enclosing two drawers, the sliding top fitted with a pen drawer to the side above a slide and three graduated drawers, on gadrooned bun-feet, 20½" wide.

(Christie's) **$11,228**

A fine early Victorian carved rosewood davenport, circa 1850, the desk top with a carved gallery and a hinged writing slope enclosing a well pulling forward to provide kneehole space, the frieze and sides applied all round with leafy strapwork and the front with twin caryatid supports of naked children, a door to one side enclosing four small and two long drawers veneered in satinwood, on oblong leaf-carved cushion feet, 21" wide.

(Sothebys) **$18,287**

A fine and rare classical mahogany and bird's-eye maple secretaire a abattant, Philadelphia, 1820-1830, the tapering rectangular plinth above a frieze with one long drawer flanked by applied ormolu figures over burlwood columns flanking a fielded panel drop-front opening to a fitted interior with bird's-eye maple veneer centering an arch flanked by applied colonettes, pigeonholes, and short drawers, 61" high.

(Christie's) **$46,200**

Rare Charles Rohlfs carved drop front desk with swivel base, Buffalo, New York, 1900, the Gothic style carved finials on peaked form with carved and shaped sides, drop front and scrolled lid support over panel with three pierced stylized motifs housing four drawers on one side and cabinet door on the other, 50½" high.

(Skinner Inc) **$12,000**

A 19th century French bronze model of the setter called 'Cora', cast from a model by Isidore Bonheur, on naturalistic base, signed *I. Bonheur* and stamped *Peyrol*, 32cm. x 74cm.
(Christie's) **$6,376**

A 19th century ivory stirrup cup, carved in the form of a dog's head with inset glass eyes, engraved with owner's name *T. Best*, 4¼" high.
(Christie's S. Ken) **$1,108**

A contemporary gilt-lined cast and chased stirrup cup modeled as the head of a bulldog wearing a studded collar, 4¼", 22.75oz.
(Christie's) **$1,925**

A Continental cold painted earthenware figure of a seated pug, with glass eyes, 15" high.
(Spencers) **$2,500**

A 19th century French bronze inkwell amusingly modeled as a hound lapping at a dish, his forepaws resting on the rim, the underside inscribed Maison Alph. Giroux, Paris, 10¼" wide.
(Christie's) **$1,828**

A short plush covered nodding Boston terrier, with pull growl and lower jaw movement, on wheels, 22" long, circa 1910, French.
(Christie's) **$557**

A Coalbrookdale cast-iron figure of a begging dog standing on his hind legs holding a riding crop in his mouth, on a circular plinth with a leaf-molded tray-base and scrolling feet, the underside of the tray with Registry mark for 1852, 23½" high.
(Christie's) **$3,742**

A papier-mâché model of Nipper with electrically operated wagging tail, 17" high, in EMI wooden dispatch case. *(Christie's)* **$682**

A good mid-19th century bronze group of a bloodhound studying the slow traverse of a tortoise, cast from a model by Henri-Alfred-Marie Jacquemart, the dog shown seated with its head bowed, on an oval base signed *A. Jaquemart*, 7 1/8" wide. *(Christie's)* **$2,106**

Arita model of a seated dog, late 17th century, 15 3/4" high. *(Christie's)* **$63,008**

Dolls are probably among the earliest playthings known to man, and carved and painted wooden figures are seen in the arms of children in the very early prints and paintings. It is worth noting however that it was not until the late 19th century that the practice began of giving pretty, well-dressed dolls to little girls. Up to then, they had to make do with rougher examples made of wood or rags, while those of finer construction were owned by rich society ladies who had them dressed in silks and satins in the fashion of the day.

This fine doll from the reign of Charles II and dated circa 1680 is probably one such, and she is the earliest known example by an unknown English doll-maker, probably working in London.

While his name is unknown, the maker's style is sufficiently characteristic to be readily recognizable, and a small number of other dolls also apparently by him still exist. In particular, the construction is thought to be unique to him, with a join between the head and neck concealing a hole through which a wire would have been threaded to make the head swivel from side to side. She has an original white horsehair wig in the color and style of the 1680's. Green was known to have been fashionable then, and her patterned silk bodice is of this color. In addition, she has a pink and cream striped overskirt and a yellow silk taffeta petticoat, the whole lavishly decorated with silver gilt braid. Braid at the ankles suggests the remains of shoe decoration, though the feet are missing. Interestingly, while her body is painted cream, the legs below the knee are painted black.

A very rare carved and painted Charles II wood doll, with bright pink rouged cheeks, the brown eyes with white dots either side of each pupil, vertical upper lashes and a single brush stroke for each eyebrow, 13" high, circa 1680. *(Christie's)* **$125,125**

The doll was formerly in one of the largest private collections in England, owned by Alice K. Early, in the 1930s and 40s, and is one of two remaining after the collection was auctioned by Christie's in 1971. The other is an early 18th century oriental carved and painted male wood figure with European features and dressed in European clothes. Mrs. Early referred to these two dolls as The Courtier and his Lady.

A bisque-headed bébé by Emile Jumeau, circa 1880, 16½" high.
(Christie's)   **$7,772**

Snow White and the Seven Dwarfs, Snow White 17" high, the dwarfs 9½" high.
(Christie's)   **$5,245**

A rare bisque headed bébé, with closed mouth, fixed blue eyes, pierced ears, cork pate and painted wooden body, 16" high, marked *1 by Bru*.
(Christie's)   **$15,801**

An English William and Mary wood doll, circa 1690, 14½" high.
(Sotheby's)   **$112,728**

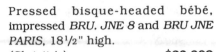

Pressed bisque-headed bébé, impressed *BRU. JNE 8* and *BRU JNE PARIS*, 18¹/₂" high. *(Christie's)* **$23,309**

Right
Bisque swivel-headed bébé, marked *BRU Jne 6*, 18¹/₂" high. *(Christie's)* **$18,533**

Far right
Long-faced bisque-headed bébé, impressed *9*, 19¹/₂" high *(Christie's)* **$15,444**

Carved and painted wooden doll, circa 1740, 18" high.
(Christie's) **$16,407**

A rare William and Mary wooden doll, circa 1690 with rouged cheeks, 12¹/₂" high.
(Phillips) **$38,880**

Industrial design Rocket Ship lawn sprinkler, manufactured by Allen Mfg. Co., Chicago, composed of cast metal in red paint with adjustable chrome nozzle, 9³/₄" high.
(Skinner Inc) **$300**

A rare tinder steel and corkscrew.
(Christie's) **$3,949**

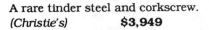

A rare Norris A11 adjustable mitre plane, the dovetailed steel stock with rosewood rear infill, figured walnut front infill, gun-metal lever, little used Norris cutter and twin-thread adjustment, the sole 10¹/₄", cutter width 6¹/₄".

Unlike the standard No. 11 mitre plane, the adjustable version reverted to the traditional box construction, with no handgrip. The adjustment is the compact pattern also fitted to shoulder and other single-cutter planes, engaging a row of holes in the cutter itself. As few mitre planes of any kind were being sold by the 1930s, this is understandably rare. It appears to have had hardly any use, although exposed steel surfaces are discolored by normal atmospheric corrosion.
(Christie's) **$4,345**

Prancing horse tobacco cutter, America, late 19th century, cutting blade and wooden handle mounted on a swivel upon a small oak plank, blade is surmounted by a horse silhouette, painted light gray, 16½" long.
(Skinner Inc)   **$1,700**

A Louis XV ormolu mounted tortoiseshell piqué spinning wheel, the oblong base with gilt-bronze rim, with at one end a six-spoked grooved wheel set on two baluster supports with gilt bronze finials, at the other, a flyer of turned tortoiseshell and two baluster supports carrying the gilt metal and tortoiseshell piqué spindle, with tension screw to flyer, and a further turned tortoiseshell piqué rod supporting the distaff, the base piqué in gold with scrolls, foliage and diaper reserves, with grotesque marks in pearl, circa 1760, length of base 13¼".
(Christie's)   **$17,710**

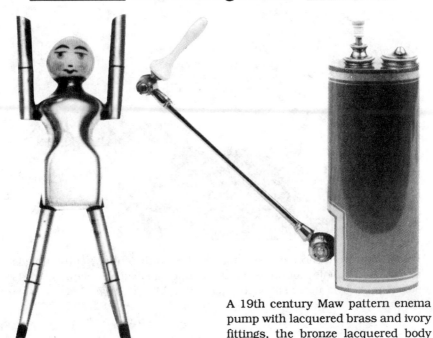

A 19th century Maw pattern enema pump with lacquered brass and ivory fittings, the bronze lacquered body decorated with gilt bands, in fitted mahogany case, 10⁷/₈" wide.
(Christie's)   **$662**

An unusual pair of sugar nips formed as a 'Dutch doll', the head enameled with a face and hair, London 1911, 3.6" high.
(Christie's)   **$841**

A pair of 16th century leather nose spectacles, 9cm. wide, discovered in the roof of a house.
(Phillips)   **$2,800**

A 19th century brass mounted tortoise-shell hearing aid with pierced grill, the oval body with extending tube, 3³/₄" long.
(Christie's)   **$264**

A 35mm. hand-cranked 'The Brunette' cinematographic projector with lens and mechanism all contained in a stylized metal case with transfers on each side.
(Christie's S. Ken)   **$739**

The electric toaster is now usually taken for granted as an everyday part of modern domestic life, and is certainly not the sort of thing that you would expect to find making headlines at an antiques sale. Early models, however, are rapidly becoming established as popular collectibles with an international market. Auction Team Koeln recently sold an example of the first known electric toaster, the Eclipse. It was made in England, has a ceramic housing, and dates from as far back as 1893. The price? A toasting $2,350.

It's comforting to know, however, that you can still find models from the 40s and 50s which will set you back less than $100, and seem set to become an excellent investment.

The first highly skilled figure maker who worked for Doulton was George Tinworth, the Lambeth sculptor, but his figure output was small.

However in 1889 Charles J. Noke left the Royal Worcester Company where he was already showing his prodigious talent as a sculptor and went to work for Doulton's at Burslem. The son of an antique dealer who appreciated the fine vases and figures made by Derby, Bow, Chelsea, Meissen and Sevres, he was fired with the ambition of recreating the once greatly admired Staffordshire figure making industry. For the Chicago Exhibition of 1893 he made several figures including 'Jack Point' and Lady Jester'.

During the next five years more figures followed including Noke's 'Pierrot'; 'Geisha' and the double figures 'Oh Law!' and 'Double Jester'. The latter figure today sells for $3,000 because it was only produced in small numbers.

These figures, though finely modeled, were of dull colors and did not sell well so Noke's figure making was suspended until around 1912 when he re-introduced a figure range which was released to the public in 1913 after Queen Mary, on a visit to Burslem, exclaimed "What a Darling!" at the sight of a figure called 'Bedtime' modeled by Charles Vyse.

'Bedtime' was re-christened 'Darling' and proved to be one of the most popular Doulton figures ever produced. It is still in production.

Royal Doulton figure 'Flower Sellers Children', HN 1406 designed by L. Harradine, issued 1930-1938, 6½" high, with color variation.
(Abridge)   **$560**

The colors of the new figures were bolder and a group of very talented sculptors worked on them. One of the most notable was Harry Tittensor, (1914-21), a local art master.

MYFANWY JONES, HN 39, designed by E.W. Light, issued 1914–1938, 12" high.
(Abridge)   **$1,750**

The work of Leslie Harradine, who began his career at the Lambeth Studio before emigrating to Canada but returned to work at Burslem after World War One, was filled with vitality. His 'Contentment' and 'The Goose Girl' showed his ability to capture movement and he also had a great talent for picking subjects which caught the public fancy. His 'Old Balloon Seller' is still in production today and is one of the most popular Doulton figures ever.

GLEANER, HN 1302, issued 1928–1938, 14½" high.
(Abridge)   **$2,625**

FRUIT GATHERING, HN 707, designed
by L. Harradine, issued 1925–1938,
7 1/4" high.
(Abridge) **$1,300**

PROMENADE, HN 2076, designed by
M. Davies, issued 1951–1953, 8" high.
(Abridge) **$1,400**

maximum number in each edition was 1,000 and each jug or cup bore a certificate of authenticity.

Some were produced to coincide with significant dates like the one made in 1932 for George Washington's birth bicentenary which was designed for the American market. In 1953 a loving cup was issued for the coronation of Queen Elizabeth II by Cecil Noke and in 1977 another edition of only 250 was produced by Richard Johnson for her Silver Jubilee.

The George Washington Bicentenary Jug designed by C.J. Noke and H. Fenton 10³/₄" high, issued 1932 in a limited edition of 1,000 with a color variation on the handle is now worth $7,200.

One of Charles J. Noke's greatest talents was giving the public what it wanted and in 1930 he hit upon the idea of producing a range of limited editions of loving cups and jugs, ornately embossed and decorated to a certain theme.

They were modeled on the slip cast relief jugs which had been made in Staffordshire during Victorian times but were much more intricate and colorful.

The first one produced was 'The Master of Foxhounds Presentation Jug'. It was modeled in low relief with rich glowing colors painted by William Grace and it set the style of the lip and handle of the jug or cup continuing the theme.

The following year 'The Regency Coach Jug' appeared and it was followed by a new one each year including the 'Dickens Dream Jug'; 'The Shakespeare Jug' and 'Robin Hood and His Merry Men'. The

A Royal Doulton George Washington Bicentenary limited edition jug by Noke and Fenton, 10³/₄" high, with colored variation on the handle. *(Abridge Auctions)*
$7,200

Dr Christopher Dresser was born in Glasgow in 1834. He studied at the London School of Design at Somerset House, and then trained and lectured as a botanist. Both these interests came together in the articles he wrote in the 1850s for Art Journal, in which he examined the significance to design of the relationship between structure and function in plants.

By the 1860s he was designing silver, and his inspirations were characterized by their simplicity of form and the careful consideration of the function of each piece, for example the handling and pouring properties of jugs, teapots etc.

He was also an enthusiastic collector of Japanese art, and its influence on his work is most clearly seen in some of his designs for handles.

During his career, his name was associated with a host of different manufacturers. For the electroplaters Hukin & Heath he designed among other things, tureens, claret jugs and tea services. 'Designed by Dr. C. Dresser' sometimes appears beside the manufacturers' mark on these. For J. Dixon, around 1880, his designs include a silver tea service of round shape, with the cast metal feet held by rivets. These bear his facsimile signature in the mark. For Elkington & Co. in the mid 1880s, he produced severe, often angular designs, while for Benham & Froud he designed firedogs, kettles etc. in copper and sometimes brass. His name is also associated with wallpaper and tiles. He even produced a cast iron hall stand for the Coalbrookdale Co.

Dresser was a prime mover in the establishment of the Linthorpe Pottery in 1879, for which he supplied many designs based on Egyptian, Greek and Roman originals and a wide range of native cultures. His work for them was impressed *Chr. Dresser*. Though his active participation in the pottery stopped in 1882, during the 1890's he designed pottery for W. Ault's factory, which often incorporated animal or grotesque masks. He collaborated too on the designs of Clutha glass vases and bowls.

In 1880 Dresser opened his own studio, and throughout his career published many books expressing his stylistic theories. He died in 1904.

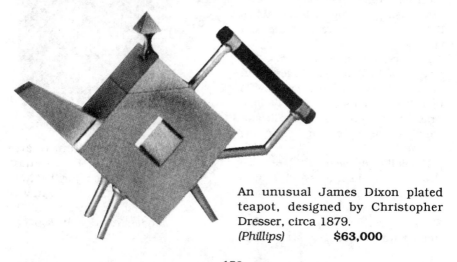

An unusual James Dixon plated teapot, designed by Christopher Dresser, circa 1879.
(Phillips)   **$63,000**

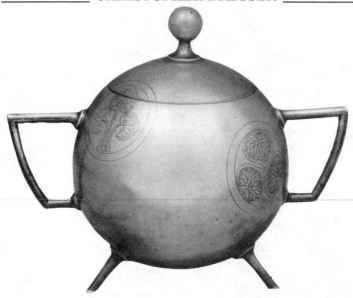

A Hukin and Heath electroplated two handled bowl with hinged cover decorated with four engraved roundels of stylized floral motifs, designed by Dr C. Dresser and date code for 26th March 1879, 19.1cm. high.
(Christie's) **$16,830**

A Hukin & Heath electroplated six-piece cruet and stand designed by Dr. Christopher Dresser, the stand with six faceted compartments and galleried sides, with central T-shaped handle, on hexagonal section feet, registration mark for 6th May 1878, 23.1cm. high.
(Christie's) **$7,392**

An Elkington & Co. plated claret jug, designed by Christopher Dresser, with almost conical lower body embellished with horizontal banding, the slender neck flaring to an oval top with hinged cover and curved angular handle with banded embellishment, 24.20cm. high, date letter for 1885.
(Phillips) **$44,000**

A rare James Dixon & Sons electroplated toastrack designed by Dr. Christopher Dresser, the rectangular frame with seven triangular supports, each with angular wire decoration, on four spike feet and with raised vertical handle, stamped with maker's marks and facsimile signature *Chr. Dresser*, 16.4cm. high.
(Christie's) **$24,167**

A rare Queen Anne figured maple dressing table, Delaware River Valley, 1750-1770, the rectangular thumb molded top with cusped corners above four thumb molded short drawers flanked by canted fluted pilasters over a shaped skirt with a pierced heart, on square tapering cabriole legs with Spanish feet, 39" wide.
(Christie's) **$41,800**

Rare and important Chippendale walnut block-front carved dressing table, Massachusetts, circa 1750, 33⅝" wide.
(Skinner Inc) **$325,000**

A fine Queen Anne carved mahogany dressing table, Salem, Massachusetts, 1740-1760, the rectangular top with molded edge above a case with thumb molded long drawer over three similar short drawers above a shaped apron centering a concave-carved shell, on cabriole legs with pad feet, 34" wide. *(Christie's)* **$66,000**

A fine and rare Chippendale carved mahogany dressing table, Philadelphia, 1760–1780, the thumb-molded rectangular top with cusped corners above one long drawer over three short drawers, the center drawer with an elaborately carved concave shell with trailing leaf tendrils flanked by fluted quarter columns, 36" wide.
(Christie's) **$121,000**

18th century Dutch dummy board figure in the form of a lady seated at her needlework. Dummy boards in the form of cut-out figures were usually placed in the halls of large houses and date from the late 17th century to mid 18th century.
(Woolley & Wallis) **$4,025**

A dummy board figure of a girl in 17th century costume standing with a lapdog and a dummy board figure of a young man wearing a hat, a maroon doublet and breeches, painted on canvas, 36" and 39" high.
(Christie's) **$4,138**

A Ron Arad 'Rolling Volume' sheet steel armchair, with rounded back and sides polished and acid-painted to give black patina.
(Christie's) **$9,240**

An Indian carved mahogany state chair commissioned by the Marquess of Dalhousie as a facsimile of Ranjit Singh's golden throne, circa 1850, of octagonal form, the three-quarters back with a carved scrollwork and foliate cresting rail, the cusped seat and conforming base carved with stylized acanthus, upholstered in yellow and crimson velvet, with loose seat cushion and two side pillows.

The original golden throne of Ranjit Singh was shipped to England by Lord Dalhousie to be deposited in the India Office Museum in 1853 and eventually transferred to the Victoria & Albert Museum where it is currently on view. This throne described as Lahore, about 1830, is composed of sheets of embossed gold over a core of wood and resin and it was evidently Lord Dalhousie's intention for the facsimile to be gilded as the original.

According to the India Office Library & Records the rate of exchange in 1854 was on average about 10 rupees

to $1 which would have made the original cost of the replica throne about $100.
(Sothebys) **$11,550**

A George I walnut-framed wing armchair upholstered in lozenge-pattern needlework, the tall rectangular back with shaped wings continuing into outscrolled arms, the seat with a loose squab, on lappet-headed cabriole legs with leaf carved pad feet.
(Bearnes) **$29,920**

A George III mahogany invalid's chair attributed to John Joseph Merlin, the winged buttoned back, arms and padded seat upholstered in close-nailed burgundy hide on square tapering legs joined by stretchers with brass wheels operated by turned handles. A design for a chair with the same mechanism, but in the Regency style, with the caption 'Merlin's Mechanical Chair' is illustrated in Ackermann's Repository of October 1811.
(Christie's) **$3,128**

A George I walnut wing armchair with padded back, outward-scrolling arms and bowed seat upholstered in associated early 18th century petit point needlework, the back with a panel woven with a Chinese lady seated by a fountain in a garden and woven overall with foliage and flowerheads.
(Christie's) **$77,500**

A fine Regency carved mahogany and brass mounted library Bergère armchair, with curved bar toprail and scroll upright with anthemion scroll and flower head, the scroll arm supports with gadrooned scroll ornament, on foliate tapered legs with reeded gaiters.
(Phillips) **$22,200**

A Swiss enameled gold oval snuff-box, for the Turkish market, painted with reserves of flowers on pink and blue grounds bordered by swags, circa 1820, 8.5cm. long.
(Christie's) **$9,000**

A Viennese enamel cornucopia with silver and gilt metal mounts, raised with jeweled bosses, supported by a merman, painted all over with classical and mythological scenes, 16" high.
(Christie's) **$9,862**

An Ando Jubei ovoid moriage cloisonne vase decorated in various colored enamels on a gray-green ground, with persimmons growing from a leafy branch, silver mounts, Ando mark, Meiji period (1868-1912), 32cm. high.
(Christie's) **$40,414**

A 19th century 'Blackamoor' half length figure of a man wearing a wide brimmed straw hat and dressed in an open necked striped shirt and holding an oval basket, 2ft. 4¹/₂" high.
(Greenslades) **$1,672**

A Nymphenburg figure of an egg-seller modeled by Franz Anton Bustelli, holding her white apron with her left hand and leaning over a naturalistically painted crate of eggs, on flat rococo scroll base enriched with gilding, impressed Bavarian shield mark to the rococo scroll and Dreher's mark *i*, circa 1755, 14.5cm. high.
(Christie's) **$66,220**

A Hittite pottery horse rhyton, the cylindrical neck of the vessel on its back, the two spouts at its front hooves, the simple rounded form enhanced by curvilinear designs painted in brick-red and umber on the buff ground, 26cm. high, 2000-1500 B.C.
(Phillips) **$17,710**

A German shaped circular Trompe L'Oeil plate molded with leaves and applied with wild strawberries naturalistically colored, scattered flowers to the border within a gilt rim, circa 1765, 23cm. diameter.
(Christie's) **$3,227**

A pair of KPM Berlin rectangular plaques, one painted by F Zapf with a girl in an interior arranging flowers in a molded baluster vase on a table, the other painted with a girl wearing a gold fringed blue drape feeding a parrot with a peach, 19th century, 12$\frac{1}{2}$" high x 10" wide.
(Christie's) **$42,350**

A Chantilly green-ground two-handled pot-pourri, the waisted campana body applied with swags of flowers, the stepped foot with gadroons, twin S-scroll handles, the pierced cover molded with flowerheads, enriched in blue, manganese, green orange and yellow, circa 1750, 19cm. high.
(Christie's)   **$8,965**

An amusing Goldscheider painted group modeled as three young black boys each wearing short trousers, 56.5cm. high.
(Phillips)   **$2,400**

A pair of Höchst figures of street vendors modeled by Laurentius Russinger as a map-seller and a trinket-seller, standing on scrolling treestump bases edged in gold and puce, circa 1760, 19cm. high.
(Christie's)   **$19,866**

A Strasbourg Faience cauliflower tureen and cover, circa 1750.
(Christie's) **$8,250**

A Vienna Du Paquier large circular Jagd service dish finely painted in schwarzlot, imitating the engraved source with a putto seated on a stone bench feeding a buck and two does within a border of Laub und Bandelwerk with diaper panels, foliage and four birds enriched with gilding, circa 1740, 37cm. diameter.
(Christie's) **$19,700**

A Castelli armorial plate painted by Aurelio Grue after a print from the 'Hunt Series' by Antonio Tempesta, the center with a huntsman at rest beneath a tree with his dog and horse laden with a bear and a deer, before distant figures and buildings, the yellow ground border painted with en grisaille putti and baroque scrolls entwined with rose garlands, circa 1725, 29cm. diameter.
(Christie's) **$21,516**

A Thuringian eye bath modeled as the head of a man wearing a yellow hat, his hair extending over his buttoned waistcoat painted with sprays of flowers which form the bowl, last quarter of the 18th century, 8cm. long.
(Christie's) **$753**

A Dagoty Paris ewer and basin, the ewer with matt blue ground, decorated in white relief with acanthus leaf borders and swan neck griffins below tooled gold shoulders, the basin with tooled gold foliate interior and classical border in white relief, 31cm. high, the jug with gold painted mark, the basin stenciled in red.
(Phillips) **$4,629**

One of a pair of Dresden groups of children playing round a wine press and a barrel, 30cm. and 34cm.
(Lawrence Fine Art) **$8,551**

A Doccia white portrait plaque of the Marquis Carlo Ginori, probably modeled by Gaspera Bruschi, the high relief half-length profile to sinister with lace collar and flowing curled wig, with the inscription *CAR.MARC. COM.GINORI.SEN.FLOR.LIBVRN. PRAES.*, the reeded circular medallion with rococo scroll cartouches, circa 1760, 17cm. high.
(Christie's) **$14,775**

A superb Berlin 'KPM' plaque of rectangular form, painted by Wagner after Delaroche with the 'Martyre Chretiènne', the bound maiden with tranquil expression depicted floating in a moonlit lake, impressed *KPM* and *scepter mark*, panel size 14¹/₂" x 20¹/₂", set within an impressive brass frame bordered with Zsolnay type panels decorated with simulated champlevé arabesque and strapwork motifs.

(Bonhams) **$16,625**

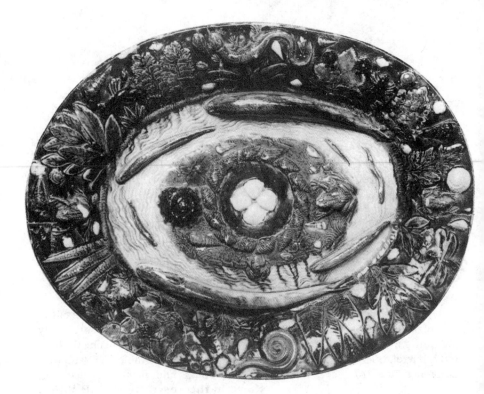

A Pallisy oval dish molded in relief with fishes swimming on a pale blue wavy ground about an island encrusted with molluscs and frogs, the dark blue ground border further encrusted with leaves, shells and other aquatic fauna, 16th century, 49.5cm. wide.

(Christie's) **$4,461**

An Italian molded dish, the center with a twin-tailed mermaid holding a tail in each of her outstretched arms, painted in green and yellow flanked by the manganese initials *M.P.*, the well with lappets painted with alternating open and closed flowerheads, the scale-molded rim enriched with green, orange, blue and yellow, late 17th/early 18th century, probably Angarano, 47cm. diameter.
(Christie's) **$5,115**

'Hercules and the Hydra', a stoneware vase by Jean Mayodon, covered in a mottled iris-blue glaze with gilt marbling and decorated in turquoise relief with the hero in combat with the serpent, 35.1cm. high.
(Christie's) **$6,500**

'Victory of the Nile' celebratory
mug 1798, 5¹/4" high.
(Christie's) **$43,288**

A Naples royal portrait
medallion with the heads of
King Ferdinando IV and Queen
Maria Caroline in profile to the
right, naturalistically colored
on a brown ground, 6.5cm.
diameter, circa 1790.
(Christie's) **$3,414**

Paris porcelain American historical pitcher, France, circa 1862, of bulbous
shape, enamel decorated portraits of Grant and Farragut in military dress,
flanking a three-quarter portrait of Lady Liberty surrounded by Old Glory,
background in gilt with stars throughout, 8³/8" high.
(Skinner Inc) **$21,000**

A Wedgwood Fairyland lustre bowl 'Poplar Trees' pattern, gold Portland Vase mark, circa 1925, Z4968, 10¹/₂" diameter.
(Warren & Wignall) **$2,625**

A Wedgwood **Fairyland** lustre malfrey pot and cover designed by Daisy Makeig-Jones and decorated with pixies and elves and with phoenix in flight among trees with pendant foliage, 22cm. diameter, circa 1920.
(Christie's) **$9,680**

Springfield, Feby 25th 1847.

Dear Johnston:

Yours of the 2nd of Decr was duly delivered to me by Mr Williams. To say the least, I am not at all displeased with your proposal to publish the poetry, or doggerel, or whatever else it may be called, which I sent you. I consent

Abraham Lincoln, autograph letter about three of his poems to Andrew Johnston of Quincy, quarto, Illinois, 25 February 1847.
(Christie's)   **$143,000**

Dear Brother,   *Philadelphia July 10th 1776*

I am extremely obliged to you for your repeated Favours, and am glad to find that amidst yours Misfortunes, and our common Calamities you preserve so much Fortitude of Mind. We have lived to see a Period which a few years ago human forecast could have imagined. We have lived to see these Colonies shake off, or rather declare themselves independent of a State which they once gloried to call their Parent. I said declare themselves independent, for it is One Thing for Colonies to declare themselves

William Ellery, autograph letter signed to his brother Benjamin Ellery concerning the signing of the Declaration of Independence, two pages, quarto, Philadelphia, 10 July 1776.
(Christie's)   **$121,000**

A gold and enamel sleeve button, mid 19th century, oval, with a gold gothic letter *L* set in black enamel, surrounded by a gold frame, with engraved detail and a gold backing; together with a fitted silver box with a beveled glass cover, engraved with an inscription and dated 1908.

The box is inscribed: *Abraham Lincoln April 14th 1865* on the cover, and on the reverse: *Enclosed sleeve button worn by President Lincoln April 14 1865 was given by Mrs. Lincoln to Dr. Taft, an attending surgeon who had removed it in search for wound.*

It is accompanied by a note card with the statement of Dr. Taft, written in his own hand with the following inscription: *This cuff button, with the initial L set in black enamel was removed by me from President Lincoln's cuff, when taking off his shirt in the box* *at Ford's Theater, the night he was assassinated April 14 1865. Charles Sabin Taft, Attending Surgeon.* (Christie's)   **$9,350**

A pair of bowler hats used by Stan Laurel and Oliver Hardy, both with *Hal Roach Studios Wardrobe Department* ink stamp on inside leather band, accompanied by a typescript letter, signed, dated February 2nd 1938 on 'Hal Roach Studio Inc.' illustrated and headed paper, to Mr Oscar A. Doob from Mary on behalf of Dorothy Callahan of the Hal Roach Studios Wardrobe Department, telling him *Mr Frank Seltzer has asked me to select costume hats for Mr Laurel and Mr Hardy to be sent to your attention.* (Christie's)   **$17,380**

George Washington, a lock of his hair matted and framed under glass with statement of provenance.

'The lock of Hair accompanying this statement is from the head of General Washington. It was cut soon after his inauguration to the Presidency of the United States, and was given to his niece, Jane Washington, who married her half first cousin, Colonel William Augustine Washington. It was incased in a gold brooch and worn by Jane Washington until her death, when it was inherited by her son, Colonel George Corbin Washington, my great grandfather. He gave it to his niece, Frances Washington.

Frances Washington was the youngest child of Bushrod Washington, a brother of George Corbin Washington, who, upon the death of her father in 1880, when she was two years old, was taken into the home of her uncle, George Corbin Washington, and reared as one of his own children, and where she remained a member of his household until his death in 1884. George Corbin Washington having but one living child at the time of his death, namely, Colonel Lewis William Washington, divided the relics of General Washington, that he had inherited, between him and Frances Washington, the latter receiving the above described brooch containing General Washington's hair and other relics.

Frances Washington died childless and without direct issue in 1909, and, a few years prior thereto, she gave the relics she had received from George Corbin Washington, including this brooch and hair, to his grandson, Major James Washington, my father. As this lock of hair was of extensive proportions, my father removed some of it from the brooch and divided it into several smaller lots, some of which I inherited, and of which the above is one.'

William Lanier Washington 2/11/ 1921.

(Du Mouchelles)   **$2,500**

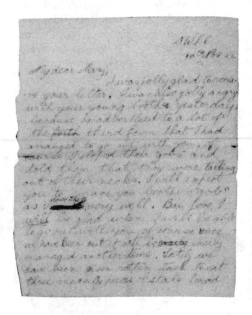

A rare collection of six autograph letters, each written by South West London College schoolboy Errol Flynn to Mary White the sister of a colleague, majority written by Flynn at the age of thirteen, various dates 8-17th November 1922, and 24th January 1924. *'My dear Mary...I was jolly angry with your brother yesterday because*

he advertised to a lot of the third form that I had arranged to go out with you, of course I slaped their "gobs"...Will you come up to the football pitch on Saturday...' signed 'With love from your faithful Errol, 1,000 times, xxxxxxxxxxxx'. Another letter dated 13.11.22 S.W.L.C., Castelnau 'My dear Mary...You struck the right thing about those kisses, there is not much in them on paper, but they are all right when they are real, by jove I know, don't you, I should think you would..' signed 'from yours truly Errol...Flynn xxxxxxxxxxxx'. Errol Flynn spent two years at South West London College 1922-1924.
(Christie's)   **$4,519**

Babe Ruth 700th home run ball, autographed by the team, dated July 13, 1934 with a King Gum colored baseball card.
(Du Mouchelles)   **$8,500**

One of the interesting developments recently has been the rise in interest for the clothing and belongings of famous people. The world gasped when Charlie Chaplin's hat and cane which he used in his film 'The Great Dictator' was sold by Christie's for $148,500. His boots went to a Swiss museum for $69,000.

A rare articulated fan, the silk leaf painted with an allegory of a milliner's shop, inscribed *La Folie l'a inventé et la Mode l'a adopté*, with a jester giving a hat to the Milliner whilst a cleric arranges another hat on an elegant customer watched by Cupid, 11", French, circa 1775.
(Christie's) **$9,625**

A fan, the leaf painted with the surrender of General Lord Blakeney at Port Mahon, Minorca, the verso painted with Spanish ships, the tortoiseshell sticks of Battoire type, carved, pierced, silvered and gilt with a lady at the the altar of love and doves, one guardstick set with monogram A.C.?, the other with an early 19th century portrait miniature of a lady, 11", probably French for the Spanish market, 1756.
(Christie's) **$4,453**

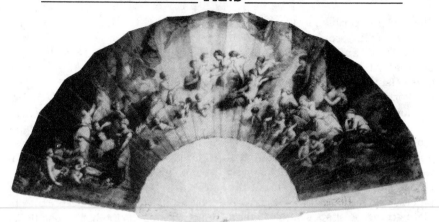

A fine fan, the leaf painted with nymphs and putti, signed in red *J. Calamatta 1870* verso signed *Alexandre*, the mother of pearl sticks finely carved and pierced with nymphs and putti and monogram H.W. crowned, in velvet box of similar date by Duvelleroy with monogram L.M. with coronet above. *(Christie's)* **$8,906**

The twentieth birthday of Le Grand Dauphin, a rare unmounted fan leaf painted in bodycolor with Louis XIV, seated beside the Queen, Marie Therese, whilst a figure dressed in blue decorated with gold fleurs de lys showers a basket of gold coins at the feet of Le Grand Dauphin, their son, dressed in blue who stands beside them, beside him stands his wife, holding a fan, there are twenty other figures in the scene, probably all members of the Royal family, the leaf has been extended to form a rectangle, 11" x 21", French, circa 1681, framed and glazed, the frame circa 1710. *(Christie's)* **$20,240**

The Federal period in US furniture design falls roughly between 1780–1820 and is basically the equivalent of European Neo-Classicism. It was a reaction against the floridity of the preceding Rococo fashion and took its direct inspiration from the excavation of ancient monuments in Herculaneum, Pompeii and elsewhere. Its main characteristics were a delicacy of decoration, often using classical motifs such as the patera, and a simplicity of line, with plain geometric shapes supported on tapered columnar legs.

At this time two seminal design books were published, Hepplewhite's 'Cabinet-maker and Upholsterer's Guide' (1788) and Sheraton's 'Cabinet Maker and Upholsterer's Drawing Book' (1791–4) and while it is difficult to assess just how much American designers relied on these, there has been a tendency to divide the furniture of the Federal era into Hepplewhite and Sheraton design, though in fact there are no substantial differences between them. Influences on the later phase of Federal style included a more literal borrowing of Graeco-Roman forms and furniture designed by Napoleon's architects Percier and Fontaine. These influences came to America through English translations, and were copied in a more restrained form by American craftsmen, who were equally influenced by English Regency design.

The actual pieces being made were also changing, and new forms included

A rare small Federal carved mahogany settee, Salem, Massachusetts, 1800-1815, with serpentine molded crest-rail centering a C-scroll bordered arched tablet carved with a basket of foliage and fruit, on square tapering legs, 73" long. This sofa is one of five or six known related examples. *(Christie's)* **$52,800**

work tables, decorative side tables and large dining tables (as the fashion for a separate dining room came in) which could often be extended or dismantled into smaller tables. Chair designs after 1800 became heavier than in the earlier Federal period, and were based more closely on the ancient klismos model, with a thick curved toprail and a curved horizontal slat across the back, while sofa styles became simpler and more delicate. The classical Grecian couch was reformed, too, into the chaise.

The man responsible for many of the most stylish examples of American Neo-Classicism was Duncan Phyfe, who was influenced first by Sheraton and later by classical French designs.

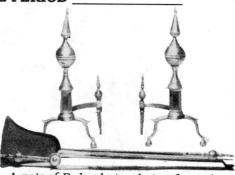

A pair of Federal steeple-top faceted plinth brass andirons with matching shovel and tongs, New York, 1790-1810. Each with faceted steeple finial above a turned-ball with beaded midband over a faceted hexagonal plinth on spur-arched legs with ball feet. 23¼" high, firetools 37" long. *(Christie's N York)* **$9,680**

A rare Federal grain-painted step-back cupboard, Vermont, early 19th century, with coved and molded cornice lifting above a stepback cupboard fitted with three shelves above a rectangular top over two cupboard doors opening to two shelves, the entire surface painted olive with brown sponge-painted grain decoration, 63½" wide. *(Christie's N. York)* **$44,000**

FIRE BUCKETS

Painted and decorated leather fire bucket, New England, 1806, decorated with oval reserve, having draped figure of Mercury blowing a trumpet against a smoke filled sky above a landscape enclosed border, inscribed *J. Peirce Active 1806*, 12³/₄" high.
(Skinner Inc)   **$27,000**

Leather firebucket, New England, early 19th century, painted dark green and decorated in polychrome with full-length figure of George Washington holding a globe topped with an eagle and a scroll inscribed *Legacy* under the inscription *Deo Et Patria*, dated *1800*, 12¹/₂" high.
(Skinner Inc)   **$10,000**

FIRE HATS

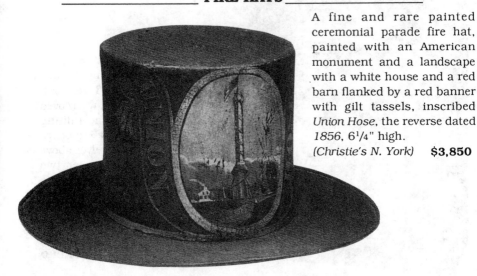

A fine and rare painted ceremonial parade fire hat, painted with an American monument and a landscape with a white house and a red barn flanked by a red banner with gilt tassels, inscribed *Union Hose*, the reverse dated *1856*, 6¹/₄" high.
(Christie's N. York)   **$3,850**

Painted and decorated parade fire hat, Philadelphia, circa 1854, the pressed felt top hat painted red and decorated with a central medallion depicting William Rush's figure 'Water Nymph and Bittern' flanked by black banners inscribed in gilt *Fair, Mount*, the reverse gilt decorated with a wood fire hydrant flanked by the letters *F, A*, the crown inscribed in gilt with the owner's initials *S.G.T.*, the underbrim painted green, the interior embossed with the name of the manufacturer *Archer 943 Ridge Avenue above Vine, Philadelphia*, 6" high.

Painted and decorated parade fire hat, probably Pennsylvania, last half 19th century, the pressed felt top hat painted black with red banners inscribed in gilt *Franklin Fire Co.* and crossed American flags all centering a gilt shield inscribed with the numeral 4, the reverse decorated with a gilt numeral 4 entwined with a red banner inscribed in gilt *Haste to the Rescue*, the underbrim painted red, 5" high. *(Skinner Inc)* **$4,000**

The original figure of 'Water Nymph and Bittern' by William Rush (1756-1833) was carved in pine and placed in Fairmount Park, Philadelphia in 1809. The figure was removed in 1854 when William Rush made a bronze casting from it which was then substituted at Fairmount Park in the center of the fountain by Latrobe. The original carved wooden figure has not survived. This parade hat commemorates this event and the work of William Rush, considered the 'Father of American Sculpture'. *(Skinner Inc)* **$8,500**

Painted and decorated parade fire hat, America, last half 19th century, the pressed felt top hat painted black and decorated with banners inscribed in gilt *Northern No 1 Liberty*, the reverse gilt decorated with wooden fire hydrant flanked by the letters *F A*, the crown inscribed *1756* in black block letters on a gilt ground, 6" high. *(Skinner Inc)* **$3,300**

Painted pine fireboard, possibly central Massachusetts, circa 1815, depicting fruit and flowering boughs in a vase within a fireplace opening, 37½" wide. *(Skinner Inc)* **$20,000**

A fine and rare painted fireboard, Maine or New Hampshire, early 19th century, centering a blue-painted classical urn embellished with gold griffins and draped swags filled with red roses on a blue plinth with a classical wave flanked by painted trees on a green ground. *(Christie's N. York)*   **$18,700**

Before 1830 there was no municipal fire brigade and when a fire broke out in a private residence, the occupants had to put it out themselves or else look for help from one of the crews employed by insurance companies which offered cover in those days. Before an insurance company fire engine would tackle your blaze however, they had to be sure that you were one of their subscribers and the way they did this was to look to see if there was a firemark attached to the wall of your home. Originally these were lead crests bearing the name of the company and your policy number but many of them must have melted in the heat of the conflagration and later ones were made of copper, tin or zinc and occasionally of terracotta or porcelain. Those which have survived in situ are jealously guarded by the house owners and there is a great interest in collecting them.

Royal Exchange Assurance, lead, raised Royal Exchange building, policy no. 570 on panel below, issued circa 1721.
(Phillips) **$6,336**

FIREPLACE FURNITURE

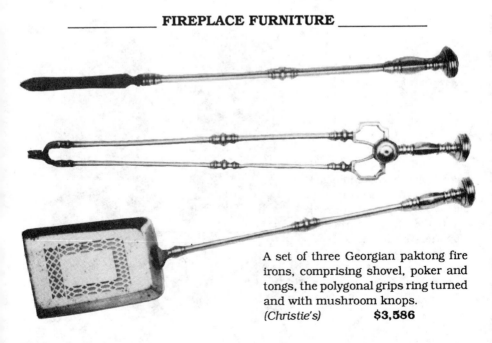

A set of three Georgian paktong fire irons, comprising shovel, poker and tongs, the polygonal grips ring turned and with mushroom knops.
(Christie's) **$3,586**

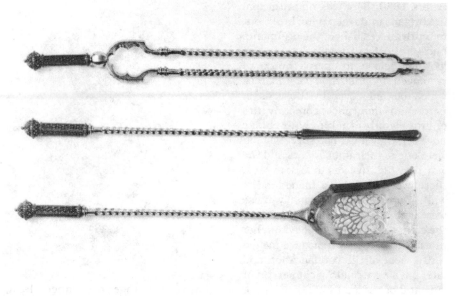

A set of three Regency steel and brass fire-irons, comprising a poker, tongs and pierced shovel, each with square faceted handle and spiral shaft, 29" long.
(Christie's)   **$6,072**

A pair of polychrome enameled bronze andirons cast in low relief with a Royal coat-of-arms within the Garter borne by supporters surmounted by a crown and standing lion, supported by naked figures, 24" high.
(Christie's)   **$4,089**

A Regency blackened-iron fire surround and grate, the molded uprights and lintel with beaded borders, the pierced basket with vase finials and geometric apron 43" wide. *(Christie's)* **$4,731**

Art Nouveau cast iron fire surrounds, measurements 72" x 36".
(Lots Road Galleries) **$4,725**

A George III steel and brass fire-grate, the shaped arched backplate with a molded circular panel, the basket with serpentine front surmounted by finials, the pierced apron decorated with dragons and foliage on pierced supports surmounted by obelisks, 38" wide.
(Christie's) **$21,252**

FISHING REELS

A rare Hardy Bros. 2¹/₂" perfect brass fly reel of 1891 pattern.
(Phillips) **$4,725**

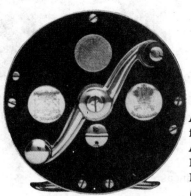

A rare Hardy Cascapedia multiplying fly reel affixed with two circular 'By Appointment' plaques, one being the Royal Coat of Arms and the other the Prince of Wales feathers, circa 1930.
(Sothebys) **$12,250**

A fine George II Kentian carved and gilded architectural tabernacle frame, with eared corners, the architrave carved with an egg-and-dart design and embellished with vitruvian scroll surmounted by an opened scallop-shell finial, 79³/₄" x 57³/₄".

The frame is most likely to have been designed by Henry Flitcroft (1697-1769), known as 'Burlington Harry', who trained as a joiner before becoming Lord Burlington's architectural assistant and Clerk of Works to George II's palaces of Whitehall, Westminster and St. James's.

(Christie's) **$57,750**

An early 16th century Venetian carved and gilded tabernacle frame, 18³/₄" x 15¹/₂".
(Bonhams) **$31,500**

A late Victorian satinwood revolving bookcase painted overall with molded circular top on column support above three circular graduated tiers, on tripod base with downswept legs and brass claw feet, 55$^{1}/_{2}$" high.
(Christie's) **$13,090**

A George III mahogany cutlery-tray of octagonal shape, the interior with central divide and carrying-handle, the ends with lion-mask ring-handles, on a later mahogany stand with square legs and X-shaped stretcher, 35" wide.
(Christie's) **$10,600**

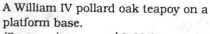

A William IV pollard oak teapoy on a platform base.
(Spencers) **$3,325**

One of a pair of George III mahogany night commodes, the pierced gallery tops above tambour shutter compartments, pull out pot holders with ebony stringing and brass swan neck handles, on square legs, 19".
(Woolley & Wallis) **$13,650**

A Biedermeier mahogany bedside cupboard with hinged rectangular top enclosing a formerly fitted interior, the fluted column base with a scrolling Ionic capital on a shaped plinth, 22" wide.
(Christie's) **$12,512**

Limbert oak window bench, Grand Rapids, Michigan, 1907, the canted flat sides with four square cut outs each centering seat, with original leather cushion, branded mark, 24" wide.

(Skinner Inc) **$11,000**

A brass-bound mahogany stick stand with carved circular border and gilt lion-mask and ring handles, the molded base carved with egg-and-dart, 25" high.

(Christie's) **$3,850**

Adirondack style sideboard, circa 1915, constructed of logs, twigs and bark, two small cabinets flanking central opening, set back on rectangular top above three drawers over central opening flanked by cabinet doors, 43" wide.

(Skinner Inc) **$750**

A most attractive 19th century satinwood duet stand, 48" high.
(Phillips Manchester)   **$6,300**

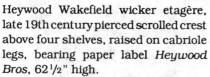

Heywood Wakefield wicker etagère, late 19th century pierced scrolled crest above four shelves, raised on cabriole legs, bearing paper label *Heywood Bros*, 62½" high.
(Skinner Inc)   **$1,200**

A set of Regency mahogany library steps with column supports, molded rectangular open base, splayed feet and brass caps, 30½" wide.
(Christie's)   **$19,360**

An Irish George III mahogany wine-waiter of rectangular shape with divided and undulating galleried top, the central divide pierced with a handle, on cabriole legs and paw-feet carved with foliage, 26" wide.
(Christie's) **$13,783**

A George III tulipwood and kingwood marquetry commode attributed to Pierre Langlois, of bombe outline, inlaid with end-cut flowersprays on a crossbanded quartered mirror-figured ground, 57" wide.
(Christie's) **$141,900**

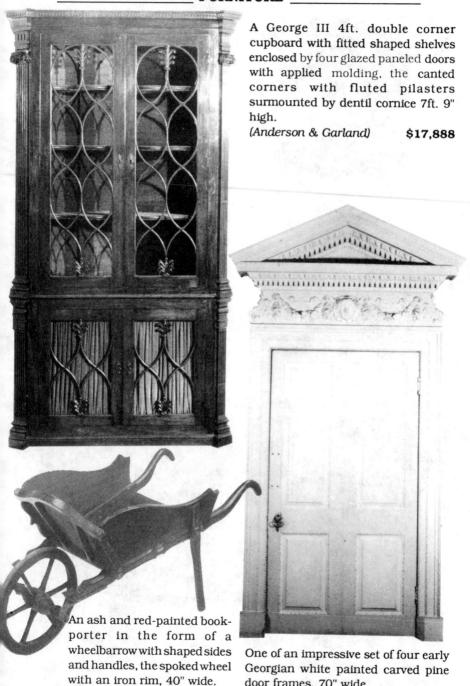

A George III 4ft. double corner cupboard with fitted shaped shelves enclosed by four glazed paneled doors with applied molding, the canted corners with fluted pilasters surmounted by dentil cornice 7ft. 9" high.

(Anderson & Garland) **$17,888**

An ash and red-painted bookporter in the form of a wheelbarrow with shaped sides and handles, the spoked wheel with an iron rim, 40" wide.
(Christie's) **$3,080**

One of an impressive set of four early Georgian white painted carved pine door frames, 70" wide.
(Bonhams) **$25,500**

A Biedermeier mahogany teapoy with hinged octagonal lid inlaid with boxwood and ebonized lines enclosing a fitted interior with lidded compartments, 31" high.
(Christie's) **$2,970**

A classical carved and gilt mahogany piano stool, Baltimore, 1820-1830, with curved and bird's-eye maple veneered tablet crestrail above a scroll and rosette-carved horizontal medial splat, 32⅞" high.
(Christie's) **$2,420**

George III ormolu-mounted mahogany oval wine-cooler with the Williams-Wynn 'Snowdonian' eagle crest, the design attributed to Robert Adam, 34" wide. *(Christie's)* **$88,000**

A rare George II walnut reading stand, the hinged top quarter veneered, crossbanded and featherbanded, with a drawer at one side and fitted with two small slides, adjustable in height on a square wooden stem in a cylindrical column and on three S scroll square section supports, 22" wide.
(Lawrence Fine Art)   **$11,297**

A fine and rare Chippendale carved mahogany highpost bedstead, Newport, Rhode Island, 1760–1780, the tapering, turned and stop-fluted footposts on square stop-fluted legs with block-molded feet joined by pegged side rails and foot rail, on square stop-fluted legs with block-molded feet centering a serpentine-shaped headboard, surmounted by a flat pine tester, 61" wide.
(Christie's)   **$88,000**

Emile Gallé (1846–1904) established his glass factory in Nancy in 1874. Initially he also made earthenware and then experimented with stoneware and porcelain, decorated often with heraldic motifs and scenes reminiscent of delft ware. It is, however, for his glassware that he is chiefly remembered, as one of the chief Art Nouveau craftsmen in glass, using flowing designs of foliage, flowers, birds or female figures.

Gallé evolved many new techniques such as marqueterie de verre and experimented with the addition of metal oxides to glass melt, coloring glass in imitation of precious stones.

By 1889 he had perfected both enameled and colored glass techniques with a wide range of colors and effects. Cameo glass was another of his characteristic styles, and his designs were often inspired by Oriental influences. In 1899 this was being produced on a commercial scale at Nancy, and he also began decorating lighting glass, producing lamps in flower forms, with the light fittings concealed by the half-open petals.

All his own work as well as that of his flourishing factory (by then with 300 employees) was signed. His personal signature, however, is sometimes to be found hidden among the foliage, and naturally adds an enormous cachet to a piece. The firm continued after his death, and finally closed in 1935.

It seems that now the great painters of the 1900's have been discovered and rendered unaffordable, it may well be the turn of the great craftsmen of the period, with a noticeable increase in interest especially from the Far East. Anything by Gallé is likely to be a sound investment. A private

Gallé 74cm. monumental vase.
(Habsburg, Feldman)   **$568,750**

collection which was changing hands for the first time since it left Gallé's workshops was sold recently by Habsburg Feldman in Geneva. This included a series of monumental vases, claimed to be the largest ever produced at Nancy. The tallest of them all, standing 74cm. high, with a magnificent design of overlaid and inlaid glass depicting blue hydrangeas, fetched a new Gallé world record of Sfr 929,500 ($568,750).

From the 1880's, Gallé had also designed furniture, often based on 18th century forms and characterized by its simple lines and naturalistic decoration. Plant forms are again much in evidence, even for limbs and cross-section moldings, and he made much of marquetry decoration in natural fruitwoods. All these characteristics are seen in a superb Art Nouveau buffet which Feldman sold at the same sale. for a Gallé furniture record of Sfr 418,000 ($277,640).

A Gallé triple-overlay cameo glass and Emile Guillaume gilt-bronze table lamp, the pale acid-textured glass of compressed form, speckled with blue and overlaid in white, butterscotch and amber with flowering peonies, with carved signature *Gallé*, the bronze pedestal molded with swags, scrolls, foliate motifs and images of Art Nouveau maidens, signed *Emile Guillaume*, 70cm. high. *(Christie's)*   **$64,548**

A Gallé faience model of a cat, dated to the 1880s, with a silly smile and green glass eyes, seated in traditional pose wearing a gilt chain and a pendant enclosing a portrait of a dog, its blue and white striped body decorated with scattered flower sprays, 13" high, signed.
(Sothebys) **$9,100**

A Gallé enameled rectangular glass casket on four button feet, 14.5cm. wide.
(Christie's) **$28,172**

A good Gallé 'Artichoke' vase, the pale mutton-fat colored body having pale brown vertical stripe, decorated with marquetrie sur-verre artichoke flowers with wheel-carved detailing, mold-blown in the form of an artichoke and supported on a spreading circular base simulating agate, 20.5cm. high.
(Phillips) **$97,800**

'La Giroflée De Muraille', a fine quality Gallé marquetrie-sur-verre and wheel-carved glass vase of almost conical shape, the clear body suffused with fine bubbles and tinted deep amber, the neck divided into three straps forming a common aperture at the top, applied with colored stems and blooms with foil inclusions and wheel-carved detailing, 20.5cm. high
(Phillips) **$122,250**

'L'Hippocampe', an artistic Gallé vase with marquetry, engraved and applied decoration, of a sea-horse, sea-weed and red veining, 29cm. high.
(Christie's Monaco) **$92,000**

A Gallé carved, acid-etched and cased glass flacon and stopper, of compressed rectangular form with short cylindrical neck and mushroom cap stopper, on oval foot, the yellow glass cased in clear and overlaid in dark amber with chrysanthemums, 11.2cm. high.
(Christie's) **$4,800**

'Cala-Lily', a Gallé molded-blown, carved and acid-etched double-overlay vase of flared baluster form with everted rim, the translucent yellow glass overlaid in red and amber with large flowering Cala-Lilies, with carved signature *Gallé*, 37cm. high.
(Christie's) **$37,180**

Emile Gallé engraved, carved and enameled vase, the bulbous amber handled jardiniere of transparent ruby red cased to colorless glass carved back with broad lily blossoms, buds and long curving stems against an etched, whittled and hammered martele surface; the four main blossoms also enameled in brilliant shades of blue, purple and red, then muted with metallic wash, a naturalistic dragonfly at one side, foliate enameled border above, signed in gold enamel on base Emile Gallé Nancy, 10" high.
(Skinner Inc) **$45,000**

Emile Gallé medievalist verrerie parlante cameo vase, the octagonally crimped heavy-walled smoky blue-gray vessel layered with amethyst, cameo carved in delicate blossoming leafy vines against a hammered martele surface and having nine cabochons of amethyst and amber glass applied over metallic foil inclusions; the phrase *Ne Mobiez Mie* is elaborately carved around the flared base, embellished and silvered as in an illuminated manuscript; signed in cameo and highlighted in gold Emile Gallé with the cross of Lorraine, 10¼" high.
(Skinner Inc) **$47,500**

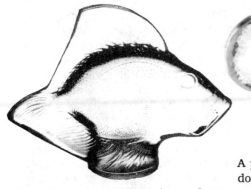

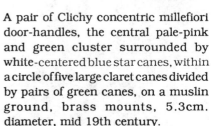

'Gros Poisson', a large Lalique glass model of a carp, its body forming an arc and molded with scale and fin details, resting on a circular base, 31.3cm. high, signed *R. Lalique, France.*
(Phillips)   **$5,216**

A pair of Clichy concentric millefiori door-handles, the central pale-pink and green cluster surrounded by white-centered blue star canes, within a circle of five large claret canes divided by pairs of green canes, on a muslin ground, brass mounts, 5.3cm. diameter, mid 19th century.
(Christie's)   **$1,215**

A Venetian enameled dish, the depressed well rising to a central point with gadrooned underside and applied footrim, the border embellished with enameled dots in green, blue and white on a wide gilt-scale band beneath a folded rim with blue filigree edge, circa 1500, 25cm. diameter.
(Christie's)   **$24,310**

A late Victorian silver mounted claret jug fashioned as a drake, the removable silver head set with realistic colored glass eyes, the hinged upper beak enclosing a spout, the silver neck mount, tail and webbed feet with engraved and chased naturalistic textures, London 1892, maker F.E., 14" high.

(Spencers) **$10,175**

A Lalique glass 'Capricorne' scent bottle and stopper, 8cm high.
(Spencers) **$8,000**

A finely engraved Nurnberg wine ewer, the flattened pear shaped body engraved on one side with a putto kneeling and holding a basket of fruit above scrolls and flanked by comports of fruit, below a draped baldaquin, the reverse with a putto fishing amidst bulrushes, with Nurnberg marked silver gilt mount to foot and handle, the hinged cover with central flower head within gadrooned border, ball thumbpiece, 33.5cm. high.

(Phillips) **$34,000**

An Almeric Walter pâte-de-verre circular bowl modeled by Henri Bergé, the mottled orange, brown and green body decorated with a band of russet beetles with long delicate antennae, amongst pale green foliage, *molded A Walter Nancy and Bergé Sc*, 7" diameter.

(Christie's) **$3,080**

A Gabriel Argy-Rousseau pâte-de-verre vase of flaring form with knopped neck, molded decoration in green and red with stylized thistles against a mottled amethyst, green and yellow ground, 15.5cm. high.

(Christie's) **$7,172**

A Mount Washington magnum pink dahlia weight, 4 1/4" diameter. *(Christie's)* **$28,600**

A Clutha glass jug of compressed hemispherical form with flared neck and pulled lip, the tinted lime green glass striated with pink and with silver foil inclusions, etched mark *JC & S, Clutha, Registered,* 18.2cm. high
(Christie's) **$6,468**

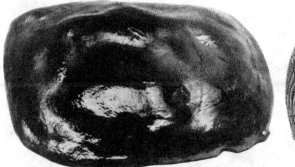

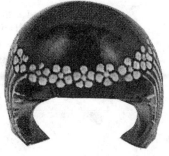

Tiffany Favrile glass red turtleback tile, extraordinary crimson color, of rounded rectangular form with iridized surface, approximately 5³/₄" x 4¹/₂".
(Skinner Inc)   **$1,200**

A rare enameled Lalique glass ring, of blue color with domed cabochon top, 2.5cm. wide.
(Phillips)   **$2,992**

'Cléo de Mérode' pâte de verre mask, by Georges Despret, circa 1907, 12¹/₄" long.
(Christie's)   **$63,000**

A dated enameled carafe, the opaque white panel inscribed *Thos. Worrall 1757*, 22cm. high.
(Christie's)   **$8,393**

A gilt-decorated opaque opaline flared tumbler from the atelier of James Giles, decorated with paterae and bucrania within entwined garlands of husk ornament, the facet cut lower part with flowerhead, foliate and mosaic motifs, the rim gilt, circa 1770, 10cm. high.
(Christie's)   **$5,236**

A green roemer (berkemeyer) of dark tint and with lightly fluted sides, the bowl with flared upper part merging into a cylindrical stem applied with a large flattened prunts, with kick-in base and on a trailed conical foot, Germany, circa 1600, 14.5cm. high.
(Christie's)   **$67,280**

An important transparent-enameled and signed topographical beaker by Samuel Mohn, the cylindrical body painted with a view of the Brandenburg Gate entitled 'Ansicht in Berlin' and with figures in the foreground, in a black-line bordered panel signed *S. Mohn*, 10cm. high. In 1811 Mohn advertized 18 beakers, each with a view of a city and with an oak-leaf border, at prices ranging from 6 to 12 thalers, floral borders cost between 2 and 4 thalers more.
(Phillips)   **$26,250**

An opaque flared tumbler finely painted in a brilliant palette with a bouquet of flowers including a pink rose, a dishevelled striped tulip, passion flower, convolvulus and auricula, a multi-colored butterfly hovering slightly to one side above, perhaps London, 1760–65, 10cm. high.
(Christie's) **$53,757**

A Vienna transparent-enameled topographical cylindrical beaker, painted by Anton Kothgasser with a view of the entrance to Schlofs Schönbrun, within a rectangular amber band cartouche enriched in iron-red, named in black script flanked by anthemion on a matt band below, signed with A.K. initials on the footrim, circa 1815, 9.5cm. high.
(Christie's) **$8,448**

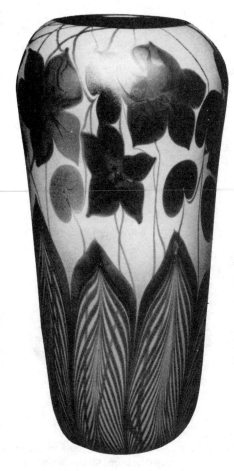

Quezal Monumental Art glass vase, the swelled ovoid form of dark red amber cased with opal white and decorated with green and gold pulled feather design in eight repeats below intricate blossom, with extraordinary iridescence and pink-blue-lavender lustrous highlights, 18" high.
(Skinner Inc)   **$12,000**

An unusual Beijing glass yellow and dark blue overlay slender pear-shaped bottle vase with incised Qianlong four-character mark within a square, cut through with a continuous band of peony, prunus and lotus growing from jagged rockwork, pierced boulders and breaking waves, 9¼" high. The combination of dark blue and yellow overlay glass would appear uncommon.
(Christie's)   **$5,600**

A German amber-tinted ring-beaker (Ringelbecher), the slender conical bowl with a gadrooned collar to the lower part beneath a milled spiraling band and applied with three small lugs, 17th century, 16.5cm. high.
(Christie's) **$14,960**

'Serpent', a fine amber glass vase, of heavily walled oviform shape, a serpent coiled around the body, the head with gaping jaws, poised on the neck of the vessel, 9⁷/₈".
(Bonhams) **$13,280**

Bronze mounted vase by René Lalique, 10¹/₄" high.
(Christie's) **$162,000**

'Archers', a Lalique vivid-blue glass vase, the oviform vessel molded in shallow relief with the naked figures of male archers, aiming their bows at birds in flight above, 26.5cm. high, impress-molded *R. Lalique*.
(Phillips) **$29,920**

English cameo glass portrait vase, with raised flared rim on classic oval vessel set upon a flat pedestal foot, the bright royal blue body layered with white, cameo cut and meticulously carved all around with a scenic portrait of a nude woman, presumably Eve, with long flowing hair, posed with one hand outstretched, the other shading her searching eyes. She stands in a Garden of Eden setting with naturalistic sculptured palm trees, tall ferns, broad leafed plants, and, at ground level, a profusion of grasses, flowers and spreading ground covers, 9" high. Although unsigned, the vase is attributed because of the extraordinary quality of the workmanship to the Stourbridge school, headed by John Northwood from whom George and Thomas Woodall, Frederick Carder, Joshua Hodgetts and others learned the techniques of the art of cameo carving.
(Skinner Inc) **$24,000**

A rare Almeric Walter pate-de-verre paperweight, designed by H. Berge, 8cm. high.
(Christie's) **$15,334**

An Argy-Rousseau pâte-de-verre bowl, with molded decoration of three reserves with a ballerina in white taking her bow, surrounded by stylized rose border, on a mottled yellow ground, 6.3cm. high.
(Christie's) **$5,984**

GLOBES

A rare pair of 18th century 12" table globes by John Sennex and James Ferguson, made by Benjamin Martin, circa 1757.
(Christie's) **$28,875**

Pair of terrestrial and celestial globes by C. Smith of London, circa 1825. The 18" diameter globes are in very good unrestored condition and mounted on simple pedestal stands with splay legs centering compasses.
(Michael Newman) **$45,500**

A fine pair of early 19th century terrestrial and celestial globes on brass azimuth rings and original matching mahogany stands with turned reeded legs. The terrestrial signed *J.W. Cary* and dated 1812, the celestial signed *J. & W. Cary* and dated 1799.
(Michael Newman)   **$91,000**

One of a pair of mid-Victorian terrestrial and celestial globes by Malby's, 56" high, 46" diameter.
(Christie's)   **$311,850**

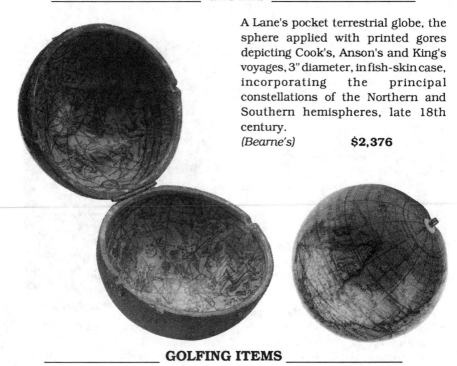

A Lane's pocket terrestrial globe, the sphere applied with printed gores depicting Cook's, Anson's and King's voyages, 3" diameter, in fish-skin case, incorporating the principal constellations of the Northern and Southern hemispheres, late 18th century.
(Bearne's) **$2,376**

GOLFING ITEMS

There is no doubt that golf has proved one of the most popular and enduring games of all time, and its popularity has carried over to influence the value of any golf-related items – not just old clubs and balls, but golfing ashtrays, teasets, clocks, inkwells, hatpins – just about everything in fact. Many auction houses now hold regular sales of golf equipment, books and related memorabilia and these attract large numbers of people and even larger bids.

For the purist, however, it is probably the equipment which is going to prove of most interest. The original golf clubs were made for much rougher fairways and greens than would be acceptable today. The earliest had shafts of ash or hazel; later, American hickory became the dominant wood, with persimmon, also from America, used for the wooden heads. In the 1920s, however, the steel shaft was introduced, and, in most recent times, these can also be made of carbon fiber. The rise in importance of iron-headed clubs, and the increase in popularity of brass and aluminium headed putters coincided with the demise of the feather stuffed ball.

The standard measure for "featheries' was a top-hat full of feathers, which were boiled down (the feathers, not the hat!) and stuffed into a leather casing which was then hammered round and painted white. In 1845, the gutta percha ball was introduced by a Dr Paterson of St Andrews. Early 'gutties' were smooth, but it was found that they flew off the club better when dented, and so they were then textured, at first by hand and subsequently in the molds in which they were made. Gutties in turn were superseded in 1900 by the rubber core ball introduced by Coburn Haskell, in which a narrow strip of rubber was wound round a central core and covered with gutta percha. This new invention was seen to be as durable as its forerunner, and in addition it was softer and did not damage club faces. It forms the basis of modern design.

Feather balls are now rare and often damaged, but good examples will regularly attract four figure prices. One, in near mint condition and made by Allan Robertson around 1840, sold for an amazing $27,500 when auctioned by Christies at St Andrews.

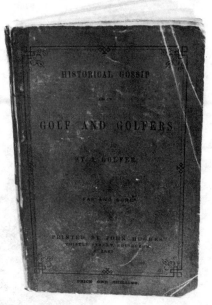

'Historical Gossip about Golf and Golfers', 1863.
(Phillips Chester)   **$20,720**

Another possible golf-related collecting theme is books, which are legion and can be quite valuable. Early 19th century golf books such as Simpson's 'Art of Golf' are rare and can be expensive. 'Historical Gossip about Golf and Golfers' for example, published in 1863, fetched $20,720 at Phillips. There is a wider price range when it comes to books from the late 19th century and Edwardian era. The record, however, is the $35,000 paid also at Phillips for a 2nd edition of Thomas Mathison's 'The Goff', a heroi-comic poem in three cantos.

'The Goff An Heroi-comical Poem', by Thomas Mathison, 3rd Ed., 1793, inscribed 2nd edition, together with appendix and notes and illustrations concerning the original poem, Edinburgh 1793, printed for Peter Hill, 32 pages bound marbled boards and brown calf.
(Phillips Scotland)   **$35,000**

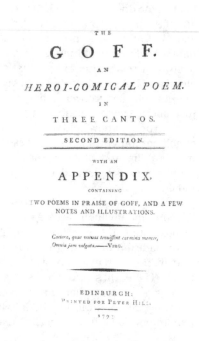

Earlier hand-made clubs are fairly hard to come by as well. These were generally of the scared head type, whereby the club head was attached to the shaft by means of a scared joint, the shaft being spliced around the head and glued, then further strengthened by binding with, for example, fishing line. About 1900 the scared head was superseded by the socket joint, and about this time too wooden clubs were being virtually mass-produced, while iron heads were forged. Collectors look for genuine makers' marks and signs of use and try to obtain authentication wherever possible. Forgeries, in the unpleasant sense of the word, are common.

Two clubs which fetched record prices when auctioned by Christies at St Andrews were late 18th century blacksmith-made track irons which sold to two Japanese collectors for $48,000 and $49,000 respectively.

A fine and unused feather-filled golf ball by Allan Robertson, stamped *Allan* and inscribed *29*, circa 1840.

Allan Robertson (1815-1859) was by common consent the supreme golfer of his era and with his assistant, Tom Morris, he manufactured feather golf balls of the highest quality.
(Christie's Scotland) **$27,500**

Rake iron (used for hitting the ball out of mud or water), circa 1910.
(Christie's) **$88,550**

Golf-related pictures overlap perhaps with the field of art, and other criteria besides their golfing interest may well determine their value. On the assumption, however, that serious art collectors will patronise picture auctions whilst those at sales of golfiana are principally golf enthusiasts, it is worth noting that J. Michael Brown's 'A Rainy Day at St Andrews' depicting the scene at the last hole in the final of the 1913 Amateur Championship sold for $132,000 at Christies St Andrews sale, again to the Japanese.

Rarity and condition have much to do with the value of golfing memorabilia. Take, for example, the Open Championship Medal for 1887, now worth $23,000. At the other end of the scale, though, there are golfing postcards or cigarette cards, which while still quite reasonably priced, seem set to be an excellent investment for the future.

London & North Eastern Railway travel poster for 'Cruden Bay' by Tom
Purvis. *(Onslow's)* **$3,000**

A Carters Poole Art
Deco tile panel,
comprising four six-
inch tiles, block printed
in yellow, blue, red,
mauve, gray and green
with a lady golfer
teeing-off and a couple
standing to one side
watching, 30.2cm.
square.
(Phillips) **$1,239**

'A Rainy Day at St. Andrews' by J. Michael Brown (fl. 1880-1916), signed, oil on canvas, 24" x 36".

This oil painting is most probably of the thirteenth hole at St. Andrews, the last hole in the Final of the Amateur Championship of 1913, played between Harold Hilton and Robert Harris, Harold Hilton winning 6 and 5. The report in 'Golf Illustrated' June 6, 1913, p. 299, of the match records: *The rain came down in thick merciless torrents. Those fortunate enough to be near the tee for the 12th ran hurriedly to shelters where players and officials sought refuge. The officials had to suspend play till the storm had spent itself. The end however was not further delayed for Mr. Harris was never in sight of a half at the 13th. After good tee shots Mr. Harris missed his second shot, while Mr. Hilton pulled his to the left of the green. Mr. Harris reached the hollow short of the green in his third. The new hole had been cut close to this end and Mr. Hilton had to pitch over a gully.*

(Christie's Scotland) **$132,275**

'Golfer', a bronze and ivory figure, cast and carved from a model by D.H. Chiparus, of a girl swinging a golf club and wearing a green-patinated skirt, jumper and hat, standing on a square black marble plinth, 36.8cm. high.

(Christie's) **$16,830**

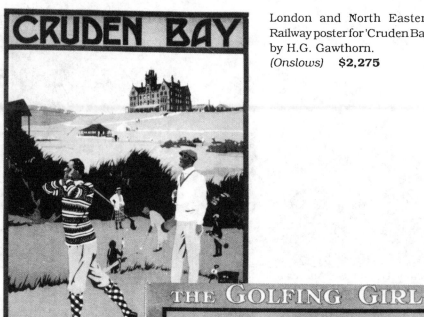

London and North Eastern Railway poster for 'Cruden Bay' by H.G. Gawthorn.
(Onslows)   **$2,275**

The Golfing Girl "Well Out On The True Line" 'The Golfing Girl and All Her Friends Play Good Golf On All The Golf Courses of The Delightful Districts Served By The Caledonian Railway', poster 102cm. x 76cm.
(Onslows)   **$5,542**

The American manufacturing silversmiths and jewelers, the Gorham Corp. was founded in 1815 in Providence, R.I. by Jabez Gorham, and from then on their history was one of constant development.

In the early days, they made jewelry with Stanton Beebe until 1831, when Henry Webster joined the firm to make silver spoons. In 1841 John Gorham joined his father in the business and it was he who installed steam machinery for finishing hand made articles. By 1861 they had opened a New York sales office and in 1868 they adopted the Sterling Standard for silverware and introduced the trade mark of a lion, an anchor and a capital G.

By 1878 they had branches in Chicago and San Francisco. In 1887 Edward Holbrook became head of the firm, and it was he who brought over the London designer, W.C. Codman.

The firm diversified, making Art Nouveau jewelry under the trade mark Martele, and they were among the first to introduce mass production techniques.

In 1925 a bronze foundry was established at Providence, where they produced figures and animals modeled by various artists. These are marked with the artist's name and stamp, a rectangle divided into three with the initials C and G flanking a panther.

The company also made Art Nouveau furniture, usually of ebony, inlaid with silver, mother of pearl and ivory.

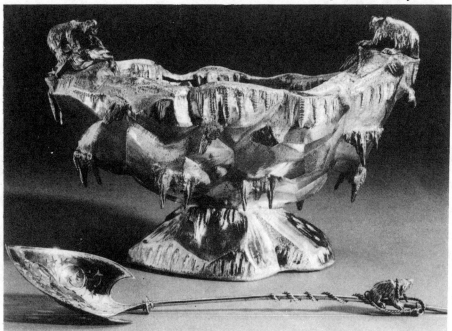

An ice bowl and spoon by Gorham, Providence, 1871, the oval bowl in the form of blocks of ice suspending cast icicles, on a similarly-decorated oval foot, the cast handles in the form of polar bears, 10¾" long, 33oz. 10dwt. *(Christie's)* **$44,000**

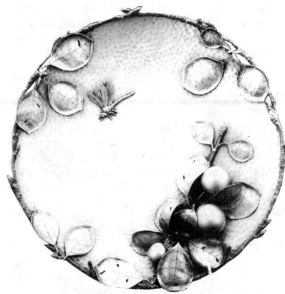

A mixed-metal tazza by Gorham, Providence, 1881, with a bronze applied rim in the form of an apple branch, the hammer-faceted surface applied with a bronze dragonfly and a silver apple branch with three fully-modeled apples, 12" diameter, gross weight 38oz. 10dwt.

(Christie's) **$26,400**

Gorham sterling and mixed metal punch bowl and ladle, Providence, Rhode Island, 1882, with round hammered textured bowl, life size bunches of grapes and leaves on either side of rim, bronze vine form base, ladle has textured handle and applied bunch of grapes, bronze stem, inscription under base and handle, approximately 100 troy ozs.

(Skinner Inc) **$17,000**

The firm of W.H. Goss was established in Stoke on Trent in 1858. It is now principally remembered for the miniature souvenir pieces designed for the new Victorian 'trippers' to take home as a memento of their day out. In fact, it was only after William Goss's eldest son Adolphus joined the company that this potential market was identified and exploited. During its early years, the company had specialized in the parian ware which had first been produced at the Copeland Works in 1846 where William Goss had risen to become chief artist and designer prior to starting his own factory. These were difficult and costly to produce, however, and William supplemented his income in the early days by selling colored enamels to other potteries for decorating china.

Goss model of a Falkland Islands penguin.
(Goss & Crested China Ltd)
$600

This rare oviform vase, containing 597 jewels, was made personally by William Henry, and is probably the most exquisite piece of Goss china ever made. It stands 155mm. high and was produced in 1877, when Goss had perfected the process for producing jeweled porcelain. This method had been patented in 1872, but jeweled ware ceased to be made after 1885. It too has remained in the Goss family until recent years, and is currently valued at $10,000.

The Alhambra vase was made by William Henry Goss in person as a trial piece in his early days. He was fascinated by Moorish design and made this copy of the original in the Alhambra in Granada for the Crystal Palace Exhibition in 1861. It remained in his possession throughout his life, when it passed to other members of his family. Standing 516mm. high, it is currently worth around $20,000.

Other early Goss specialities included jeweled scent bottles and vases. These were produced from pierced and fretted parian, with inset cut glass jewels in the Sevres style.

A very rare W.H. Goss porcelain figure of 'The Trusty Servant', 20cm. high, which supposedly represents all the various attributes desirable in a servant.
(Spencers) **$2,210**

William Henry Goss, a Londoner, born in 1833, started business in 1858 producing fine china in the Copeland style. He might have gone on forever as just another china man had he not been interested in heraldry, and had his eldest son, Adolphus, not had a passion for archaeology. By combining his manufacturing talent and those two great interests, Goss hit upon a unique and highly successful formula for souvenirs for the holiday trade.

The best china shops of the time had shelves crammed with his miniature models of Roman vases, tombs and lighthouses, together with detailed replicas of famous buildings, which are amongst the most sought after pieces of Goss available today.

He made models of 51 cottages between 1893 and 1929, all of which (bar the Massachusetts Hall and Holden Chapel) were British, the two exceptions having been made specifically at the request of his Boston (U.S.) agent.

The firm traded under the name of W.H. Goss & Sons and later W.H. Goss Ltd. Printed marks include W.H. Goss, with goshawk, wings outstretched.

The Feathers Hotel, Ledbury, 114mm. long.
(Goss & Crested China Ltd) **$1,750**

Sulgrave Manor, Northamptonshire, 125mm. long.
(Goss & Crested China Ltd) **$2,187**

First and Last House in England with Annexe, 140mm. long.
(Goss & Crested China Ltd)
$1,500

Hop Kiln, Headcorn, Kent, 89mm. high.
(Goss & Crested China Ltd)
$2,500

Priest's House, Prestbury, 90mm. long.
(Goss & Crested China Ltd)
$2,275

Holden Chapel, Harvard University, Boston, U.S.A., 137mm. long.
(Goss & Crested China Ltd)
$4,500

William H. Grueby (1867–1925) was an American potter who in 1894 formed the Grueby Faience Co. in East Boston, MA. During his training he had worked at the tile factory of J.G. Low, and had also been a partner in an ill-fated company making tin-glazed earthenware for architectural use. The development of glazes fascinated him, and he was able to draw on all these experiences in his new company, which produced tiles, often in the Hispano-Moresque style, and plaques inspired by the designs of the Della Robbia family.

Vases were another of their lines, and from 1898 Grueby used matt glazes of opaque enamel in shades of yellow, brown, blue and sometimes red. The most characteristic of all, however, was a dark green with a veined effect. These vases tended to be hand thrown and were either plain or with simple geometric patterns and decorated with plant forms in low relief. From 1904 scarab shaped paperweights were added to the range.

Grueby pottery two-tile scenic frieze, Boston, circa 1902, depicting four cows in various states of grazing and repose in landscape with trees and river on the horizon, done in brown, cream, shades of green and gray-blue, unsigned, 12¼" square.
(Skinner Inc) **$6,250**

The influence of the Art Nouveau style is also visible in Grueby's tile design. These were hand decorated with images of flowers, animals, knights and forest scenes etc.

From 1899, art pottery was made under the name of Grueby Pottery and this was incorporated in a separate entity in 1907. Sadly, however, the Grueby Faience Co. was soon in difficulties and by the following year was bankrupt, though a new firm, the Grueby Faience and Tile Co., continued making architectural ware. Vase production had completely ceased before the outbreak of war in 1914, while the tile interest was sold in 1919 and finally went out of business in 1930. Grueby was a contemporary of Stickley, (q.v.) and the simplicity, not to say severity, of many of their designs suggests that they had much in common. A Stickley table, decorated with twelve 4-inch green Grueby tiles is an irresistible example of the combination of their two talents.

Grueby pottery polar bear tile, Boston, rectangular-form with molded decoration of polar bear in white with deep blue background, unmarked, 5⅝" x 7".
(Skinner Inc) **$350**

Tiffany leaded glass and Grueby pottery table lamp, circa 1910, the Tiffany pomegranate shade in colors of yellow and orange in a mottled green field, broad leaf Grueby base in matte blue green glaze, shade signed *Tiffany Studios/New York/ 1561-24,* artist's initials on paper label partially obscured, probably *Ruth Erickson,* impressed *Grueby* mark on base and remnants of various paper labels, 15" high.
(Skinner Inc)   **$7,500**

Gustav Stickley table with twelve Grueby tiles, circa 1902–04, with four flat rails framing 12 four-inch green tiles over arched skirt and lower rectangular shelf with keyed tenons, slight splay to legs, signed with large red decal, 24" wide.
(Skinner Inc)   **$29,000**

'Le Tennis' a crepe handkerchief, printed in green with figures playing tennis, with an orange border, signed *Raoul Dufy*, 15" square, circa 1918-1924.
(Christie's)   **$1,533**

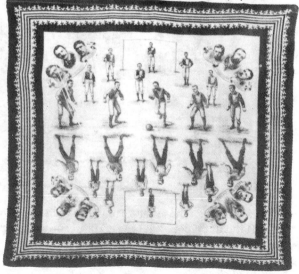

A commemorative cotton handkerchief printed with two football teams in play formation, with various team captains commemorated on the four corners, including A. Hunter, Aston Villa, Birmingham; W. Sudell Esq, Preston; J. Mills, Swinton, Manchester; and W. Draper, Old Boys, Liverpool, with wide purple and brown patterned border, 1890's, 26$\frac{1}{2}$" x 28$\frac{1}{2}$".
(Christie's)   **$612**

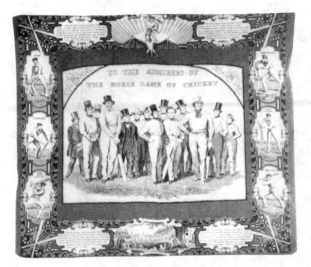

To the Admirers of the Noble Game of Cricket, a commemorative cotton handkerchief, printed with the England XI of 1847, after the watercolor by Felix, the wide red border interspersed with extracts from the laws of cricket, vignettes of a batsman in various poses and a village game, surmounted by the figure of the same batsman riding a bat (mammal), 26¹/₂" x 32¹/₂". *(Christie's)* **$489**

'Lawn Tennis. Those Who This Pleasant Game Would Try Should be Quick of Hand and Foot and Eye', a 19th century cotton handkerchief printed in black and red depicting 4 children playing lawn tennis with caption beneath, 13¹/₂" x 14".
(Christie's) **$721**

Pair of Continental agate and lapis candlesticks, probably German, 18th/19th century, the octagonal knopped stems mounted with lapis plaques, spreading molded base, carnelian feet, 9" high.
(Skinner Inc) **$4,250**

A fine bloodstone model of a carronade, the tapering multi-form barrel decorated with relief moldings, plain trunions and cascabel, on artillery-type carriage, with spoked wheels and with turned agate ram-rod, second half of the 18th century, 9½" long.

Robert Bell (1761-1844), then a Major of the Honble. East India Company's Madras Artillery, led fifty artillery men, with a proportion of gun lascars in the attack on the Fort of Seringapatam. Following the success of the attack Major Bell was one of the Commissioners of Prizes and acquired this model for himself. *(Christie's)* **$12,166**

A very rare calcified jade figure of a seated man, the knees folded with both hands resting on them, the face very well carved with a smiling contented expression, the large ears and the crisp outline of his hat clearly defined, Han Dynasty, 5.5cm. high. Human figures occur very rarely in Han jades.
(Christie's) **$79,640**

A gold table-seal, the handle chased and engraved overall with putti climbing amongst vines, the twisted trunk surrounded by two putti with baskets of grapes on plain gold mount, the white agate matrix engraved with a coat-of-arms and motto, probably French, circa 1830, 3¹/₄" high.
(Christie's) **$13,475**

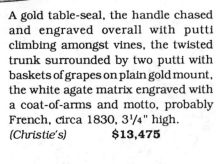

A hardstone model of a spray of lily-of-the-valley with nephrite leaves and gilt-metal stem in a rock-crystal vase, circa 1910, in fitted Cartier case, 5" high.
(Christie's) **$14,437**

An English gold-mounted hardstone rectangular necessaire, on four shell feet, the walls of panels of striated agate over a painted ground, mounted in a cage-work of gold chased with flowers and scrolls, a stag and two hounds, the hinged cover with later pine-cone finial, containing two gold-mounted cut-glass scent-bottles, a gold-mounted mirror, a pair of ivory tablets, gold-mounted scissors, earpick and various steel implements, circa 1760, 4³/₈" high.
(Christie's) **$4,866**

A fine and rare Imperial German officers helmet of the Saxon Guard Reiter regiment. Tombak skull with fine helmet plate of silvered rayed star with Landwehr cross and Saxony arms, German silver edge strip trim, gilt leather backed chinscales, both cockades, lobster tail neck guard, with silvered lion parade crest, supporting shield with Royal cypher, silk and leather lining.
(Wallis & Wallis) **$17,300**

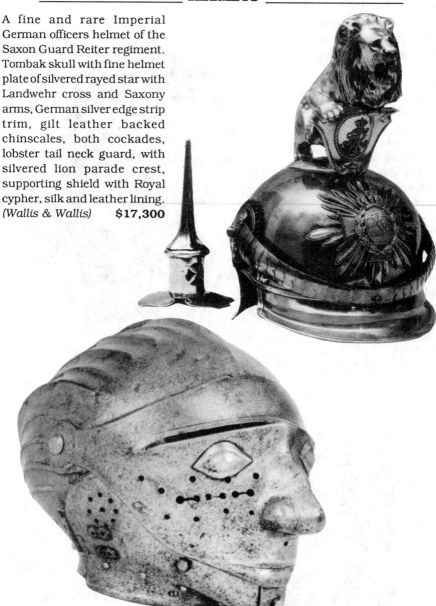

Armet in the manner of Hans Seusenhofer of Innsbruck, circa 1515-20, 9¼" high.

This item belongs to the well-known group of helmets with grotesque visors produced in the Innsbruck Court Workshop by Konrad Seusenhofer and his brother Hans.
(Christie's) **$55,407**

HELMETS

A rare Saxon Electoral Guard comb morion of one piece with roped comb and brim, the base of the skull encircled by sixteen gilt-brass lion-masks capping the lining rivets, the surface decorated with gilt etching against a blued ground comprising figures of Mutius Scaevola and of Marcus Curtius leaping into the gulf, with the Nuremberg mark, circa 1580, 11 1/2" high. This belongs to the group of helmets made for the Trabantan Guard of the Electors of Saxony.

(Christie's)   **$21,175**

HORSE MUZZLE

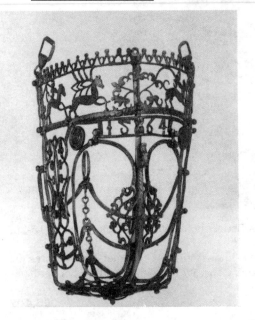

A rare German tinned iron horse-muzzle, constructed of slender riveted bars framing panels of foliated scrollwork, the upper borders involving stags pursued by hounds, surmounted by pierced triangular cresting, the front with applied dragon between the nostril openings and below a panel framing the date 1564, 10 1/2" x 11".

(Christie's S. Ken)
$9,625

HUMPEN

A German dated enameled Reichsadler humpen of greenish tint, enameled in colors with the crowned Imperial Eagle, its breast bearing a portrait within an oval cartouche inscribed above *Römisher Kaÿser* and its wings with named portraits of the seven Electors, with kick-in base, perhaps Franconia 1662, 20.5cm. high.

(Christie's) **$18,480**

A German enameled dated wagoner's guild humpen of pale greenish-gray tinted metal, enameled in colors with five draught-horses drawing a cart bearing barrels and driven by a wagoner holding a long whip, on a wide band spiraling round the slightly tapering cylindrical body. The upper part including the inscription *Allmein thun und anfang midtell undt endeß rthet allein in Gotteß handt • 'Gott un unß'* (All my doing and beginning, middle and end rests solely in God's hand. 'God and us') above the date 1660, the lower part inscribed *Drinck und iß Gott nicht vergiß* (Drink and do not forget God), with kick-in base, Franconia or Bohemia, 1660, 17cm. high.

(Christie's) **$24,156**

261

A four-case Kinji Inro richly decorated in Shibayama-style with an elaborately caparisoned elephant attended by two karako, a group of karako playing musical instruments on the reverse, signed *Yutokusai*, 19th century, with an attached turquoise ojime, 8.7cm. *(Christie's)* **$12,870**

A fine kinji ground slender five-case inro decorated in gold and silver hiramakie, takamakie, kirigane and takazogan with Ushiwakamaru playing a flute outside the residence of Joruri hime, the reverse with a veranda of a mansion with koto and a candle-holder, signed *Hasegawa Shigeyoshi saku* and *Ryumin*, early 19th century, 9.6cm. high. *(Christie's)* **$12,727**

INSTRUMENTS

Early scientific instruments have become very popular collectibles, and more and more are coming on to the market as they are replaced by modern electronic gadgets which do the job but are not nearly as decorative. There are plenty available from the 19th century, and the best examples of telescopes, microscopes etc, should be of brass or at least brass mounted. Good pieces will fetch sums comfortably into four figures, while the sky is literally the limit for some of the astrolabes and other items dating from earlier times.

A brass astrolabe, signed *Georgivs Hartman Norenberge Faciebat Anno MDXXXII*, 137mm. diameter.
(Christie's) **$26,400**

An early George III mahogany angle barometer with thermometer framing a perpetual calendar by F. Watkins, London, the angled barometric tube with signed silvered register plate and sliding recorder, the cistern cover turned and fluted, the alcohol thermometer with similar recorder and corresponding bulb cover, 41" x 25".
(Phillips) **$37,840**

Early scientific instruments have long had a devoted following, and one of the most sought after pieces among these is the astrolabe, a medieval device for measuring altitude. This fine example was made by Regio Montanus or Johannes Muller in 1462 and was dedicated to Cardinal Bessarion, the Papal Legate in Venice. When auctioned at Christie's South Kensington it was sold for $355,000.

A magnificent late 18th century silver George Adams 'Variable' microscope.
(Christie's) **$38,500**

A fine late 18th century French lacquered brass theodolite signed *Lenoir à Paris*, with carrying case.
(Christie's) **$19,250**

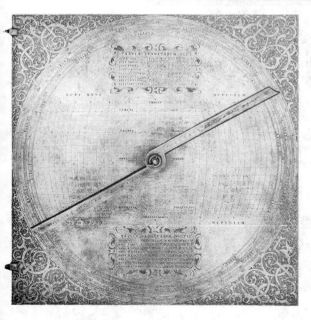

A rare and important 16th century gilt-copper astrolabe quadrant signed *Christophorvs Schissler* and dated 1576.
(Christie's) **$327,250**

A fine and rare mid 19th century Islamic celestial globe from the workshop of Lalah Balhumal Lahuri.
(Christie's) **$13,475**

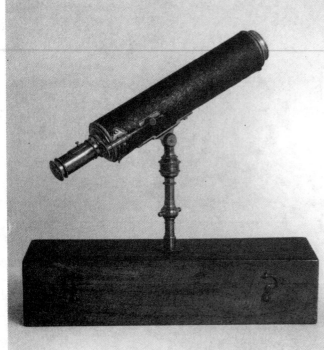

An 18th century brass and simulated leather 1¾" reflecting telescope by George Friedrich Brander.
(Christie's) **$5,000**

A rare and unusual carved ivory mirrorback, mid 14th century, Paris school.
(Spencers) **$49,000**

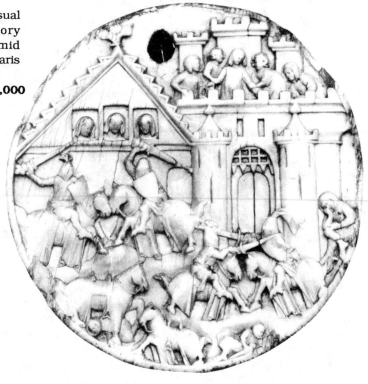

An impressive ivory carving of a mass of rats clustered on a group of nuts and bean pods, their eyes inset in pale horn, signed Nobukazu, late 19th century, 23cm. long.
(Christie's) **$34,650**

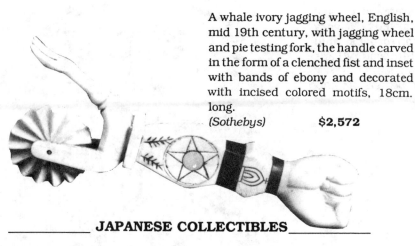

A whale ivory jagging wheel, English, mid 19th century, with jagging wheel and pie testing fork, the handle carved in the form of a clenched fist and inset with bands of ebony and decorated with incised colored motifs, 18cm. long.
(Sothebys) **$2,572**

JAPANESE COLLECTIBLES

Japanese inros, netsukes and tsubas all appertain to traditional Japanese dress, and, as such, have no real Western counterpart. Inros are slim, rectangular, lacquered boxes used by men to carry their family seal, medicines and their tobacco. They were worn hanging from the belt beside their sword and were in general use between the 16th and 19th centuries. Most were made in three-five sections which slotted neatly together. Cords were threaded through the sides of the box and each cord was kept in place by a bead called an ojime. The knot between the inro and the belt (obi) was kept in place by a netsuke.

The simplest of these were wooden toggles, but Japanese craftsmen seized on them as a medium for their art and made them out of ivory, bone, jade, amber and horn, carving them with birds, animals, flowers or people.

Tsubas were another medium for the craftsman's art. These are the hand protectors for Japanese swords, about 2" across with a wedge shaped hole for the sword blade, often with other openings too for the sword knife and skewer. Tsubas could be made of iron, brass or copper and were often inlaid and applied with decorations in gold, silver, champleve, or cloisonne, showing landscapes and historical scenes. Like netsuke, they became a subject for **specialized craftsmen**.

An oval iron Tsuchimeji Tsuba decorated in takazogan and nunomezogan with crabs of various sizes among reeds, signed Shoami, 19th century, 7.4cm.
(Christie's) **$4,041**

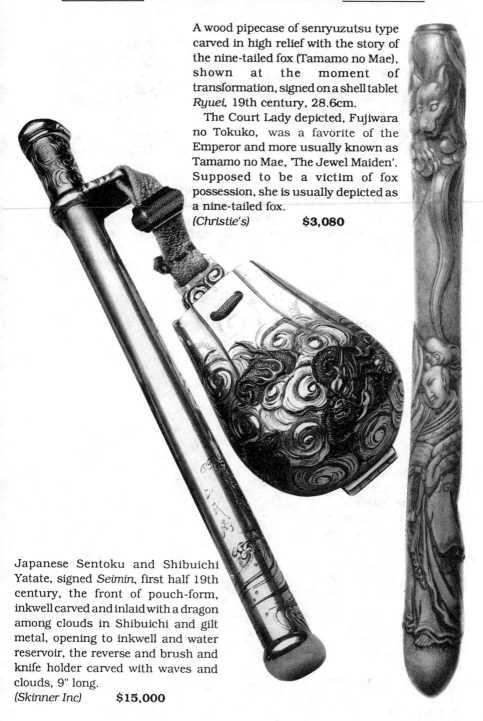

A wood pipecase of senryuzutsu type carved in high relief with the story of the nine-tailed fox (Tamamo no Mae), shown at the moment of transformation, signed on a shell tablet *Ryuei*, 19th century, 28.6cm.

The Court Lady depicted, Fujiwara no Tokuko, was a favorite of the Emperor and more usually known as Tamamo no Mae, 'The Jewel Maiden'. Supposed to be a victim of fox possession, she is usually depicted as a nine-tailed fox.

(Christie's)   **$3,080**

Japanese Sentoku and Shibuichi Yatate, signed *Seimin*, first half 19th century, the front of pouch-form, inkwell carved and inlaid with a dragon among clouds in Shibuichi and gilt metal, opening to inkwell and water reservoir, the reverse and brush and knife holder carved with waves and clouds, 9" long.

(Skinner Inc)   **$15,000**

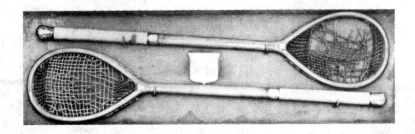

A pair of Jefferies Racquets, the oval heads with stringing, the necks with small applied silver shield shaped plaques, the handles with silver mounts and terminals, chased and engraved with foliage, wrapped in blue linen, 30³/₄" long, applied with a silver shield-shaped plaque inscribed *J.P. Rodger, Winner of the Single Racquets, Eton 1869.*
(Christie's)   **$2,695**

KAKIEMON

A highly important Kakiemon circular deep bowl decorated in iron-red, green, yellow, blue and black enamels, the interior with branches of pomegranates, peaches and finger citron, circa 1680, 31.5cm. diameter.

Bowls such as this show the Kakiemon style at its best, and emphasize its special brilliance of design. This particular example is one of the largest known, and has on its outside an elegant arrangement of tree peonies and a crested long-tailed pheasant.
(Christie's) **$1,102,200**

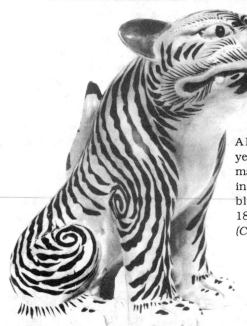

A Kakiemon model of a seated tiger its yellow body painted with brown fur markings, the mouth and ears detailed in iron-red, the eyes in green with black pupils, late 17th century, 18.5cm. high.

(Christie's) **$61,600**

LACQUER

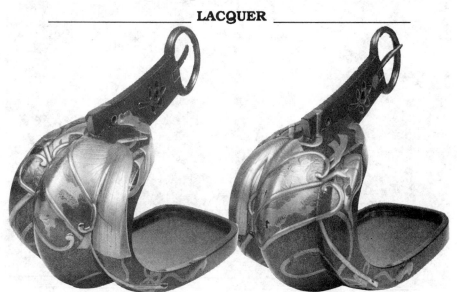

A pair of iron stirrups decorated in takamakie, hiramakie and heidatsu with sahari, hossu and gunsen, the last decorated with dragons in clouds, all on a nashiji ground, the inner surfaces lacquered red, unsigned, 19th century, each 29cm. long.

(Christie's) **$5,214**

LACQUER

A Ming carved red lacquer dish with shallow rounded sides rising to a stepped rim, the interior carved with a peacock standing on rockwork with wings and tail feathers fully extended amidst lotus sprays, the reverse with a continuous floral meander, probably 16th century, 17cm. diameter.
(Christie's) **$67,375**

LAMPS

Rare Limbert copper and mica Prairie School table lamp, Michigan, circa 1913, the trapezoidal copper framed shade with cut out vine silhouette lined with mica on oak double pedestal standard and cross-base, branded on foot, 24" wide.
(Skinner Inc) **$50,000**

The urge to create light in the darkness must be one of the most primitive and atavistic of man's desires and all sorts of subconscious, emotional reasons may therefore have contributed to the enormous popularity of lamps as collectibles.

There is a ready market in all lamps, even the functional Tilley and brass carbide varieties. The lamp maker's art, however, found its greatest exponents in the great glass makers of the late 19th/early 20th century. Daum, Gallé, Lalique, Handel, Loetz all turned their genius to creating magnificent examples now worth many thousands of dollars, while the Tiffany shade has become almost a generic term in its own right.

'Batwomen', a large and unusual painted bronze and ivory figural table lamp cast and carved from a model by Roland Paris the base adorned with three Batwomen each wearing a bat-cape, red cap and a mask, they stand with their hands linked beneath the original pagoda-style shade, 93cm. high.
(Phillips) **$12,600**

'Peony' triple overlay glass table lamp by the firm of Emile Gallé, 24¹/₂" high; the shade 18¹/₈" diameter.
(Christie's) **$242,000**

Rare Pairpoint blown-out puffy apple tree lamp with extraordinary large blown glass shade handpainted on the interior to depict alternating seasons of the apple tree, spring blossoms, summer leaves with butterflies and bumble bees, and autumn fruits, all in brilliant primary colors enhanced by light from within, diameter 15½", raised on conforming four-arm holder.
(Skinner Inc) **$25,000**

'Rosebush' leaded glass and bronze table lamp by Tiffany Studios, 29½" high.
(Christie's) **$363,000**

'Pond Lily' leaded glass and bronze table lamp by Tiffany Studios, 26" high.
(Christie's) **$550,000**

A rare rose engine by Holtzapffel & Co., No. 1637 with mahogany double frame, massive iron bed, treadle, crankshaft and flywheel, eight drawer full-length mahogany cabinet under bed, hand crank drive at front of bed to work via treadle wheel to large pulley on mandrel tail, long heavy headstock trunnioned under bed to swing with worm adjustable spring centering device and lock to secure headstock for plain turning, 54" wide x 51" high, 6" center, mandrel 1 1/16" x 9.45 t.p.i.

There are believed to be only six of these machines made of which all are thought to survive. The most famous is that belonging to the Society of Ornamental Turners, and the sister to this one is in the Ogden collection in USA. 1637 was first supplied to William Peters Nov. 1838, and early in the present century was in the possession of the Royal Mint. It was subsequently owned in Australia and America. It appears to have been little used in modern times.

(Christie's) **$40,000**

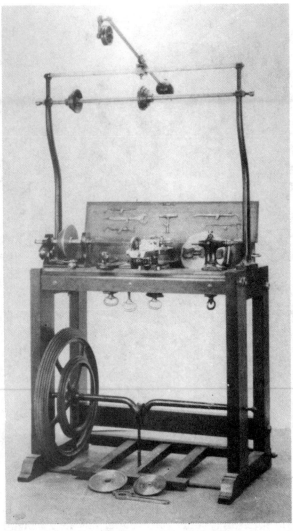

An ornamental lathe by Holtzapffel number 2333, with double mahogany frame, iron bed, treadle gear, crankshaft and flywheel, double standard overhead of Evans pattern, traversing mandrel headstock with brass pulley, six rows of divisions, index, screw barrel tailstock, hand rest base with three tees, boring collar and stand, ornamental slide rest, spiral apparatus with face spiral fittings, Bennett's die chuck and key, twenty-three various brass work-chucks, vertical cutting frame, eccentric cutting frame, horizontal cutting frame, drill spindle, various keys, spanners and sundries, and long fitted mahogany back box, 45" long x 84" high.

Number 2333 was originally supplied in 1879.

(Christie's) **$8,894**

The doyen of model figure production was undoubtedly William Britain, who launched his invention of hollow cast lead figures on the UK toy market in 1894. They were made from simple casts, came in a wide range of typical military poses and remained pre-eminent until the use of lead was banned on health grounds in 1962. Once discontinued (replaced by plastic), they immediately became collectors' items and now change hands for sums that are quite amazing, especially considering their original cost.

Though the paintwork was fairly basic, detail was surprisingly good. Early figures had no identifying marks and were cast on oval bases. Between 1900–1912 the bases were stamped 'William Britain', between 1912–17 the mark was 'Britain's Ltd' and after that 'England' was added.

The range grew steadily and bases became square in shape. Some early figures were withdrawn and reintroduced much later with different numbers. Interestingly, a few rich customers were willing to pay an extra few cents to have their set painted by a more skilful craftsman, and such sets of course command particularly high prices.

Britains also introduced display boxed sets, which proved very popular. The mounted regiments of the British Army, introduced in the first year of production, are amongst the most desirable, as are foreign sets, such as the South African Mounted Infantry. More unusual sets such as the Salvation Army Bandsmen can also sell for sums in excess of $1,700.

The world's most expensive set of toy soldiers however, was sold by Phillips in London. This was a rare set of 281 figures, (the largest ever made by Britains) including infantrymen, bandsmen, sailors and Camel Corps soldiers in original box with two lift-out trays. This set, no. 131, fetched $17,500.

Heyde for Märklin, hand-painted cast lead German Naval band of 19 pieces, circa 1912.
(Christie's S. Ken) **$7,172**

Large display box Set 93, containing Coldstream Guards with mounted officer, four pioneers, thirteen-piece band, two officers, twelve marching, twelve running, two trumpeters, six troopers and fifteen normal troopers, 1938, Britain's.
(Phillips) **$11,550**

An early Britains set 149, American Soldiers, 'Military Display and Game', in original box, circa 1907.
(Christie's) **$2,695**

Britains extremely rare set 1645, Walt Disney's Mickey Mouse, with Minnie Mouse, Goofy, Clarabelle Cow, Donald Duck and Pluto, 1939.
(Phillips)   **$3,652   £2,200**

Rare Britains Set 1339, Royal Horse Artillery at the gallop, in the original box.
(Phillips)   **$11,550**

'The Royal Horse Artillery' in Service Dress with peaked caps and khaki uniform, by Britain's. set 318.
(Phillips) **$10,725**

LIBERTY

The English retail firm of Liberty & Co. was established in 1875 by Arthur Lasenby Liberty, who had formerly been a manager of the London Oriental warehouse in Regent Street. From the 1880's the company was commissioning a range of Art fabrics and goods using designs by many of the graduates from the Royal Academy of Art which had been opened in the 1850's. Liberty was a foremost promoter of the Art Nouveau style, and sold furniture, for example, which showed a marked Arts & Crafts influence. They also sold and popularized art pottery by such names as Brannam and Moorcroft. Unsurprisingly, in view of the background of the founder, Oriental and Moorish influences were also discernible in their designs.

A very unusual pair of Art Nouveau hair ornaments of asymmetrical design, hammered finish yellow metal tops each set with a single drop shape opaline glass, circa 1900, fitted Liberty case.
(Bonhams) **$6,460**

One Otto Von Guericke, a contemporary of Robert Boyle, is generally regarded as producing the first light from electricity back in the 17th century when he discovered that by holding the hands firmly against a revolving ball of sulphur, the friction produced a dull glow. It wasn't, however, until the electric arc was discovered early in the 19th century by Sir Humphrey Davy, that a practical source of artificial light was established.

Light bulbs themselves date from about 1841 when an American inventor named Starr found that a bright light could be produced by sending an electric current through a piece of carbon.

The first successful incandescent electric lamps produced in the U.K. were made by J.W. Swan of Newcastle and subsequently by several other inventors and pioneers including St. George Lane Fox, while in America the market was dominated by T.A. Edison.

All these manufacturers used carbonized material as the filament, such as a cotton thread (Swan), a fiber of grass (Lane Fox) or a sliver of bamboo (Edison). Such light was regarded with fascination and carbon filament lamps were tremendously popular from 1880 until the turn of the century.

The big breakthrough came in 1906 when the General Electric Company found that by using a tungsten filament sealed in a glass bulb, it not only produced a clear white light but used very little electricity as well.

This revolutionized the whole industry and created a massive demand, though doubts were expressed at the time as to the adverse effect all this powerful light would have on the eyesight of future generations.

Early light bulbs are now commanding healthy prices. This English Swan 'Pipless' light bulb dating from 1882, is now worth **$600**

Late 19th century 'Sunbeam Lamp' electric light bulb, with lobed element, 11" high. **$600**

A Louis Vuitton shaped motor car trunk, covered in black material, interior with three matching fitted suitcases, each with white cotton interiors and straps, all labeled *Louis Vuitton Paris, Nice, Lille, London,* No's 190383 to 190386, the suitcases with monogram locks, the trunk with brass drop strap loops each end, 85cm. x 65cm. x 50cm.
(Onslows) **$6,475**

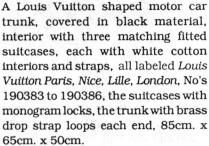

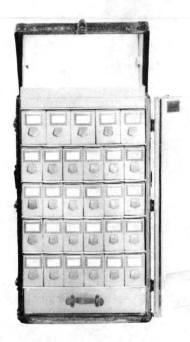

The only drawback to period luggage is its weight. Air travelers are forced to stick to lightweight cases for practicality but it is difficult to beat the old ones for style and appearance. In the days when weight did not matter, there was a huge market for suitcases and bags of all sorts made from real leather. The steamship cases made by Vuitton can sometimes be seen in films set on ocean liners, huge upstanding things like wardrobes.

A Louis Vuitton shoe secretaire, covered in LV material, on castors, bound in brass and leather with brass carrying handles, fitted with thirty shoe boxes with lids, two large drawers top and bottom and tray, all lined in white felt, labeled inside *Louis Vuitton Paris, London No 778790 bought from Saks & Company Fifth Avenue New York,* lock No 064055 with key, 112cm. x 64cm. x 40cm.
(Onslows) **$11,470**

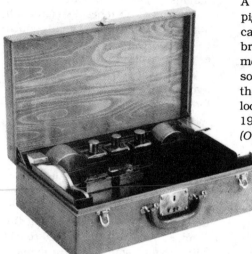

A Louis Vuitton special order tan pigskin gentleman's fitted dressing case, accessories include silver tooth brush, soap and talc containers, silver mounted hair and clothes brushes, some pieces stamped *LV*, the inside of the case stamped in gilt No 790855 lock No 074213, 54cm. x 32cm., circa 1930.
(Onslows) **$4,625**

A Louis Vuitton 'Sac Chauffeur', the two circular halves covered in black material, the lower section watertight, marked *Sac Chauffeur Vuitton London Paris*, with three brass strap rings and replacement straps, 89cm. diameter, circa 1905. This model was designed to fit inside spare tyres.
(Onslows) **$5,550**

A Louis Vuitton Johnny Walker whisky travelling drinks case, covered in LV material, with leather carrying handle, the light brown pigskin interior stamped Louis Vuitton fitted for one bottle of whisky, two bottles of mineral water, one packet of cheese biscuits, two glasses and ice container.
(Onslows) **$3,700**

An ebonized oak ladderback chair designed by Charles Rennie Mackintosh for the Willow Tearooms, Glasgow, the chair stamped number 24, the seat number 3, circa 1903, 41 1/2" high.
(Christie's Glasgow) **$40,000**

The Willow Tearooms on Sauchiehall Street in Glasgow, for which this chair was designed, were the most prestigious of all the Glasgow tearooms run by Miss Catherine Cranston, the famous Glasgow restaurant owner. They opened in October 1904 although Mackintosh had been commissioned to work on designs for the establishment since the spring of 1903. It was his only commission for a tearoom for which he was responsible for the complete design of the facades, interiors, furniture and fittings.

Mackintosh devised a decorative theme based loosely on willow-trees for the restaurant, as 'Sauchiehall' means 'avenue of willows' in Gaelic. However, he did not adhere to this idea to the exclusion of all other decorative devices, and he rang the changes in each of the several rooms with varying themes based principally on light-colored interiors and dark-stained furniture, although some furniture was painted either white or silver, primarily in the 'Room de Luxe'. The dark-stained ladderback chairs were an ubiquitous feature of each room, apart from the 'Room de Luxe', these being the Front Saloon, Back Saloon, and the Gallery. The ladderback chair can be seen therefore as the workhorse of the Willow Tearoom, intended to be strong and basic enough for prolonged use, as well as of sufficiently sophisticated design to be an important element of the elegant overall decorative theme.

Mackintosh had designed other ladderback chairs, notably in 1893 and 1901; this particular one was intended to be primarily functional and secondarily, decorative. One hundred and thirty-seven of the chairs were supplied to the restaurant by Alex Martin, the cabinet maker who carried out many of Mackintosh's furniture designs, and these were paid for in December 1903 for the sum of £0.17.6d. each. Unfortunately the chairs proved to be slightly less sturdy than intended and a further support had to be fixed at the top of the two main uprights, forming an additional top rail behind the ladder rungs, giving the chairs a distinctive originality and character.

After the sale of the tearooms in the 1920's the chairs were dispersed by auction, some being acquired by the Grosvenor Restaurant. These two chairs were purchased by the present owner from a Glasgow antique shop in the early 1950s for $15.

At the present time there are still approximately thirty chairs unaccounted for.

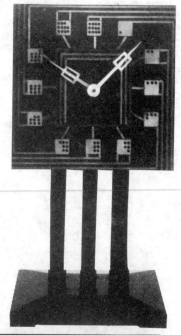

The Sturrock Domino clock, designed by Charles Rennie Mackintosh as a wedding present to Alex Sturrock and Mary Newbery, 25cm. high.
(Phillips)   **$73,500**

A stained oak cabinet designed by Charles Rennie Mackintosh, with beaten brass door panels signed by Margaret Macdonald and dated 1899, 182cm. wide.
(Phillips)   **$210,000**

A.D.W. Hislop set of four silver spoons and forks designed by Charles Rennie Mackintosh, the two spoons with deep bowls, incised junctions and slender tapering stems, stamped with maker's marks and Glasgow hallmarks for 1902. The silver cutlery was one of twelve sets designed by Mackintosh in 1902 for Francis Newbury, headmaster of The Glasgow School of Art. *(Christie's)*   **$36,960**

DONALD MCGILL

Donald McGill, the 'King of Sauce' had the last laugh when a collection of his original watercolors and postcards, including ones used as evidence in obscenity trials, made double the estimated amount when sold at auction.

Tim Heath, Spencer's auctioneer, who conducted the sale said "it was ironic that the artist had died in reduced circumstances because of his art when now it is so keenly sought after."

Frantic competition resulted in the highest price of the day being paid for a watercolor depicting a bathroom scene with a chamber maid bursting in on a large, and almost naked, gentleman. This sold for $1,665 and funnily enough was taken from a real-life situation in which McGill had once found himself – he turned embarrassment into amusement.

An original comic postcard design framed with corresponding postcard captioned 'Why The Devil Did'nt You Knock?' 'Its Alright Sir. I Looked Through the Keyhole Just to Make Sure You Wasn't In Your Bath'. Signed, watercolor, 19.5cm. x 14.5cm.

(Spencers) **$1,665**

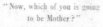

An original comic postcard design framed with corresponding postcard captioned 'Now, Which Of You is Going to be Mother?'. Signed, watercolor, 18.5cm. x 14cm. *(Spencers)* **$1,500**

An important white marble urn in the manner of Thomas Hope, with a domed cover and gadrooned body, on a concave-sided triangular base carved with anthemia, husks, feathery wings and lion's paw feet, circa 1807, 38" high.

The handles on this urn are almost identical to those illustrated on an urn on plate XXXIV of Hope's Household Furniture & Interior Decoration, 1807, whilst the body and overall form, excepting the sophisticated triangular base is almost identical to plate XLVIII, No. 3, which is described as 'a copy of a vase in the Barbarini Collection'.

(Hy Duke & Son)   **$24,500**

A white marble trough, of rectangular form, the front and sides carved with cherubs, riding chariots, raised on winged sphinx supports, 45½" wide.
(Christie's)   **$14,080**

A 19th century Greek sculpted white marble figure of a naked, smiling young boy, in a bath tub, inscribed in Greek *D. Filippoteos, Tenios, Made in Athens, 1885*, on a cylindrical and stepped marble column, 34" high overall.
(Christie's)   **$18,300**

An Italian porphyry and red marble tazza with shallow oval body, the turned spreading base with molded black marble plinth, possibly associated, early 19th century.
(Christie's) **$2,763**

A pair of white marble urns-on-pedestals, each urn of ovoid shape, the ribbed body divided by a band of interlaced guilloché, the waisted neck edged with egg-and-dart flanked by scrolling foliate handles with swans, the covers with cone finials, each pedestal with lappeted leaves and berries on turned bases, circa 1800, 82" high.

"These neo-grec vases on sepulchral cippi columns were conceived around 1800 by the francophile connoisseur, collector, patron and designer Thomas Hope (1769-1831) in his romantic grecian manner to serve like cinerary urns in honour of his Scottish ancestry, with perhaps, a claim of descent from the Trojan tribe that escaped from Greek captivity."
(Christie's) **$149,600**

Bubble gum came to Britain in 1942 with the US forces who were stationed there after America's entry into World War II. Despite its instant popularity however, it was not until the early 1950s that a domestic industry emerged, with A & BC becoming rapidly established as market leader.

Manufacturers gave away cards with their wares and also designed colorful wrappers of waxed paper, printed with pictures of TV and pop stars, Wild West heroes and the like. New designs were launched every few weeks, and many wrappers are therefore quite rare.

In 1957 the launch of the Sputnik caused new themes of space travel and science fiction to be introduced, and these quickly became among the most popular.

The heyday of the wrapper in the UK spans the two decades from 1953-73, though earlier examples from as far

back as the 1930s can be found from American brands. The ultimate bubble gum wrapper prize is, however, Mars Attacks, issued in 1962 and quickly withdrawn following complaints that some of the lurid designs frightened children. One of these will now fetch $200.

MARTINWARE

A rare and highly unusual Martin Brothers Stoneware bird, modeled as a likeness of the British Prime Minister Benjamin Disraeli, the creature has a distinctly hooked beak/nose and small goatee beard, heavy brows and piercing gaze, 37cm. high, signed on neck and base *R.W. Martin & Brothers, London & Southall dated V-1889.*

(Phillips) **$14,960**

MARTINWARE

A Martin Brothers 'John Barleycorn jug, the ovoid body modeled with grinning face amid hops and foliage, with mottled glaze, the eyes in black and white, 18cm. high, incised mark and 6-1911.
(Lawrence Fine Art) **$880**

MASKS

Northwest coast hawk mask of polychromed alder wood, 9½" high, 8" wide.
(Skinner Inc) **$41,000**

Northwest coast mask, Bella/Bella Coola, of polychrome cedar wood, 12⅝" high.
(Skinner Inc) **$49,000**

Northwest coast portrait mask of polychrome carved and incised cedar, pre 1884, 10½" high.
(Skinner Inc) **$25,000**

About the same time as gramophones and phonographs were beginning to appear, Paul Lochmann invented his polyphone which was a development of the musical box. He founded the Symphonion Company Leipzig in 1885 and, together with Gustav Brachausen, started producing the machines. In 1894 Brachausen emigrated to America where he began manufacturing polyphones at his Regina Company in New Jersey. Like music boxes, the sound from polyphones was produced by projecting metal pegs in a disc pinging against the teeth of a metal comb. The disc was set in such a way that when it was revolved it reproduced the music of operas or songs from music halls. Polyphones came in a variety of sizes, the smaller ones had discs which were about eight inches in diameter and were intended to be played in the home while machines with 24 inch discs were for public performance.

One of the rarest for home use is the Orphenion, produced in 1895, an example of which recently sold at Auction Team Koeln in Germany for $7,000.

Thomas Alva Edison launched the phonograph in America in 1876 and in 1887 Emile Berliner patented the first gramophone, also in the U.S.A. The first machines were jerky because of hand cranked powering but in 1896 the techniques of clockwork mechanisms were worked out and shellac discs replaced the old zinc coated rubber discs.

One of the first commercially produced gramophones was the H.M.V., His Masters Voice, from 1903, examples of which now sell for about $2,000. *(Auction Team Koeln)*

Fine 'Mikado' polyphon hall clock, 104^1/$_2$" high.
(Christie's)   **$39,131**

An American Wurlitzer Model 1015 1948 style juke box, with domed mahogany casing, visible electric record selector for twenty-four 78 r.p.m. records, record index, illuminating perspex pilasters, illuminating coin entry slots and latticed speaker grill cover, 59^7/$_8$" high.
(Christie's)   **$12,192**

A rare Libellion musical box with twin combs and spring motor in walnut case with simulated inlaid panels to sides. The Libellion was patented by F.A. Richter, of Rudolstadt, Germany between 1893 and 1900, and uses a system of levers to pluck the comb, as found also on the same maker's Imperator disc musical box. This example takes a card book 9³/₄" wide.
(Christie's) **$4,114**

A Thorens No 17 folding portable gramophone in the form of a folding camera in brown and yellow crackled enamel casing, 11" wide.
(Andrew Hartley) **$315**

A Symphonion 'Eroica' triple-disc musical box in walnut case with clock backed fretwork door, small disc storage chute in base and balustraded top, 80" high, with sixteen sets of discs.
(Christie's) **$21,175**

A Mikiphone pocket gramophone in the form of a large pocket watch with Mikiphone sound box and black composition resonator in nickel plated casing, 4½" in diameter.
(Andrew Hartley) **$297**

'RCA Victor Special' portable phonograph, John Vassos, circa 1935, manufactured by RCA, New York, aluminium and various metals.
(Skinner Inc) **$3,100**

A Polyphon style No. 62 ('Geisha') longcase clock with 15⅝" double comb movement in base, two-train clock movement with exposed brass-cased weights and pendulum, in walnut case with quarter-veneered back panel and applied pilasters, consoles and finials – 108" high, with eight discs.
(Christie's) **$32,725**

An His Master's Voice model 203 mahogany cabinet gramophone No. 2030000108, with re-entrant tone chamber, 5a soundbox No. 52 motor with lubricator and gilt fittings, 50" high, 1930.
(Christie's) $10,587

A 24¹/₂" Lochmanns 'Original' coin-operated disc musical box with twelve-bar glockenspiel, left or right hand wind, manual overide stop/start control and varnished walnut case with glazed door, fretted pediment of Art Nouveau design, coin drawer and disc-bin stand with hinged door and sixteen discs, 90" high.
(Christie's) $15,928

A Meissen candlestick from the Swan service modeled by J.F. Eberlein and J.J. Kändler for Count Brühl, and his wife Anna von Kolowrat Kratkowska formed as two entwined putti supporting a reed molded holder beside two cartouches bearing the coats-of-arms, circa 1739, 24cm. high. *(Christie's)* **$52,767**

A Meissen figure of a seated ape modeled by Johann Gottlieb Kirchner naturalistically modeled, holding a fruit in its right forepaw, its long tail curling round the shaped rockwork base, with blue-black hair, tail and paws, white body, blue crossed swords mark to rear of base, circa 1735, 25cm. high.
(Christie's) **$11,352**

A Meissen portrait pipe-bowl of the Court Jester Fröhlich modeled by J.J. Kändler, wearing a yellow broad-brimmed hat, his features naturalistically colored, the neck with blue and red ruffs terminating in a fantastic animal head, circa 1742, 8.5cm. long.
(Christie's) **$7,946**

A Meissen chinoiserie salt from the Brühlsche Plat de Ménage modeled by J.J. Kändler as a laughing Chinaman, wearing a blue-brimmed hat, yellow-lined robe with scattered indianische Blumen and yellow pointed shoes, seated astride a shell enriched with gilding, crossed swords mark, circa 1737, gilt metal cover, 19cm. high.
(Christie's) **$8,745**

A Meissen pipe-bowl modeled as a seated pug-dog by J.J. Kändler, the nostrils, ears and mouth pierced, the coat and features naturalistically painted, blue crossed swords mark, circa 1745, 8cm. long.
(Christie's) **$16,082**

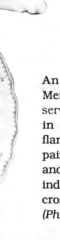

An important and large Meissen dish from the Swan service, molded with a swan in flight above two swans flanked by bulrushes, the rim painted with the arms of Brühl and Kolowrat-Kratkowska and indianische Blumen, 30cm., crossed swords mark.
(Phillips) **$26,250**

MICRO-MOSAICS

An Italian rectangular silver-gilt mounted hardstone snuff-box, veneered in malachite, the cover set with a Roman micro-mosaic of Pliny's Capitoline doves, within plain molded silver frame, Rome, circa 1815, 3³/₈" long.
(Christie's) **$5,346**

Italian micro-mosaic and bronze jewel casket, 19th century, shaped corner square form on scrolled feet, scenes of Rome around box, pigeons drinking from a basin on cover, 8³/₈" square.
(Skinner Inc) **$11,000**

A fine Roman circular micro-mosaic plaque depicting a goldfinch on a branch, the reverse inscribed: *Giacomo Raffaelli Fece Roma 1789*, 2³/₄" diameter.

Giacomo Raffaelli (1743-1836), one of the most talented mosaicists of his time, was possibly the first to work in micro-mosaic, about 1775. His work was highly regarded by the Vatican and foreign courts for whom he worked, although he refused a commission in Russia.
(Christie's) **$4,235**

19th century Italian, micro-mosaic and gilt casket, 13cm. long.
(Phillips) **$2,362**

A Roman micro-mosaic picture with a view of the Piazza San Giovanni in Laterano, Rome, signed *R.F. di S.P. A. Bonifazi*, last quarter 19th century, 15" x 20".

Eugenio Bonifazi, Via Margutta 17, Rome, worked under the patronage of the Reverende Fabrica di San Pietro (RF di SP), active 1876. Micro-mosaics were created by the Vatican Studio by private ateliers and catered increasingly for the growing souvenir trade as the 19th century progressed and had attained an astonishing level of technical perfection by the middle of the century.

This view depicts the Lateran Palace, built by Sixtus V and the largest Egyptian obelisk in Rome, transported to the city in AD 357. The Baptistery was built by the Emperor Constantine and restored by the notorious Pope Francesco Barbarini, Urban VIII, in 1637.

(Christie's) **$29,400**

A George IV silver-gilt snuff box, the cover set with micro-mosaic panel depicting an angry bull goring a vicious-looking dog, whilst another attacks it, a stream in the background, the raised border and thumbpiece of shell, scroll and floral designs, by John Linnit, 1825, 7.4cm x 5.3cm.

(Phillips) **$7,612**

A rare 14th century blue and white slip-decorated stemcup, late Yuan Dynasty/Hongwu. The cup flaring out sharply to an everted rim, resting on a spreading stem with five horizontal ribbed sections, painted on the exterior with a striding three-clawed dragon chasing a flaming pearl, 4½" diameter.

Based on excavations around the precincts of the Hongwu Palace in Nanjing in 1970, a whole group of porcelains, including stemcups, have been reassessed and their former attribution to the Yuan Dynasty has now been revised.
(Christie's Hong Kong) **$352,564**

An important large early Ming blue and white dish vividly painted in 'heaped and piled' strong cobalt tones with two carp swimming amongst aquatic fern and weeds at the center, the cavetto with a continuous floral scroll comprising hibiscus, peony, pomegranate, chrysanthemum and lotus below elongated horizontal floral sprays at the rim, Yongle, 53.6cm. diameter.
(Christie's) **$378,200**

An early Ming blue and white double-gourd moon flask, Bianping Xuande six-character mark below the rim and of the period. Following a Near Eastern prototype with flattened circular body and baluster-shaped neck, rising from a rectangular foot, painted in inky-blue tones to one face with an eight-point star-burst radiating from a central yinyang symbol, the foliate points interspersed with palmette ornaments encircled by a half-diaper circular band, 9⁷/₈" high.
(Christie's Hong Kong)   **$521,794**

A rare Ming double gourd vase, painted in underglaze cobalt blue of strong purple tone with four immortals riding alternatively a phoenix or a crane amongst cloud scrolls upon the upper pear shaped section. The broad concave waist decorated with four auspicious objects between two rows of small flowerheads. Six character mark of Jiajing written in line encircling the lip and of the period, 9.75".

No other vase of this pattern appears to be recorded, but a vase of this shape and size also with the Neinhao around the lip, but with the more common decoration of a lotus meander is in the Percival David Foundation Catalogue, section three, number A655.

(Woolley & Wallis) **$14,700**

William Grimaldi (1751-1830), after Sir Joshua Reynolds, P.R.A. (1723-1792), H.R.H. Frederick Duke of York, three quarter length, full face, wearing the Regalia of the Order of the Garter, signed in full on reverse with the address 2, *Albemarle Street*, gilt-metal frame, oval, 4³/4" high.

Grimaldi painted this portrait as a duplicate for himself, the original miniature painted in 1790, was presented to the Princess Royal of Prussia on her marriage with the Duke. The original painting by Reynolds, in the Royal Collection, was painted in 1787.

(Christie's) **$24,640**

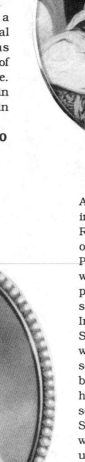

An extremely fine and important miniature of Major Richard Gomonde, in the staff officer's uniform of the Madras Presidency, with white waistcoat and frilled cravat, powdered hair en queue, signed with initials and I for India, and dated 1790, by John Smart (1742–1811), gold frame with pearl border, the reverse set with plaited hair within blue glass border, oval, 2¹/2" high. Major Richard Gomonde served as Town Major of Fort St. George, Madras, when he would have worn the staff uniform seen in this portrait. He married Susannah, daughter of Ellerker of Rieseby Park York, whose miniature was also painted by Smart in the same year as her husband.

(Christie's) **$26,180**

Richard Gibson (1615-1690), Sir Henry Blount, facing right, in black doublet and white lawn collar, fair curly hair on vellum, inscribed *Sir H B/Aetat/58*, gold frame with pierced spiral cresting, the reverse enameled with a black and white rosette on blue field with scalloped border, oval, 2¼" high.
(Christie's)   **$35,838**

Miniature of three children and a cat, American School, 19th century. Unsigned. Watercolor on ivory, 4¾" x 3¾", framed.
(Skinner Inc)   **$16,000**

John Hoskins (fl. circa 1645), Lady Mary Glemham, facing right, in low-cut black dress trimmed with white lace and brooch at corsage, wearing pearl necklace and earrings, her brown hair dressed in curls, landscape background, on vellum, signed with initials and dated 1648, gilt-metal frame, oval, 2⅛" high.
(Christie's)   **$35,838**

A Minton 'Majolica' garden-seat modeled as a crouching monkey holding a yellow pomegranate with green foliage in one hand, a second pomegranate in his other hand and supporting a royal blue square padded cushion on his head. circa 1870, 47cm. high.

(Christie's) **$12,512**

Minton 'majolica' peacock after the model by P. Comolera, circa 1875, 60¼" high.

(Christie's) **$30,518**

A Charles II stump-work and walnut mirror with beveled rectangular plate in a molded slip, the cushion frame worked with flowers, butter-flies, insects and birds with a King and Queen to either side, each corner with a roundel depicting a lion, a leopard, a stag and a unicorn, 35½" x 29".
(Christie's) **$17,661**

A Flemish giltwood and tortoiseshell mirror with rectangular plate and foliate slip, the frame carved with putto masks, foliage and flowerheads, the cresting with Venus and Cupid within a cartouche, early 17th century, 50" x 37".
(Christie's) **$18,287**

A rare Chippendale carved mahogany dressing mirror, Boston, 1765-1775, the rectangular mirror with molded and gilt frame surmounted by an open scrolled leafage cartouche suspended between two canted double-bead molded supports with diamond finials over a coffer-molded top base with single drawer. 16³/₈" high.

Eighteenth century Amertican examples of dressing or toilet mirrors are not common, but of a small number known, the majority appear to be of Boston origin. **$6,050**
(Christie's)

One of an important pair of George I gilt mirrors of large size, 85" high x 45" wide.
(Bonhams) **$78,750**
One of a pair of George III giltwood pier-glasses with Chinese mirror pictures, 79" x 45".
(Christie's) **$379,280**

Anything to do with cars means money, as those confronted by their latest garage service bill doubtless have cause to reflect! In the collecting world, though, it's the same story, from the millions of pounds which are now being paid for even non-vintage models of the greatest marques, down to the equally interesting prices, in relative terms, which people will pay for boxed models in the toy sense of the word. Entire auctions are now being devoted to Dinky cars, and, perhaps because such things call up again that obscure, nostalgic link with our childhood, it seems unlikely that this will be just a passing phase.

The Dinky is perhaps the best known brand-name for such models, but other older types to look out for are Märklin and Carette. Pre-First World War examples will fetch the most. Condition is always important, and they should, if possible be accompanied by their original box to really command a premium.

One of the most sought-after Dinkys is the No 24 set, comprising a Vogue saloon, sports tourer 4-seater and 2-seater, which if boxed and in good condition, will fetch around $10,000.

An early hand enameled tinplate De Dion car by Bing, circa 1904, 7³/₄" long, the car with clockwork mechanism, operating handbrake, painted spoked wheels, white rubber tyres, steering wheel and front headlamp, in original paintwork.
(Christie's S. Ken)   **$3,360**

A Richardson and Allwin painted wood and metal model Bullnose Morris
pedal car, with folding hood, measuring 3ft 9" long.
(Hobbs & Chambers) **$7,000**

A Continental pottery centerpiece modeled as a vintage car with a lady
passenger and a gentleman passenger in Edwardian dress, signed W.
Lachner, 1906, 17½" long.
(Christie's) **$14,600**

A rare hand painted tinplate four seater open tourer steam car by Doll & Co., circa 1924. *(Christie's)* **$5,750**

An early hand enameled four-seater open tourer, No. 3358/21, by Carette, circa 1911, 21cm. long, with clockwork mechanism driving rear axle, operating brake, adjustable front metal spoke wheels, white rubber tyres and composition painted chauffeur.
(Christie's S. Ken) **$5,759**

A German tinplate clockwork limousine by Märklin, circa 1907, length 16¹/₂". *(Sotheby's)* **$29,920**

An early French hand-painted tinplate limousine, with clockwork mechanism driving rear axle, adjustable front spoked wheels, white rubber tyres, steering wheel with horn, opening rear doors, glass window, remains of simulated button leather upholstery, circa 1903, 15" long. *(Christie's)* **$6,160**

A 3" scale model Foden 'C' type twin cylinder steam lorry entitled 'Patricia', measuring 6ft long and 2ft 5" wide.
(Hobbs & Chambers)   **$5,425**

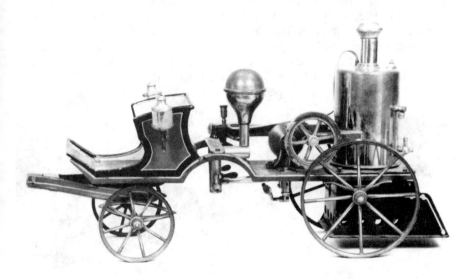

A fine and rare Märklin spirit-fired fire-engine, catalogue No. 4067, German, circa 1902, finished in bright scarlet with black and yellow lining, with vertical copper boiler, spirit burner below, 7cm. flywheel driving horizontally mounted single cylinder, 21" long.
(Sothebys)   **$27,300**

MODEL ENGINES

Märklin, a large well engineered steam plant boiler with pressure gauge, safety valve, single cylinder with governor, the flywheel driving dynamo. The cylinder having steps and handrail, the whole mounted on a tinplate base board, 53cm. x 45cm.
(Phillips)   **$5,500**

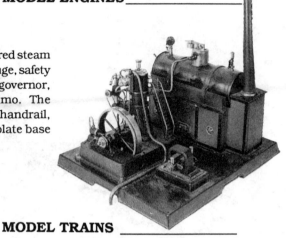

MODEL TRAINS

Most of us have at some stage owned a train set. In some cases the enthusiasm carries on unabated into adulthood, though few would carry it so far as Count Antonio Coluzzi who, first inspired by the sight of the Blue Train steaming south to the Cote d'Azur in the 1920's, went on to form a magnificent collection and then his own company to produce quality models. Some of his collection was sold by Christie's and a few of the most important pieces are featured here.

The major firms in the production of model trains are the German companies of Märklin and Bing, the French Carette, and, of course, the English Hornby and Basset Lowke trade marks. The marks to look out for on models are GMC for Märklin, GBN for Bing, and GC for Carette. Good examples by all of these can be worth serious money.

A rare Märklin Jubilee Set No. Ar12930/35/3 comprising a gauge 0 (3-rail) electric model of the 2-2-2 'Planet' locomotive and tender 'Der Adler', two stage-coach type coaches, with opening doors and an open carriage, with a driver and twenty composition lady and gentleman passengers, three holding parasols, all in original paintwork, circa 1935.
(Christie's)   **$6,725**

A rake of three very rare gauge 1 Central London Railway four wheel passenger coaches, all with opening side doors and roofs, to reveal benches, by Märklin, circa 1903.
(Christie's S. Ken) **$11,313**

A rare and early Märklin gauge 1 clockwork model of the Central London Railway 'Steeplecab' 0-4-0 electric locomotive, in original green and dark green paintwork, black chassis, orange and pale green lining, circa 1901.
(Christie's S. Ken) **$4,114**

Märklin 75mm. gauge steam, 'Wurttemberg', circa 1912, fitted with electric light and battery compartment under tender.
(Christie's)   **$48,411**

J.P. Hartmann 3¾" gauge painted metal CIWL teak sleeping car, circa 1921, with external body and chassis details, fully fitted and beautifully executed interior, electrically-operated automaton figures en déshabillé, compartment lighting, and removable roof and side, 132cm. long.
(Christie's)   **$21,516**

A rare Märklin hand painted District Railway twin bogie passenger coach, with side opening sliding doors, in original paintwork, circa 1902. (Christie's)   **$7,000**

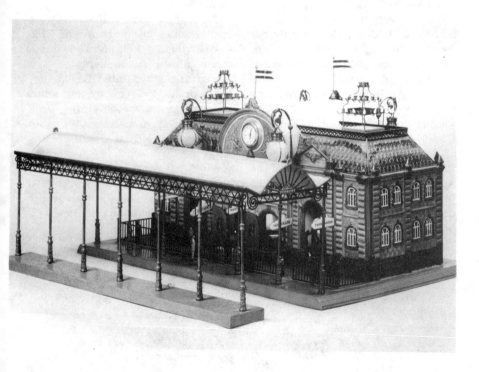

Märklin, Grand Station, with track canopy, interior and exterior fittings, working clocks and electric lighting, circa 1909, 92cm. wide, 54cm. high. (Christie's)   **$26,895**

When Mr Leslie Weller, Managing Director of Sotheby's, Billingshurst visited a Sussex home on a probate valuation, he did not anticipate finding a major antique discovery in the bathroom. Hidden underneath the old fashioned wrought iron bath tub was a model of a ship, beautifully carved in fruitwood and revealing minute detail.

The boat was discovered to be a very rare Admiralty model of a 6th Rate Ship-of-the-Line produced in Great Britain in the 18th century. This type of boat, often a hull only, without rigging, was built for members of the Admiralty Board to convey the general proportions, appearance and construction of a ship. The three dimensional form was an ideal method of illustrating the merits of such a ship, especially to the layman who may have found drawings and plans highly technical.

The highest quality materials were used, such as lime and boxwood. This model which is half-planked, has a single gun deck with twenty ports, a carved and gilt painted lion figure-head, ornate bell canopy and ships bell, capstan, boxwood grating deck with stairway and stern with cabin windows, and decorated with wreaths and putti.

When the model was entered for auction at a Sotheby's sale it surprised all present in the saleroom by realizing $217,800 – a world record price for a model ship.

Märklin electric, 'Kaiser Wilhelm Der Grosse', circa 1909, 117cm. long. This model was the largest Märklin liner and would run with two 4 volt batteries for seven hours.
(Christie's S. Ken) **$53,790**

An extremely fine contemporary early 19th century French prisoner-of-war bone and horn model of a forty-six gun Royal Naval frigate, 10" x 13½". Complete with bound masts, yards with stun's'l booms, detailed standing and running rigging with standards at the mastheads and White Ensign at the mizzen and deck details including carved and painted figurehead, carved hair-rails, brass anchors with bone stocks, catheads, belaying rails, capstan, gratings, companionway, double ship's wheel, upper deck guns in slides and three ship's boats with thwarts, one in stern davits.
(Christie's) **$27,885**

A finely carved and detailed early 19th century French prisoner of war bone and horn model of a 104-gun Royal Naval Man-of-War, 8½" x 11½", complete with full running and standing rigging including gold leaf mast binding and ebony stun's'l booms. The case bears the legend *this little 82-gun frigate was made by Captain Francis Langley during a 13 year imprisonment (as a war captive) in the French Bastille.*
(Christie's) **$25,000**

Lutz for Märklin Clockwork, 'Toulouse', circa 1880, 61cm. long.
(Christie's) **$19,723**

Märklin Clockwork, 'Connecticut', first series, circa 1900, 72cm. long.
(Christie's) **$18,827**

1794 half-dime. One of perhaps 15 surviving mint state examples. *(Christie's)* **$50,600**

1879 mint state *Stella* or four-dollars. *(Christie's)* **$46,200**

1907 high relief double-eagle. *(Christie's)* **$37,400**

1834 choice mint state quarter-eagle. *(Christie's)* **$38,500**

Pair of Louisiana Purchase Exposition 1903 proof dollars. *(Christie's)* **$82,500**

1833 choice mint state half-eagle. *(Christie's)* **$88,000**

The one penny piece was first launched in the reign of George III, with the king's head on the front and the figure of Britannia on the reverse. The format continued more or less unchanged until its final demise with the coming of decimalisation.

Pennies always had a huge mintage. Even in 1797 over 8.5 million were coined; in 1917 mintage totalled almost 108 million, and the final issue of 1967 totalled a staggering 654.5 million coins. It is therefore hardly surprising that most examples, even if perfect and uncirculated, will seldom fetch more than a few hundred dollars.

The notable exceptions, however, are pennies dated 1933 and 1954. In these years trial samples only were minted, perhaps a dozen of each. If you can find an example from either of these years you could have a coin worth $40,000.

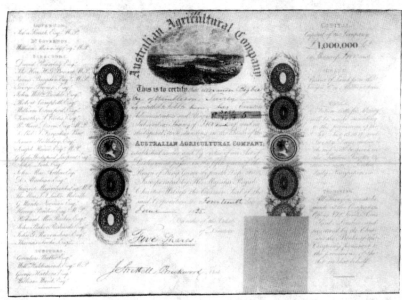

Australian Agricultural Company, incorporated by Royal Charter in 1824, certificate for 5 x £100 shares dated 14th June, 1825. Elegant and decorative piece with a vignette of Sydney Harbour from the Observatory area, with fine detail of the harbour, showing the present Opera House point, Taronga Park Zoo and even showing South Head and the houses of Vaucluse in the far distance. This is one of the earliest known Australian certificates and the earliest Australian certificate with a vignette. The plan to form a large chartered company was put forward in 1804 by John Macarthur (1767-1834). Macarthur was one of the most controversial figures in early Australian history and has often been referred to as the founder of the Australian wool industry.   *(Phillips)*   **$7,110**

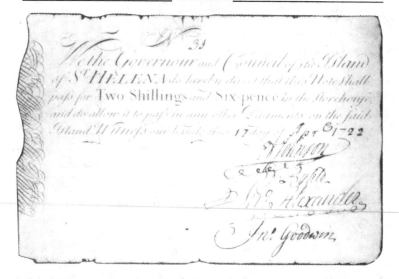

St. Helena, 1722 2/6d issued by 'The Governor and council of the Island'; the first paper currency of St. Helena was produced in 1717 for a total issue of £400, this note is believed to be the only surviving paper money of that period.   *(Phillips)*   **$8,855**

States of Guernsey: £5 essay on thin paper produced in 1836 with a covering letter to Perkins, Bacon & Petch approving the general design and requesting delivery of 2,000 notes.   *(Phillips)*   **$6,636**

Abraham Newland, £1, 2 March 1797, note number 4, first date of issue for the first £1 notes ever produced by the Bank of England.
(Phillips) **$27,370**

A Zanzibar Government 10 rupees note, 1928.
(Phillips) **$2,025**

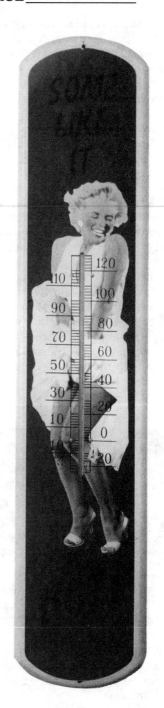

Marilyn Monroe, a polychrome film poster for 'Bus Stop', 20th Century Fox, printed in England by Stafford & Co., Nottingham and London. 30" x 20".

(Christie's) **$1,208**

A promotional thermometer for the United Artists film 'Some Like It Hot' of bright orange and white enamel and printed metal, the gauge decorated with a picture of Marilyn Monroe, her white dress blowing in the breeze, made in the U.S.A., circa 1959, 39" x 8".

(Christie's) **$6,507**

One of the most remarkable tile makers and potters of the Arts and Crafts movement in England was William de Morgan (1839-1917). He was a friend of William Morris and collaborated with him to produce tile designs including flowers, fish, ships and mythical birds and beasts. He also worked with Joe Juster, Halsey Ricardo and Frederick and Charles Passenger. De Morgan had a pottery and showroom at Cheyne Row, Chelsea and later, at Merton Abbey, he and Morris made tiles, dishes and vases with predominantly purple, blue and green colors which imitated 15th and 16th century Iznik tiles. He established a factory in Fulham which produced pottery, tiles, panels and murals. After 1892 De Morgan spent a great deal of time in Italy where he was influenced by the work of Florentine artists. His marks include DM, a tulip and leaves, a Tudor rose or an A forming the steeple of a ruined abbey.

A De Morgan charger, decorated by Chas. Passenger, 1890s, 41.5cm. diameter.
(Sothebys) **$9,223**

A William de Morgan tile panel composed of twenty-four square tiles painted with red lustre, twelve of which are larger, and decorated with various animals on waved white backgrounds, in a wooden frame, 59cm. x 126cm.
(Christie's) **$9,350**

A William de Morgan 'Persian-style' pottery vase, early Fulham period, possibly painted by Halsey Ricardo, of globular form with swollen neck and twin handles depicting in greens, brown and mauve, fish swimming against a deep-blue ground, with scrolls on the neck and foliage on the handles, 25cm. high, impressed *flower and DM mark*.

(Phillips) **$6,520**

MOLDS

Walnut pastry mold, *S.Y. Watkins*, New York, first half of 19th century, carved with an American eagle perched on a shield, enclosed by fruit-filled cornucopias and foliage, within a crosshatched border, impressed *S.Y. Watkins N.Y.*, 10³/₄" x 11¹/₄".
(Skinner Inc) **$1,300**

Carved wooden gingerbread mold, probably Continental, late 18th century, one side with the caricatured figure of a gentleman wearing a wig, patterned long coat and knee breeches and carrying a walking stick, the reverse with the caricatured figure of a lady wearing a floral patterned dress, 27" high.
(Skinner Inc) **$1,100**

The manuscript full score of 'Elijah', annotated throughout by Mendelssohn, sent by him in instalments from Leipzig to London in preparation for the first performance of the oratorio, given at the Town Hall, Birmingham, on 26 August 1846, and used by the organist, Henry Gauntlett. This long-lost manuscript of Mendelssohn's Magnum Opus provides the only complete surviving record of the greatest of all 19th century oratorios in the form as it was first heard, and before it was subjected to drastic revision.
(Phillips)   **$134,640**

Sullivan (Sir Arthur) the autographed full score of Sullivan's symphony in E (The Irish), with extensive passages deleted, numerous overlays and autograph revisions to the score, marked up for conducting in blue crayon, 'Copyright, 1902 by Novello & Co. Ltd.

Sullivan composed the symphony in 1863 when only twenty-one years old. It was conceived while on holiday in Northern Ireland; he wrote to his mother at the time: *'I feel my ideas assuming a newer and fresher colour.*
(Phillips)

$26,010

Painted and decorated tambourine, America, late 19th/early 20th century, painted in polychrome, pressed brass bells, 9½" diameter.
(Skinner Inc) **$1,400**

The Anaconda, the only known example of a contra-bass C serpent by Joseph and Richard Wood in Upper Heaton, Yorks, circa 1840, overall length 475cm. The body of wood, covered black fabric with brass supports and mounts, ten brass keys with circular flaps, the low C sharp key on pillars, with long brass crook and mouthpiece.

Joseph and Richard Wood were hand loom weavers. They made the instrument and played it for some 20 years in Almondbury Church and on festive occasions in York Minster.
(Phillips) **$8,700**

Large painted and decorated parade bass drum, inscribed William Bridget Maker & Painter, Belfast, Maine, late 19th century, decorated in polychrome, with stretched hide heads, 37" diameter.
(Skinner Inc) **$4,250**

A Tanzbaer automatic accordion with trigger-operated twenty-eight key mechanism, in grained wood casing, with fourteen rolls.
(Christie's) **$3,272**

Columnar alto recorder by Hans Rauch von Schratt (enbach), mid 16th century, total length 20¹/₈".
(Christie's) **$81,180**

A very fine Italian violin by Domenico Montagnana, labeled Dominicus *Montagnana sub Si-/gnum Cremonae Venetiis 1727*; the two-piece back of small curl, the ribs of broader figure, the scroll of faint curl, the table of medium grain, the varnish of a deep red color over a golden ground, the length of back 14¹/₈".
(Christie's) **$235,620**

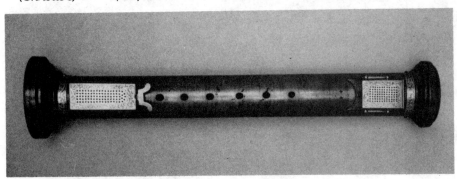

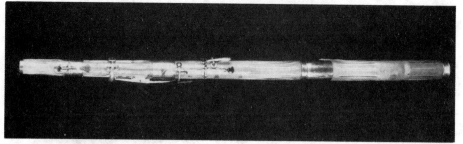

A six-keyed glass flute by Claude Laurent engraved *C. Laurent à Paris 1819/Brevete*; silver keys and end-cap, set with colored glass, silver mounts, sounding length 21⁵/₁₆".
(Christie's) **$11,919**

An important violin by Antonio Stradivari labelled *Antonio Stradivari Cremonensis/Faciebat Anno 1720*; the two-piece back of handsome medium to broad curl descending from the center joint, the ribs and scroll similar, the table of medium grain, the varnish of a rich red color over a golden ground, the length of back 13¹⁵/₁₆". (35.5cm)
(Christie's) **$1,776,940**

A good single-manual harpsichord, the nameboard inscribed *Jacobus et Abraham Kirckman Londini Fecerunt 1790*; in a mahogany case with brass escutcheon hinges and a birchwood interior, the soundboard with a King David rose with initials *AK*, on trestle stand, 87¹/₂" x 34¹/₄".
(Christie's) **$28,600**

A dress fez worn by Mussolini as First
Honorary Corporal of the MVSN, black
fur skull with large gold bullion
embroidered eagle and fasces to front,
a similar smaller eagle to left side with
four metal fasces above, fixed red cord
to right side, black hanging tassel to
top, leather and silk lining with maker's
logos of *S.V. Presciutti, Roma Via
Leccosa 4.*
(Phillips)   **$69,080**

Identity cards carried by Mussolini, comprising that of Commandante
Generale MVSN, with photo of Mussolini, card of the Associazione Nazionale
Combattenti 1945, a card of the Presidenza Nazionale of the Opera and a
card of the Istituto Nazionale Di Cultura Fascista.
(Phillips)   **$9,734**

NETSUKE

An ivory netsuke of a kirin sitting gazing upwards, unsigned, circa 1800, 9cm. high.
(Christie's) **$9,037**

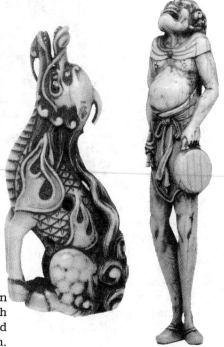

A fine boxwood Netsuke of a human skull entwined by a snake, which emerges from the right orbit, signed *Hogen Rantei*, 19th century, 4cm. high.
(Christie's) **$5,214**

An important ivory netsuke of a South Sea Island drummer standing holding a drum and drum-stick, his hair in tightly coiled ringlets, his chest and abdomen partly covered by a figured cloth held by a coral clasp at the throat, signed *Shugetsu*, 18th century, 14.5cm.

Awarded the title Hogen for his work as a painter in Kano style, Hara Shugetsu lived in Osaka and is mentioned in the Soken Kisho.
(Christie's) **$90,500**

A highly unusual Okimono-style netsuke depicting two South Sea Islanders on the ocean bed struggling to free a large piece of coral surrounded by seashells and an octopus, the materials comprising natural red coral, shakudo for the kurombo, the body of the netsuke in umimatsu, the base in silver formed as high breaking waves, the octopus in copper with gilt eyes, various seashells inlaid in copper-gilt and aogai, the base with a cord attachment, signed *Shoshi*, 19th century, 6cm. wide.
(Christie's) **$13,475**

A Fantascope optical toy comprising a fitted mahogany box with drawer containing fifteen picture discs, some printed *Ackermann & Co., 96 Strand*, viewing mirror, stand and paper label.
(Christie's) **$8,662**

An 'International Mutoscope Reel Co., Inc.' What-the-butler-saw machine, with 'Vanishing Violet' drum.
(David Lay) **$2,035**

Ernst Planck, Germany, a hot-air powered Praxinoscope comprising a removable spirit burner, condensing pistons and 6" diameter praxinoscope drum with three picture strips all mounted on a wooden base with maker's label. *(Christie's)* **$6,737**

A Doucai globular jar and cover delicately painted with eight roundels, each containing two chrysanthemum heads, interspersed with formal sprays of scrolling lotus all between underglaze-blue bands of ruyi-lappets at the foot and shoulders, 4 3/4" high. *(Christie's)* **$67,000**

A large Satsuma vase decorated in various colored enamels and gilt with Taira no Kiyomori visiting the Itsukushima shrine and praying for the prosperity of his descendants, the shoulder with a coiled dragon molded in relief, signed *Hotoda sei*, late 19th century, 57.5cm. high.
(Christie's) **$10,600**

A fine and large Doucai jardiniere, finely painted on the exterior with Mughal-style lotus medallions surmounted by feathery foliate plumes, divided by interlocked ruyi-head and feathery foliate wreaths between lotus panels around the foot, the nianhao within a countersunk disc, 13" diameter.
(Christie's)
$105,769

A famille rose tureen and cover of chamfered rectangular form with rabbit mask handles and rococo scroll knop, Ch'ien Lung, 13¹/₂" wide. *(Lawrence Fine Arts)* **$6,098**

A rare Arita model of a seated horse following a Dutch Delft original, decorated in iron-red and black enamels and gilt on underglaze blue, its saddle-cloth with flowers and foliage, the base with scrolling foliage, circa 1700, 18cm. long. *(Christie's)* **$13,035**

A rare large Imari model of a cockerel, its plumage painted in underglaze blue, iron-red, black, green enamel and gilt, perched on a decaying tree stump with fungus growing from its sides, 10¼" high, Genroku period.

(Bonhams) **$14,000**

A rare painted red pottery figure of a matron, the corpulent figure standing, the legs slightly apart, feet pointed in opposite direction, the robes with incised folds caught with a belt below the generous waist, Tang Dynasty, 45cm. high.

These pottery female figures are more usually dressed in loose shifts; it is less common to find them in belted garments, but when so dressed, the draperies are more defined and elaborately-folded.

(Christie's) **$34,320**

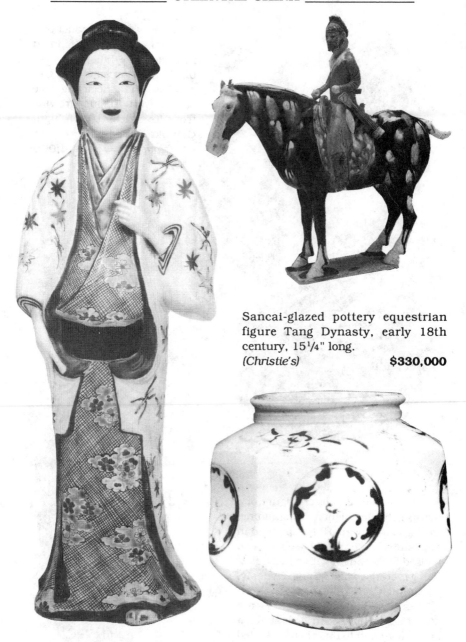

Sancai-glazed pottery equestrian figure Tang Dynasty, early 18th century, 15¼" long.
(Christie's) **$330,000**

Kakiemon model of a bijin, circa 1680, 15¼" high.
(Christie's) **$128,590**

Copper red decorated porcelain jar Yi Dynasty, 7" high.
(Christie's) **$55,000**

ARTHUR OSBORNE

Arthur Osborne set up business as a plaque maker in Faversham, Kent, in the late 1890's. He first made molds of well-known buildings or scenes in plasticene, but later on he widened his repertoire of subjects to include literary subjects, foreign scenes and historical or biblical characters. Arguably the most collectible plaques are those which commemorate special events, as is the same with pot lids such as Washington Crossing the Delaware, probably produced to commemorate the Centenary Celebrations of the American War of Independence. It is interesting to compare some of the subjects chosen by Osborne with those by W.H. Goss, Pratt and Mayer. We find Tam O'Shanter, Lady Godiva, Shakespeare's house and Burns' cottage all depicted. Judging by the influences on his work, one could say that Osborne is the 20th century equivalent of George Baxter, W.H. Goss and Felix Pratt: he was an innovator who aimed to produce mainly small, decorative objects depicting well-known subjects and scenes which would be bought by l'homme de la rue, thus bringing 'art' to within the reaches of a wide audience.

The 'Ivorex' wall plaques began life as plasticene which was coated in wax to preserve the shape, and casts were taken in plaster of Paris. The casts were then hand colored in watercolors, usually brown and rust, and then when completely dry, dipped in paraffin wax. This not only darkened the plaques to an ivory color but also gave them a waxy feel. Some plaques were then framed in ebonized wood and glazed.

Up to 440 models were used in all, but most have been broken up. The firm closed in 1964.

Mr Pickwick addressing the members of The Pickwick Club, 'the proudest moment of his existence', 48.5cm. x 65cm. *(Phillips)*   **$700**

PAPER CUT-OUTS

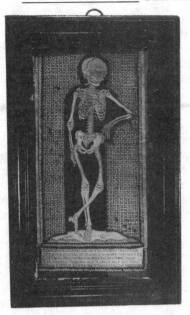

A rare 18th century Scottish paper cut-out of a skeleton, with the inscription *This representation of the human skeleton cutt with scizars by Thomas Hunter 1791 aged 82 years was presented by him to Doctor John Glendining during his residence at the University of Edinburgh*, 10" x 4³/₄".
(Christie's) **$1,540**

PENKNIVES

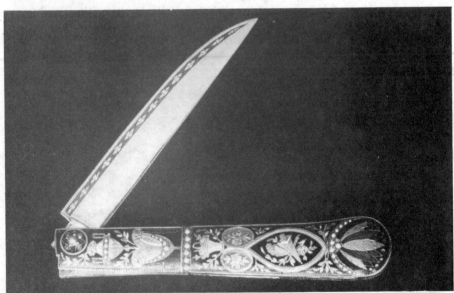

A rare Swiss jeweled enameled gold musical pen-knife, the handle chased and engraved with champlevé vases, foliage and flowers and with quivers and arrows in baskets within borders of blue, black and green enamel and set with split pearls, Geneva, circa 1810, 14.5cm. long.
(Christie's) **$27,000**

An unusual fisherman's knife with steel blade, the silver mounted handle modeled as a fish engraved with fins and scales and with red eyes, G.W. Lewis & Co., Birmingham 1923, overall length when open 6³/₄".
(Christie's) **$865**

PENCIL SHARPENERS

A 1920s 'Morrisharp' Art Deco style electric pencil sharpener of bakelite, with shavings drawer, and chrome sharpness indicator, made by Bert Morris Co., Los Angeles, California, accompanied with letters of authenticity from Peter Noble, stating that the composer Max Steiner used the pencil sharpener when writing the score for the film 'Gone With The Wind'.
(Christie's) **$313**

An Edwardian silver-mounted oblong pencil sharpener fitted with a drawer to catch the shavings, *A.B.*, London 1908, 3³/₄".
(Christie's) **$1,155**

A rare white metal/lacquer Dunhill-
Namiki fountain pen, decorated with
a twining stylized floral pattern with
flowers picked out in a palette of red,
orange and green lacquers and golden
flowers with heart shaped 'petals', lever
filled, and fitted with pilot manifold
14kt. gold nib, circa 1926–30.
(Bonham's) **$8,500**

A French tortoiseshell and enamel pen with cylindrical body, the grip
painted in opalescent guilloché enamel, bordered by pellets of opaque white,
with yellow-metal nib, by Cartier, Paris, in original fitted case, 8¼" long.
(Christie's) **$3,048**

_____ **PEWTER** _____

A fine and rare pewter
teapot by Peter Young,
New York, 1775–1785,
the domed cover with
a beaded edge and a
turned finial, the spout
scrolled, on a narrow
circular footring,
marked inside with
Laughlin touch 515,
7¼" high.
(Christie's N. York)
$30,800

United States 1918 24c. *Curtis Jenny* Airmail Invert, the unique plate number block of four.
(Christie's) **$1,100,000**

5 cents mint block of eight, 1847.
(Christie's) **$99,000**

United States circa 1846 5c. Annapolis Maryland Postmaster's Provisional. Record auction price for a US cover and for any item of postal stationery.
(Christie's) **$184,041**

A mint corner block of 12 Penny Blacks.
(Phillips) **$150,000**

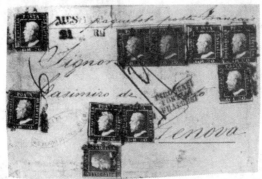

Sicily 1859 50 grana lake-brown pair used with seven single 20 grana dark slate-gray and two grana plate 1 cobalt-blue to make a rate of 242 grana.
(Phillips) **$55,000**

Great Britain 1842 'Queens Own' printed pictorial envelope used in Edinburgh to *the Hon Lady Dunfermline.*
(Phillips) **$10,500**

1856 letter to France sent at the quadruple rate bearing four 5 cents stamps.
(Christie's) **$66,000**

10 cents types II-III-IV se-tenant.
(Christie's) **$46,200**

1880 5 cents special printing.
(Christie's) **$52,800**

1892 $5 Columbian mint block of four.
(Christie's) **$21,450**

1856 issue 5 cents block of four used with 1 cent on cover addressed to France.
(Christie's) **$104,500**

1877 Buffalo balloon cover from the 18 June flight.
(Christie's) **$88,000**

United States 1846 5c. Milbury Massachusetts Postmaster's Provisional, the finest of the seven recorded covers.
(Christie's)   **$231,000**

Malaya Straits Settlements 1868 cover to New York.
(Christie's)   **$8,928**

Robert Howlett (1831-1858), albumen print of 'Isambard Kingdom Brunel and Launching Chains of the Great Eastern', 1857, 16¹/₂" x 86¹/₂", arched top, contemporary window mount, inscribed in a later hand in pencil on reverse ...*This photograph was given by Brunel to Charles Freeman*....
(Christie's)   **$14,437**

An Albumen print of Mrs. Herbert Duckworth, 1867, by Julia Margaret Cameron, 13¹/₂" x 9³/₄", mounted on gray card in original oak frame.
(Christie's) **$23,309**

Henry Peach Robinson, 'Who Could Have Sent It?', 1885, albumen print, 21¹/₂" x 16¹/₄", mounted on card, framed.
(Christie's) **$15,240**

Lewis Carroll, 'Irene at Elm Lodge', July 1863, oval albumen print, 6⁷/₈" x 8⁷/₈".
(Christie's) **$15,400**

Lewis Carroll, 'Irene (MacDonald), Flo Rankin, Mary (MacDonald) at Elm Lodge', July 1863.
(Christie's) **$16,500**

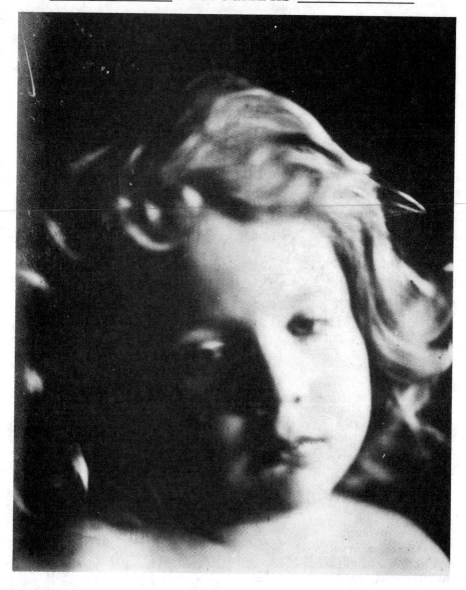

Julia Margaret Cameron, untitled, child portrait, circa 1864-65, albumen print, 11½" x 9¼", mounted on card, this trimmed, ink manuscript credit and caption *From Life not Enlarged*, on mount.
(Christie's) **$24,200**

Photograph of Xie Kitchin, 'Chinese Merchant' by Lewis Carroll, sitting on pile of chests, in Chinese costume, fan in hand, on cabinet card, 10.5cm. x 15cm., and a whole plate negative. *(Phillips)* **$4,984**

'Algerine Woman', (early 1850s), calotype, 8⅞" x 7⅛", titled in ink on mount (possibly Charles Marville). Charles Marville traveled to Algeria in 1852 and is known to have made portraits there.
(Christie's) **$25,102**

Duncan Phyfe was one the the greatest exponents of the late Federal or Neo-Classical furniture design in the USA, which corresponded broadly with the English Regency period.

Phyfe was born in Scotland, and emigrated to America with his parents in 1783–4. Within a decade he had established his own shop and was still in business in 1840, when the name of the firm was changed to D. Phyfe and Son.

His pieces are characterized, among other things, by the extremely high quality of their production. Tapered reeding on turned legs of furniture had become popular in America around 1800, and within a few years was to dominate the decorative scheme of ornament. It was Phyfe who became synonymous with this style, though many other eminent cabinet makers were also using it, and their work is at times difficult to distinguish from his. Influenced by Sheraton and by later classical French designs, Phyfe's workshop produced Empire style pieces in the 1820s and 30s. Simple, restrained elegance is the hallmark of Phyfe's products. They have been widely copied over the last 150 years by craftsmen of varying degrees of skill. Genuine pieces by Phyfe are, however, among the most valuable pieces of American furniture of the period.

A fine and rare figured mahogany veneer cellarette attributed to Duncan Phyfe, New York, 1815–1825 of sarcophagus-form, the hinged lid with a banded edge opening to a mahogany interior fitted to hold four bottles, 25¼" high.
(Christie's N. York)
$13,200

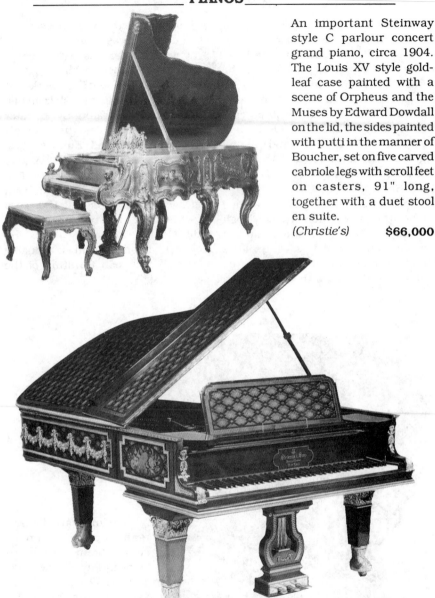

An important Steinway style C parlour concert grand piano, circa 1904. The Louis XV style gold-leaf case painted with a scene of Orpheus and the Muses by Edward Dowdall on the lid, the sides painted with putti in the manner of Boucher, set on five carved cabriole legs with scroll feet on casters, 91" long, together with a duet stool en suite.
(Christie's) **$66,000**

An ormolu-mounted harewood, bois clair and mahogany marquetry overstrung grand piano by Steinway and Sons, New York, the case inlaid with flowerheads within a trellis with oval musical trophies to the sides and top, the borders chased with foliage and tongue-and-dart, the sides hung with ribbon-tied swags of roses, the square tapering legs with foliate capitals, circa 1882, 83" wide. *(Christie's)* **$115,115**

A pair of Regency polychrome plaster figures of Chinese figures in court dress with nodding heads, 13¾" high. There are a number of similar, though larger, figures in the Corridor of the Royal Pavilion, Brighton.
(Christie's) **$17,028**

White painted plaster classical figure, one of a group of four from Nidd Hall, Harrogate, 86" overall height.
(Tennants) **$12,040 each**

Playing cards have been in use for many centuries and they were sufficiently popular in Florence in the 14th century for a decree to be issued prohibiting their use. The standard design of cards as we know them today, originated in Rouen during the 15th century and since then the four different suits of thirteen cards each have been fairly universal at least in Europe. However the suit signs of hearts, diamonds, spades and clubs are not universal even inside Europe for they are only used by the English and the French while Germanic countries use hearts, leaves, dumbbells and acorns and Italians prefer cups, swords, coins and sticks. Outwith Europe, Indian playing cards are circular and can have between eight and twenty suits with 12 cards in each while Chinese cards are long and narrow like book marks.

If you really strike it lucky, however, you might find something like this complete set of cards, illuminated on pasteboard, each card made up of four layers of paper pasted together. From South Flanders, possibly Lille, and dating from 1470-85, they are worth an amazing $180,000.

POST CARDS

BALLOON POST
FROM THE CLOUDS.
September 20th, 1902.

Cards to be Addressed, Stamped, and Delivered for Balloon Post to Hon. Sen., 98 John Dalton Street, on or before Friday, September 19th.

The postcard was introduced in Britain by the GPO in 1870 and was so designed to take the address only on one side with the message alongside the illustration on the other. In 1902, however, an Act of Parliament decreed that the message and address could be written on the same side, leaving the other free for a picture, and after this postcards became very much more popular. One phenomenon of the time was the 'Lifeboat Saturday' card which was delivered by Balloon Post from Manchester to Haslingden on 20 September 1902. It is now worth around $4,000.

The Tate Gallery 17 FEBRUARY-28 MARCH 1971

Warhol

An exhibition poster 'Warhol', The Tate Gallery, 17 February-28 March 1971, reproduction in colors, signed *Andy Warhol* in black felt pen, 30" x 20". *(Christie's)* **$1,075**

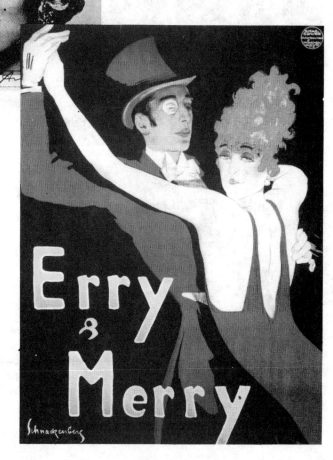

A Walter Schnackenberg poster entitled 'Erry & Merry', lithograph in colors, 50" x 37½". *(Christie's)* **$7,788**

Kenneth D. Shoesmith, Colombo Ceylon, a poster published by the Empire Marketing board, double crown 101cm. x 153cm.
(Onslows) **$5,250**

'Flirt Lefevre-Utile', 1900, signed *Mucha* in the stone, titled in gold across top, and *Biscuits/Lefevre-Utile*. Color lithograph and poster on original board with gilt edges and ribbon at the top, image area 23³/₈" x 10".
(Skinner Inc) **$2,100**

A fine pot lid depicting Holy Trinity Church, Stratford-on-Avon, with leaf and scroll border.
(Phillips) **$3,828**

Very rare Victorian pot lid 'Eastern Lady and Black Attendant'.
(Phillips) **$6,300**

FERDINAND PREISS

Art Deco found one of its most vivid expressions in the bronze and ivory, or chryselephantine, figures of F. Preiss. Virtually nothing is known about Preiss, save that he was probably born in Vienna, his forename may be Friedrich and he flourished in the late 20s and 30s. His work was closely copied by one Professor Otto Poerzl, working out of Coburg, so closely copied in fact that there is speculation that they may be one and the same.

Preiss modeled classical and modern nudes – and the Olympic figures, lithe and vibrant, glorifying the body beautiful and so much in tune with the spirit of the 1936 Olympics and the Nazi preoccupation with the physical prowess of the Aryan master race that suspicion has abounded that Preiss was an adherent of the movement.

'Autumn Dancer', a bronze and ivory figure, cast and carved from a model by F. Preiss of a dancing girl standing on tip-toe with one leg bent before her, on a black and green onyx plinth, 37.5cm. high.

(Christie's) **$34,500**

'Cabaret Girl', a bronze and ivory figure cast and carved from a model by Ferdinand Preiss of a dancing girl in silver patinated and cold-painted blue costume, on a hexagonal green onyx base, 35.3cm. high.
(Christie's)   **$17,250**

'Mandolin Player', a bronze and ivory figure cast and carved from a model by Ferdinand Preiss, the gold and silver patinated girl wearing a top-hat and loose fitting skirt, holding a mandolin under her right arm, the other hand on her hip, on a stepped black and brown striated base, 58.4cm. high.
(Christie's)   **$21,378**

Elvis Presley's outstanding white one piece stage suit decorated with gilt studs in a 'shooting star' design all over the costume, with letter of authenticity from the suit's designer Bill Belew.
(Phillips) **$44,980**

A rare set of five Elvis Presley Sun label singles comprising 'Mystery Train', 'I'm Left You're Right, She's Gone', 'Milkcow Blues Boogie', 'I Don't Care If The Sun Don't Shine' and 'That's Alright' each on the Sun label, 45 r.p.m.
(Christie's) **$3,945**

Elvis Presley, a rare single-sided acetate 'Good Rockin Tonight', Memphis Recording Service label stamped *W.H.B.Q. Memphis* accompanied by a certificate of authenticity from The Elvis Presley Museum stating that *...this Elvis Presley's 2nd recording for the Sun label is the original first copy made on the night it was recorded....*

Accompanying certificate gives the history of the acetate. *...Sam Phillips owned Sun records which was housed at his 'Memphis Recording Service' studio. Sam's brother Dewey Phillips was the D.J. in Memphis at W.H.B.Q. Radio Station. Sam sent the acetate to Dewey to air test that night. It was immediately pressed and released.*
(Christie's) **$5,775**

Elvis Presley 'That's the Way it Is' a black cotton shirt printed in shades of brown as worn in the film, circa 1971. *(Phillips)* **$10,150**

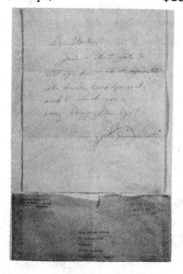

An Elvis Presley autograph letter, signed to a fan, *Dear Marlene*, with original envelope frankmarked Memphis, Tenn., January 24th 1961. *(Christie's S. Ken)* **$900**

Gibson FJ-N acoustic guitar, owned and used by Elvis Presley. *(Christie's)* **$10,578**

'St. James's Park', colored stipple engraving by Francois Davide Soiron, originally published by Colnaghi and Company, London, 1790, 455mm. x 535mm. *(Phillips)* **$7,350**

'Love's Blossom', by Louis Icart, etching and drypoint, printed in colors, signed lower right, inscribed *Parfum de fleurs, © Copyright 1937 by L. Icart Sty. N.Y.*, 44.5cm. x 64.3cm. *(Christie's)* **$8,248**

The Bloody Massacre Perpetrated in King Street Boston on March 5th 1770 by a party of the 29th Regt, engraving with hand-coloring, 1770, on laid paper, with the LVG watermark cited by Brigham, second (Final) state, with title and text, 10¼" x 9".

Brigham noted correctly that "Paul Revere's *Boston Massacre* is the most famous and desirable of all his engravings. It is the corner-stone of any American collection."

The second state of the Massacre is most commonly identified by the hands of the clock being pointed to show the time at 10.20. According to Stauffer and Brigham, impressions of the print were pulled giving the time as 8.10. The massacre, however, took place after ten o'clock and it is believed that Revere re-worked his plate to produce a more historically accurate document.

The somewhat crude but evocative hand-coloring of man of the prints is generally thought to be contemporary. Christian Remick, a mariner and artist, has generally been credited with coloring Revere's print of the Boston Massacre.
(Christie's)   **$110,000**

To the Merchants of Boston this View of the LIGHT HOUSE is most humbly presented By their Humble Servt Wm Burgis

William Burgis, mezzotint with a few touches of white heightening, 1729, on laid paper, a rich and beautiful impression of this extremely rare print known only in two copies, with the engraved title and inscription: *To the Merchants of Boston this view of the Light House is most humbly presented by their humble serv^t Wm Burgis*, with $1/2$ to $5/8$" margins, $9^7/8$" x $12^5/16$".

This is the only print known to have been engraved by Burgis himself and is the first maritime print executed in the American Colonies. The print was issued April 11, 1729, and is only the second mezzotint known to have been done in these Colonies (after Peter Pelham's *Cotton Mather*, 1728). Before the present copy was discovered, the impression belonging to The Mariner's Museum, Newport News, Virginia, was thought to be unique. Only the two impressions are known today. *(Christie's)* **$104,500**

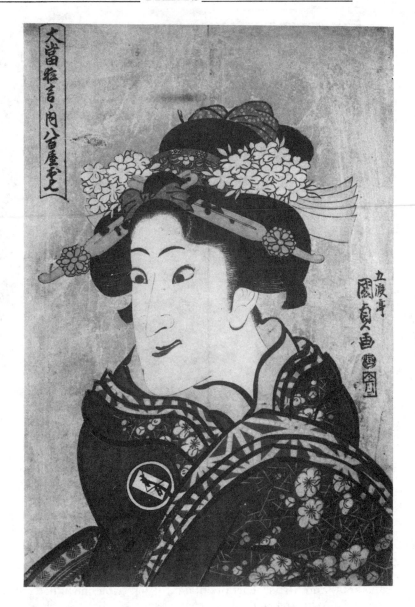

Kunisada (1786-1864) print of the actor Iwai Hanshiro V as Yaoya
Oshiel, performed in either first or seventh month of 1809, from the
series Oatari kyogen no uchi 'From famous hit performances', signed
Gototei Kunisada. This series made in 1815/1816 is considered to
be Kunisada's masterpiece of theatrical portraiture.
(Christie's)   **$16,360**

A fine and important appliqued and stuffed album quilt attributed to Mary Evans, Baltimore, Maryland, 1850, centring a large square reserve with reverse appliqued red feather border enclosing a flower-filled basket surrounded by a be-ribboned floral wreath, the inner border with twelve pictorial squares including flower baskets and urns, cornucopias, bouquets, wreaths and birds, each signed by a presenter of the quilt, 90" x 90".

This album quilt was presented to Mary Updegraff of Hagerstown, Maryland in 1850. Rather than stitching individual squares to be sewn together at a later date as was traditional, the presenters commissioned Mary Evans, a professional quiltmaker, to produce the finished product. As a result, the quilt has a unified composition and rhythm that distinguishes it from other album quilts.

The triple bowknot, reticulated baskets and careful selection of fabrics are all classic characteristics of Mary Evan's work. In this case, the quilt is personalised by individual ink inscriptions on each square from the presenters to the recipients.
(Christie's) **$132,000**

An unusual appliqued and embroidered cotton pictorial quilted coverlet, by Jennie C. Trein, Nazareth, Pennsylvania, 1932. Centring a scene depicting a family Sunday picnic with gathering guests, a house in the background, boats in the water, and the family graveyard surrounded by an inner border with 'Sunbonnet Sue' figures, 84" x 82". Mrs. Trein depicts herself twice: once on the right-hand border with her two twin daughters, Mary Ellen and Mary Elizabeth, and again on the center bottom border shaking hands with her neighbor.

(Christie's)   **$41,800**

RACE TICKETS

A George III silver race ticket, maker's mark *WC*. This ticket entitled the owner to admission in perpetuity, to the grandstand and paddock only at Doncaster racecourse.

(Spencers)   **$5,250**

369

A George III silver Doncaster race ticket, of oval form, the obverse engraved with a classical temple and inscribed *Doncaster*, the reverse numbered *150*. Makers mark *W.C.* This Ticket Entitles the Owner to Admission in Perpetuity to the Grandstand and Paddock only at Doncaster Racecourse. The owner should register the ticket at Doncaster Racecourse where badges of admission are issued annually or prior to each meeting.
(Spencers) **$6,475**

RADIOS

'Emor', a Modernist chromium plated radio formed as a globe, on a tubular stem and stepped circular foot, the tuning band around the circumference of the globe, with transfer label *Emor Quality Radio* and registered design and English patent numbers, 50.4cm. high.
(Christie's) **$865**

Sparton radio, designed by Walter Dorwin Teague, circa 1936, circular face of blue mirror glass centring circular chrome framed dial and speaker intersected by three horizontal chrome bands resting on circular blue glass reflector plate, 15" high.
(Skinner Inc) **$1,700**

A silver-mounted maple wood mazer bowl on spreading circular foot, the hammered everted rim pierced and applied with stylized foliage and wave ornament and engraved *Except the Lord build the house: their labour is but lost that build it. Except the Lord keep the city: the watchman waketh but in vain.*, the boss enameled with a coat-of-arms, by Omar Ramsden, 1937, 10¼" diameter.
(Christie's)   **$34,650**

A fine quatrefoil dish by Omar Ramsden, the center with applied medallion depicting a winged angel holding a torch, within inner girdle cast with fruiting vine, oak leaves, ears of wheat and fruit, with hammered body and with molded rim and footrim, 12" diameter, the base inscribed *Omar Ramsden me fecit* hallmarked London 1938, 29ozs.
(G.A. Canterbury Auction Galleries)
        $19,250

In 1685 Louis XIV of France revoked the Edict of Nantes, whereby almost a century earlier Henry IV had granted freedom of worship and limited civil equality to his Protestant Huguenot subjects. The renewed religious persecution which followed caused what amounted to a Huguenot diaspora to friendly Protestant countries, principally Holland, England and her colonies in the New World. Many of the refugees were skilled craftsmen, mainly weavers and silversmiths, and their new homelands benefited greatly from their industry and expertise. Among them was the silversmith Apollos Rivoire (1702–1754) who settled in Boston in 1715. His son Paul followed him in his trade, though he is principally remembered in most circles for his memorable ride of 18 April 1775 when he warned the rebellious citizens of Massachusetts that British troops were on the march. The following day the first shots of the American War of Independence were fired at Lexington.

Revere eventually opened a bell and cannon factory in Boston in 1796, though his revolutionary fervour does not, according to some critics, appear to have extended to his artistic imagination. He was, by and large, content to imitate the imported Neo-Classical style which prevailed at that time. Nevertheless, his pieces are extremely fine examples of their type, and fetch huge sums today.

A fine silver cream jug by Paul Revere II, Boston, circa 1790, of fluted urn-form, with a curving strap handle, a spreading cylindrical stem, and a square base, the rim with a stylized-leaf border above pendant swags and tassels, 7" high, 6 ozs 10 dwt.
(Christie's)   **$82,500**

A fine silver sugar urn by Paul Revere II, Boston, 1793, of fluted urn-form, with a domed cover, bud finial, flaring cylindrical foot, and square base, the shoulder engraved with fringed swags and tassels, 9" high, 13 ozs.
(Christie's)   **$49,500**

A fine silver teapot and stand by Paul Revere II, Boston, circa 1790, with a tapering cylindrical spout, a carved wood handle and an oval cover with a bud finial, the sides bright-cut engraved with floral swags centering oval shields, the conforming stand with a molded rim and four feet, gross weight 24 ozs.
(Christie's)   **$165,000**

ROBOTS

Japan came late to the toy making market, but once there swiftly all but took it over. The Japanese began making tinplate toys in the 1950's, which happened to coincide with a surge of interest in space and science fiction. By the early 60's they had begun producing battery operated or clockwork spacemen and moving robots, based on the character Robby the Robot in the 1950's film 'Forbidden Planet'. Over 90% of all such toys made were produced in Japan, with such ingenuity that they could accomplish a multitude of feats, walking, talking, turning, shooting and flashing lights while rotating at a dizzying speed. (A pure robot, it should be noted, must not have a human face behind its plastic dome.)

By the 1970's however, tinplate was abandoned in favour of, needless to say, plastic, with considerable loss of aesthetic appeal. The early models have long since achieved collectible status, and regularly crack $2,000.

Names to look out for are Lilliput, Linemar, Horikawa, Yoshiya and Ichida. One of the highest priced to date, in fact, is a battery operated immobile Answergame with flashing eyes made in the 1960's by Ichida, which executes simple mathematics, and which was sold by Christie's for $2,494.

Nando Robot by Opset, Italian, circa 1948. 5¹/₈" high.
(Christie's) **$2,200**

Answergame, printed and painted tinplate, battery operated, immobile, executes simple mathematics, flashing eyes, by Ichida, Japanese, 1960's, 35.5cm. high.
(Christie's) **$2,494**

Jupiter Robot by Yonezawa.
(Christie's) **$5,280**

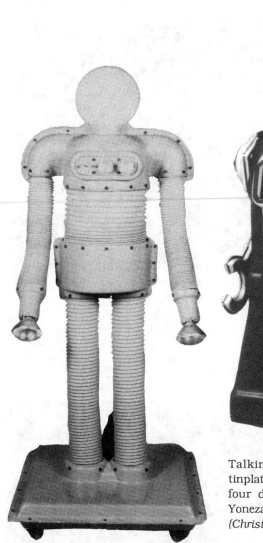

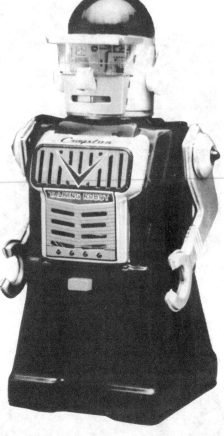

Talking robot, printed and painted tinplate, battery powered, mobile, speaks four different messages, with box, by Yonezawa, Japanese, 1950's, 28cm. high.
(Christie's)   **$1,542**

'Rudolph', a robot light fitting designed by Frank Clewett, the orange fiber-glass torso with rectangular central panel, the head formed by spherical glass shade, the adjustable arms with light bulbs forming the hands, the gray plastic concertina legs on square base with castors, 149cm. high.
(Christie's)   **$1,580**

Tekke animal-tree asmalyk, West Turkestan, early 19th century, this very fine Tekke animal-tree asmalyk is the tenth known example of this rare group which is closely related to the well-known bird asmalyks. Seven examples of animal tree asmalyks are documented in Turkoman Studies I by Pinner and Franses; the eighth is published in Antique Oriental Carpets from Austrian Collections and the ninth was sold at Rippon Boswell, Wiesbaden, May 7, 1988, 4ft. 8" x 2ft. 10".

(Skinner Inc) **$40,000**

Appliqued and embroidered table rug, America, circa 1840, with bands of figures depicting the activities of an early 19th century market day including peddlers, farmers with livestock, a militia band, entertainers and shoppers, worked with wool patches and heightened with cotton embroidery on a wool ground, 27 x 55½". *(Skinner Inc)* **$16,000**

Silk Garrus carpet, 13ft. 6" x 9ft. 3".
(Christie's London) **$151,360**

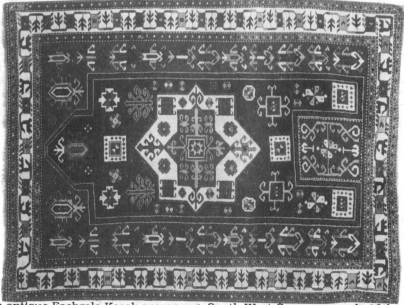

An antique Fachralo Kazak prayer rug, South West Caucasus, early 19th century, the flame-red field enclosing a deep blue mihrab decorated with a characteristic ivory and red central star. The design at the base of the mihrab is derived from an archaic emblem depicting a pair of confronting animals, 5ft. 4" x 4ft. 1". *(Phillips)* **$31,500**

A Donegal style Arts & Crafts carpet, the dark blue field woven in shades of green and beige with bold palmettes and flowering branches, 15ft x 12ft 6". *(Lawrence Fine Art)*
$31,760

Pictorial hooked rug, America, early 20th century, bearing the inscription *Old Shep* and depicting a standing dog enclosed by tulips, flowerheads, kitten and puppy within a striped border, worked with cotton and wool in bold shades of red, yellow, blue, pink, magenta and black on burlap ground, 27" x 34". *(Skinner Inc)* **$900**

RUM BARRELS

A brass bound oak rum barrel inscribed HMS Victory No. 3, 16½" high.
(Christie's) **$3,162**

William IV officer's full dress sabretache of the 3rd Dragoon Guards with belts and VR pouch.
(Wallis & Wallis) **$3,587**

SALTGLAZE

A saltglaze Bacchus teapot and cover modeled as the grotesquely overweight but youthful Bacchus scantily draped in vine, his left arm akimbo and forming the handle, seated astride a ribbed barrel, the front with a curved serpent spout, circa 1760, 16.5cm. high.
(Christie's) **$36,575**

A saltglaze molded candlestick, the tapering cylindrical double-knopped stem with flared drip-pan terminating on a scroll, foliage and shell-molded base on a dimpled ground, circa 1760, 20cm. high.
(Christie's) **$10,587**

Samplers were originally a record of embroidery patterns which could then be copied. The earliest dated one is in fact English, made in 1586, and was worked by Jane Bostock. Early examples are rare, for they were made only by the leisured upper classes. By the mid-1700s however, sampler work was spreading to all classes. By this time too printed patterns in book form were becoming more readily available, and the original function of the sampler changed to become more and more of an apprentice piece for young girls, where they could practise and display the various stitches they could execute.

On the earliest samplers, motifs tended to be embroidered at random, with little eye to proportion or harmony of form. By the mid 17th century however there were indications that greater attention was being paid to overall design. Horizontal border patterns of geometric floral motifs are typical of samplers dating from 1650–1720 and around the end of the 18th century the decorative aspect was obviously becoming increasingly important. Samplers became more and more a record of a child's name, age, home (with illustrations of a house, plants and animals,) together with, very often, an uplifting moral or religious verse or text.

Another interesting development during the late 18th and early 19th centuries was the map sampler, which could range from a very simple design to a complicated Globe map. At this time too the basic shape changed from long and narrow to square or rectangular, which were altogether more appropriate for the pictorial content.

A fine and rare needlework sampler by Alice Mather, Norwich, Connecticut, 1774, worked in green, blue, rose and white silk and metal threads, on a black background with bands of alphabets and numerals embellished with a verse 'Who can find a virtuous woman. For her price is far above rubies,' above a scene depicting a shepherdess with a flock of sheep. This needlework sampler is part of a small group of Norwich samplers, with solidly worked black backgrounds, Greek key bands and four petalled stylized flowers.
(Christie's N. York)
$49,500

In later examples, the horizontal bands that once formed the whole were now used only as a border frame for the pictorial content, and the style became simpler, with a smaller variation of stitches.

Samplers continued to be worked till the end of the 19th century and beyond, but the combination of the sewing machine and Berlin woolwork patterns really spelt their death knell. There are signs of a revival, however with needlework sampler kits being produced once more.

Many samplers survive, having been regarded from the first as family heirlooms, almost on a par with the family Bible. Generally speaking, the earlier ones fetch the most money, but it is early American samplers which really attract a premium. While others will fetch a few hundred, or even a couple of thousand, early American samplers often start at $20,000 and go on to sell for really staggering sums.

A fine needlework sampler by Elizabeth Crowninshield, probably Marblehead, Massachusetts, 1805. Worked in polychrome silk threads on linen ground with the alphabet above the maker's name and birthdate over a pious sentiment above a register with full-length silhouettes of a man and woman, 15$\frac{1}{4}$" x 17$\frac{1}{2}$".

Elizabeth Diamond Crowninshield, born September 19, 1793, was the daughter of Edward Crowninshield and Mary Dixey, Elizabeth married Francis Freeto on September 7, 1817. From this union one child survived infancy, Mary Jane, born 1825. *(Christie's)* **$24,200**

A needlework sampler probably New Jersey made by Anna Braddock, aged 14, 1826. *(Skinner Inc)* **$38,000**

Needlework sampler, Joanna Maxwell, Warren, Rhode Island, dated 1793, made by *Joanna Maxwell, born May the 8 AD 1782 at Warren* and further inscribed *Wrought at Warren, September the 12 AD 1793.* 16¹/₂" high, 13" wide. One of a rare group of samplers made in Warren, Rhode Island probably under the tutelage of the Warren school mistress Martha Pease Davis. Joanna never married. She died at the age of 60 and is buried in the Swan Point Cemetery in Providence, Rhode Island.

(Skinner Inc) **$40,000**

Sand jar, America, late 19th century, arranged in geometric patterns centering an eagle with American flag on one side and the name *Mary J. Savile* flanked by floral devices on other, 9" high.

(Skinner Inc)   **$2,100**

SCAGLIOLA

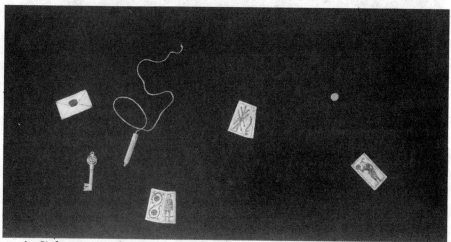

An Italian pietra dura table top decorated with a key, a coin, an envelope, five cards and a pencil on a string, the ground grey-black, 18th century, 57" x 37½".

This table belongs to a small group inlaid with playing-cards. Scagliola work has been practised in Italy since the Romans and enjoyed a notable renaissance in Tuscany early in the 18th century. The great exponents worked in the monastery of Vallombrosa under the patronage of Grand Duke Cosimo III (1670-1723). Enrico Hugford, born 1696, son of Ignatius Hugford (or Huggeford) an English Catholic exile, clockmaker to the Grand Duke, perfected the art of scagliola. He became Abbot in 1737 and his oeuvre was renowned throughout Europe. The English became his chief patrons, Horace Walpole possessed a panel.

(Christie's)   **$12,089**

An Italian scagliola rectangular table top by Laurentius Bonucelli, the black ground with playing-cards, a flute, a gold and enamel pocket watch, flowers, an open book with music and an envelope inscribed *To his dearest friend & Patrones the Lady Dorothy Marsh, London*, the knave of spades inscribed *Carte Di Genua*, the knave of hearts inscribed *Laurentius Bonuccelli*, late 17th century, 47³/₄" wide.

A persistent but unsubstantiated family tradition records that this table top, which depicts four hands of cards, represents the last hand played by a member of the D'Aeth of Narbrough family, of Knowlton, who is said to have staked his estate and chattels on one hand of cards. The hand, ace of diamonds, ace of clubs, six and seven of clubs, was capped by the banker who held the ace of spades, the ace of hearts, the king of clubs and the six of diamonds. The unfortunate gambler tore across two cards, flung down his fob and signet ring and went upstairs to shoot himself. The music is 17th century Italian and can be played. *(Christie's)* **$116,000**

A pair of cushions covered in 18th century tapestry woven in wool and silks, each with an oval, one woven with travelers in a landscape, the other with soldiers in a landscape, on a black ground woven with tulips and roses, with tasseled fringe, 22" wide.
(Christie's) $5,000

One of two tent-stitched balloon seat covers, Rooksby Crease, Boston, Massachusetts, circa 1750, each depicting a figured idyllic landscape within a bold floral border; the first with harlequin and a seated lady with lute by her side, the second with a seated lady holding a flower basket beckoning to a strolling farmer and his dog, 20" x 23".
(Skinner Inc) $67,000

SEAT COVERS

One of nine tapestry seat covers woven in wool and silk with poppies, bluebells and other flowers on a black background, 29" wide x 22" long, Continental late 17th/early 18th century.
(Christie's) **$42,350**

SEDAN CHAIRS

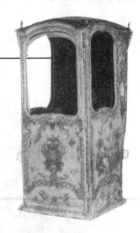

Mid 19th century North Italian parcel gilt and painted sedan chair, 30½" wide, 69" high.
(Christie's) **$14,696**

SETTEES

An early 19th century Anglo-Indian padouk double scroll-end settee, the arched backrail, arm tops and facings, seat frame and legs all profusely carved with anthemion, acanthus scrolls, paterae etc., on scroll-carved legs, 8ft. long. *(Russell Baldwin & Bright)* **$14,000**

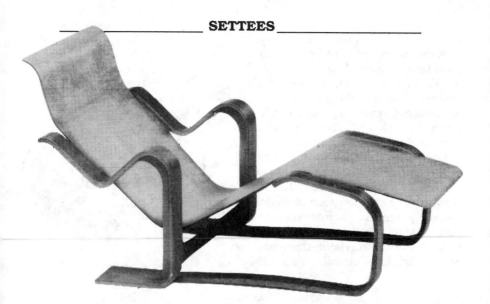

A Marcel Breuer chaise longue, made for Isokon, the curvilinear laminated beech frame supporting single molded plywood panel, 136cm. long. *(Christie's)* **$5,108**

A gilt, silver, green and black-painted grotto sociable, the S-shaped back and arms in the form of entwined scrolling dolphins, with scallop shell splats and seat on shell-encrusted cabriole legs. *(Christie's)* **$5,390**

A Sèvres porcelain chamberstick by Jean-Louis Thévenet, the sconce in the form of a chalice surrounded by a garland of flowers, the green ground border decorated in scrolling giltwork, mark *E* for 1757, between two interlaced Ls.Thévenet's marks.

Jean Louis Thévenet was a painter at the Sèvres factory between 1741-77. On 29 December 1757, Lazare Duvaux delivered a green and gilt French porcelain chamberstick to Mme la Marg. de Pompadour for 60 livres. This almost certainly that same piece. *(Christie's Monaco)*   **$25,593**

A pair of Sèvres-pattern Napoleonic giltmetal-mounted vases and covers, the tapering oviform bodies decorated by Desprez with continuous battle scenes including Napoleon Bonaparte on a white stallion between wide gilt bands reserved on royal-blue grounds gilt with foliage and applied with a giltmetal shield-shaped medallion inscribed *N* beneath an eagle, signed *Desprez Sèvres*, imitation Mre Imp^{le} de Sèvres marks, late 19th century, 100cm. high.
(Christie's)   **$21,252**

The familiar lockstitch sewing machine was invented by an American machinist, Elias Howe in 1846, and patented by Isaac Merrit Singer in 1851. In the years that followed, many firms tried to cash in on this wonderful new device, but it was the Singer Sewing Machine Co which cornered the lion's share of the market. By 1890 they turned out 10 million machines, many of which were of such high quality that they are still usable today.

The sewing machine boom even generated the spin-off invention of the sewing machine chair, a collectible in its own right, which was patented in 1871. The chair and back rest tilt forward, corresponding to the inclination of the sewer's body, giving support to the back and relieving stress on the thighs.

Collecting early machinery is becoming increasingly popular, and the sewing machine is one of the favorites. There are enough of them around, they are by and large still affordable, and they are also a convenient size to make collecting practical for most enthusiasts. Above all, they have an aesthetic appeal all of their own, for many early examples are beautifully made with mahogany covers and wonderfully embellished with gilt and mother of pearl, inlay, or even hand painting.

A rare Kimball & Morton 'Lion' treadle sewing machine, the machine head formed as a standing lion, on treadle with end standards cast with heraldic beasts, 26½" wide, with registration mark of 1868. *(Christie's S. Ken)* **$7,762**

Early examples to look out for, made by companies other than Singer, include those by the Imperial Sewing Machine Co, the Howe Sewing Machine Co (it's nice to think he made something out of his good idea!) and others imported from Germany. One of the most imaginative of these is a rare Nuremberg clown sewing machine, the seated cast iron figure with nodding head and working arms, operated by a porcelain handled crank and on an iron base with lion's paw feet. It is only 8.75 inches high and fetched $4,519 at auction. Another rare machine is one by Clemens Müller from 1873, on a decorative tripod it's worth $2,000.

Most amazing of all, however, is the Kimball & Morton Lion treadle sewing machine, the machine head formed as a standing lion. It dates from 1868, and was sold recently for $7,762.

An unusual 19th century Davenport cased sewing machine by S. Davies & Co. *(Phillips)* **$2,080**

SEWING MACHINES

A rare Nuremburg 'Clown' sewing machine, No. 4024, the seated cast-iron figure with nodding head and working arms operated by a porcelain-handled crank, on iron base with lions paw feet, 8³/4" high.
(Christie's S. Ken) **$4,519**

SHAKER

Simple, sturdy furniture and artifacts were produced in the late 18th and early 19th century by the Shaker sect in New England and New York State, originally for use by community members. Later, however, chair-making in particular developed into quite an industry supplying neighboring towns. The pieces were painted (usually dark red) but undecorated. Most typical items are rocking chairs and slat back chairs designed to be hung on a wall rail. Production declined after 1860.

Early 19th century Shaker tiger maple and cherry trestle base dining table, Canterbury, New England, 71¹/4" wide.
(Skinner Inc) **$86,000**

Four oval Shaker boxes, America, 19th century, each with fitted lid, the graduated boxes with three or four tapering fingers, each with original finish.
(Skinner Inc) **$3,100**

Shaker cherry candlestand, New Lebanon, New York, mid 19th century, 26" high. This stand was originally purchased when the New Lebanon, New York Shaker Community closed in 1948.
(Skinner Inc)   **$14,000**

Rare miniature painted Shaker box, Enfield, New Hampshire, dated *March 1836*, oval form with fitted lid and three tapering fingers, painted yellow, inscribed in pencil underside of lid *From G.A. Enfield, N.H. March 1836*, $15/16$" high x $2^7/8$" long.
(Skinner Inc)   **$23,000**

A fine Shaker maple cupboard with chest of drawers, Mount Lebanon, New York, Mid-19th century, the molded top above a paneled cupboard door opening to a single shelf over eight short drawers above a long drawer over a dressing slide above three long drawers, 94" high, 28$^1/_8$" wide, 19$^3/_8$" deep.
(Christie's)   **$22,000**

A Shaker, number 6, black-painted rocking armchair, Mt. Lebanon, New York, circa 1876, with four arched splats flanked by knopped cylindrical stiles above curved armrests with mushroom grips, 42$^1/_4$" high.
(Christie's)   **$1,870**

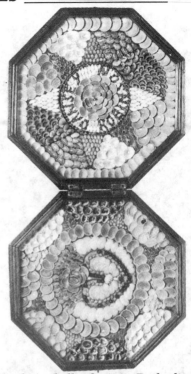

A rare Regency Gothic Revival shell model of a church, with lancet windows, the interior with a pulpit, boxed pews and an organ loft, 27" high x 21" long, in a mahogany and glazed case. It has been suggested that the church is Hampton Lucy, in Oxfordshire.

(Christie's) **$7,022**

A sailor's shell valentine, Barbadian, third quarter of the 19th century, the octagonal mahogany case with central hinge, opening to two shell pictures, one with heart design, the other lettered *Pansey Robinson*, 23cm. wide.

(Sothebys) **$882**

A finely engraved mother-of-pearl nautilus shell commemorating the building and bringing into service between England and America of the steamships 'Great Britain' and 'Great Western', engraved with water-line plans and various dimensions of each vessel, 8¹/₂" long.

Information included in the carving includes *This shell was engraved with a common penknife by C.H. Wood, who had the honour of presenting one similar to Her Most Gracious Majesty Queen Victoria, January 11th 1845.*

(Christie's) **$4,812**

Obadiah Sherratt started making Staffordshire pottery figures around 1822. While his initial work was rather coarse, he showed undoubted modeling skills, and produced some fine busts of Wesley and other notables.

One of his most important groups depicts a bull-bait, a popular diversion among the commoners of Burslem at that time, while a colorful depiction of a menagerie is another of his finer pieces.

No marked specimens of his work have been recorded so far, but the Willett Collection in the Brighton Museum contains many typical pieces. Sherratt continued to be active until the mid 1860's.

An Obadiah Sherratt group of the Death of Lieutenant Hector Monroe with a large tiger with bright yellow fur with black stripes facing to the right and with a dead officer resting to the side with his head between the tiger's jaws, on long rectangular base with six low feet entitled the Death of Munrow, circa 1815, 12½" wide.

There are two stories behind the killing of Lieutenant Hector Monroe in India on December 2nd 1792. The more flattering version was that he was out shooting deer when he was attacked by the tiger.
(Christie's) **$27,225**

An Obadiah Sherratt bull-baiting group, the chained bull painted in shades of red with a black dog falling across its back and with a yellow marked dog crouching down by its horns, a man standing to the right in brown jacket and yellow breeches holds a club up in the air, on shaped oval base molded with brightly colored feathers and blue scrolls, circa 1830, 13" wide.
(Christie's) **$6,160**

An Obadiah Sherratt group of Polito's Menagerie, the stage with an organ grinder and companion and five other musicians wearing iron-red, blue and pink clothes, flanking a central entrance surmounted by a yellow facade molded with an elephant flanked by a lion and lioness with two monkeys in trees above and inscribed around the edge *Politos Menagerie of the wonderfull burds and beasts from most part of the world..Lion & C*, circa 1830, 35cm. wide.
(Christie's) $25,168

A Staffordshire Pearlware group of The Death of Munrow of Obadiah Sherratt type, the fierce beast with bright-yellow coat with a white ruff and black markings, his tail curled over his back and with the dying officer's head in his jaws, his face cruelly gashed, circa 1820, 33.5cm. wide.
(Christie's) $17,325

The Shibayama were a family of Japanese inro artists who, in the late 18th century, developed and specialized in a style of encrusted lacquer (now known as Shibayama) in which a decorative surface was covered with minute, delicately carved encrustations of materials such as ivory, mother of pearl, coral, gold, silver and metallic alloys. They were meticulously designed and executed, with realistic patterns showing human, animal and plant forms.

Their work became very popular in the 19th century and during the Meiji period it was produced in large quantities, usually for export to the West.

Production methods were simplified, and quality suffered accordingly, with patterns being reduced to a few stereotypes, composed of shallowly inlaid pieces of precarved and tinted raden, usually on an ivory ground.

A good silver mounted Shibayama vase, the body of rectangular section decorated with four Kinji lacquer panels in mother-of-pearl, colored ivory, coconut shell and enamel with birds, flower arrangements and Kwanyin, the body of Kirikane, the shoulders with elephant masked loose ring handles, 30cm. high.
(Phillips) **$18,480**

A Japanese Shibayama tear drop box, Meiji period, decorated on fundame background, the interior and base decorated makie, the top depicting a Japanese Koy carp trainer and a bronze vessel with chrysanthemums and prunus blossoms, matching bon-bon tray decorated jay and foliage in hiramakie, 5" wide. *(Riddetts)* **$7,750**

SHIBAYAMA

A fine Japanese Shibayama-style ivory standing caparisoned elephant with trunk raised, surmounted on the top with two flowerheads, the ornate trappings inlaid in jade, mother of pearl, horn, stained ivory, turquoise and other hardstones, the saddlecloth densely overlaid, predominantly in mother of pearl, with dense flowers, signed *Toshikazu*, Meiji period, 8½" long.
(Christie's) **$11,900**

SHOES

The best-documented collector of shoes of current times must be Imelda Marcos, wife of the deposed Philippines president, who reputedly had whole rooms filled with nothing but shelves full of shoes. A psychologist would doubtless have an explanation for this collecting mania or the mere fascination with footwear which seems to affect, albeit to a lesser degree, a surprising number of people. Even Andy Warhol, for example, chose the shoe as a central subject in a number of his pictures.

It becomes relatively simple when the shoes in question have associations, such as some of these featured here. Otherwise, it is, of course, always interesting to observe what people forced their feet into in the name of fashion in bygone ages. Prices range from a few dollars to a few thousand or more, depending upon rarity and condition, and shoes seem set to become an increasingly popular collectible of the future.

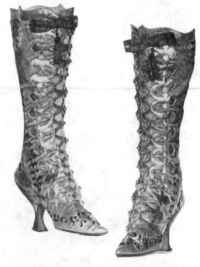

A pair of ladies' button boots, the front of gilt leather with a stitched scalloped edge, with a gilt painted Louis 4" heel, the leg of aquamarine plush, embroidered with gilt thread, trimmed with gilt leather frogging and a gilt tassel, 1880's.
(Christie's S. Ken) **$6,545**

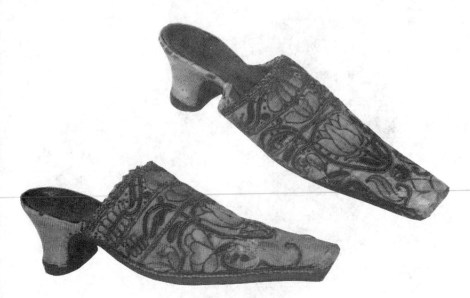

A pair of early 17th century
gentleman's mule slippers.
(Phillips) **$14,700**

Pair of 'ruby slippers' worn by Judy
Garland in the 1939 film The Wizard
of Oz.
(Christie's) **$165,000**

A superb pair of Michael Jackson's purple lace up dancing shoes heavily studded with purple glass stones.
(Phillips) **$7,480**

A lady's mule of yellow and brown silk brocade woven with abstract designs and cartouches, with an ivory kid rand, a 2¹/₂" high leather covered heel and a slightly forked toe, 10" long, circa 1660 with a label on the sole inscribed *Sarah Hammersley's shoes, Prince William III.*
(Christie's) **$25,025**

An important Chippendale carved mahogany side chair, labeled by Benjamin Randolph, Philadelphia, 1760-1770, with serpentine-eared crest above an interlaced pierced splat over a trapezoidal slip seat, on shell-carved cabriole legs with ball-and-claw feet, labeled on rear inside seat rail, 38"high. This chair, marked *VI*, is one of an original set of twelve.
(Christie's)   **$33,000**

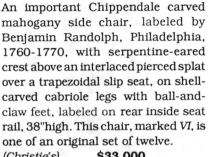

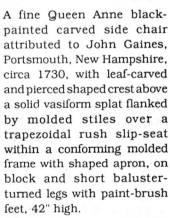

A fine Queen Anne black-painted carved side chair attributed to John Gaines, Portsmouth, New Hampshire, circa 1730, with leaf-carved and pierced shaped crest above a solid vasiform splat flanked by molded stiles over a trapezoidal rush slip-seat within a conforming molded frame with shaped apron, on block and short baluster-turned legs with paint-brush feet, 42" high.
(Christie's)   **$33,000**

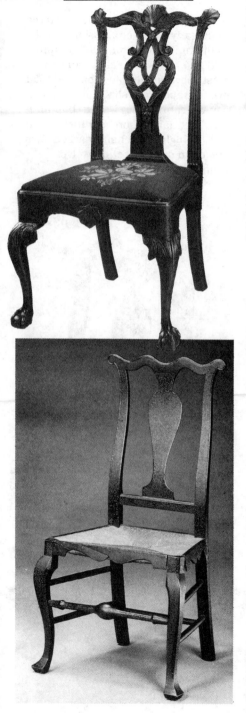

A fine Chippendale carved walnut side chair, Philadelphia, circa 1760, with a serpentine crest-rail centered by a shell flanked by foliate boughs and shell-carved ears over fluted stiles and a pierced vase-shaped splat carved with scrolling foliage and roseheads, above a trapezoidal seat within a shaped seat-rail centering a shell, on acanthus-carved cabriole legs with ball-and-claw feet, 41³/₄" high.

This chair appears to be from a set of which several examples are known. These include a chair in the Metropolitan Museum of Art illustrated in Morrison Heckscher, *American Furniture in the Metropolitan Museum of Art II* (New York, 1985), pp. 93-94, no. 48; another at the Rhode Island School of Design, illustrated in Christopher P. Monkhouse and Thomas S. Michie, *American Furniture in Pendleton House* (Providence, 1986), p. 169, no. 111, a third chair illustrated in *Antiques* (December, 1966), p. 749; and another formerly in the Howard Reifsnyder Collection, American Anderson Art Galleries, April 24-27, 1929, lot 646.
(Christie's)   **$110,000**

One of a fine pair of Chippendale maple side chairs, Philadelphia, 1755-1765, each with serpentine crest rail above a solid baluster splat over a rush seat within a scalloped-edge seat frame, on cabriole legs with spade feet joined by a ball-turned front stretcher, 40¹/₂" high.
(Christie's)   **$16,500**

A pair of William Kent carved giltwood chairs with low upholstered panel backs with scallop shell and foliate laurel leaf top rails with trailing husk carved uprights, having stuffover seats on canted scale carved legs with female masks at the knees.
(Phillips) **$45,500**

Military chair' by Gerrit Rietveld, the white painted rectangular back and seat on black painted bar frame, the seat supported on twinned bar apron, the profiles painted white, on rectangular section legs. This chair from the 'Military series' was designed in 1932. It was commissioned from Gerrit Rietveld by a military club, and has been designed so that it can be completely dismantled.
(Christie's) **$18,700**

A pair of oak side chairs designed by C.A. Voysey, the arched backs with arched back rails and tall square section finials, each back splat pierced with heart-shaped motif.
(Christie's) **$12,012**

Heywood Wakefield wicker piano chair, late 19th century, serpentine pierced back, circular carved seat, raised on cabriole legs joined by stretchers, bearing paper label *Heywood Brothers and Wakefield Company, Wakefield, Mass. U.S.A.*, 43½" high.
(Skinner Inc) **$750**

Before the era of photography, if you couldn't afford a portrait, you might sit for a silhouettist. These little black and white likenesses are named after Etienne de Silhouette, a French politician who, it seems, believed in cutting everything down to essentials. They first appeared around 1750, and were drawn either freehand or by tracing the shadow of a profile on a piece of black paper. Later, more sophisticated techniques developed. The art flourished too among amateurs and was regarded as quite a drawing-room accomplishment.

August Edouart (1788-1861), silhouette of three children with toys, cat and dog, cut paper applied to a watercolor, 17.8 x 34.6cm.
(Skinner Inc) **$2,100**

Mrs. Isabella Beetham (circa 1753-1825), Mrs. Sharland, seated half length in profile to the left, in lace trimmed dress and hat decorated with rosette, silhouette, painted on convex glass, 3⅞" high.
(Christie's) **$3,498**

A rectangular silhouette by Wm. Welling, of a husband and wife taking tea, signed and dated 1874, 28 x 38cm.
(Phillips) **$4,832**

A German parcel-gilt cylindrical tankard, on domed foot and with scroll handle applied with beading, hinged domed cover and openwork curved thumbpiece, the base, sides and cover inset with thalers, variously dated 1583, 1655 etc., the base engraved with a coat-of-arms, circa 1685, town mark G., possibly for Matthes Francke of Glogan, 7½" high, 1,483grs.
(Christie's)   **$30,294**

A George I plain spherical sponge box, on spreading circular foot, the hinged domed cover pierced with stylized strapwork and scrolls and engraved with a cypher, unmarked, circa 1720, 2¾" diameter, 6ozs.
(Christie's)   **$4,276**

A fine George II shaped-oval bread basket, each on four shell and scroll feet, pierced with scrolls, stylized shells and latticework and applied with a shell and scroll border and with similar swing handle, chased with a band of rocaille ornament, by Ayme Videau, 1741, 13½" long, 66ozs.
(Christie's)   **$30,107**

A three-piece electroplated tea-service, each piece modeled as a car, comprising: a teapot, a milk jug, and a sugar bowl, the teapot stamped *E.P.N.S.*, teapot 26cm. high.
(Christie's)   **$2,117**

A George III pudding slice, the shaped-triangular blade pierced and engraved with scrolls and with feather edge border and dolphin and spiral twist junction and turned wood handle, by William Plummer, 1774, 12¼" long.
(Christie's)   **$3,207**

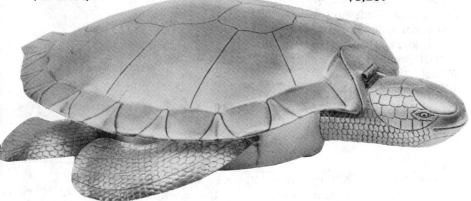

A rare Sheffield plate turtle soup tureen, life size, finely modeled, the hinged shell back forming the cover, 17cm. high x 58cm. long (apparently holds five quarts of soup), circa 1800.
(Phillips)   **$12,456**

A Victorian cornet-shaped posy holder decorated in the aesthetic taste with flowers, birds and foliage in vari-colored gilding on a frosted ground, applied with engraved shield-shaped cartouche, with chain, pin and finger loop attached, Hilliard & Thomason, Birmingham 1884, 5.7".
(Christie's) **$1,260**

A Belgian windmill cup, the bell-shaped bowl engraved with portrait busts, fruit, birds and foliage, and with spool-shaped knop, the windmill with ladder and figures, engraved with initials, probably Ghent, circa 1600, 9" high, 253grs.
(Christie's) **$51,975**

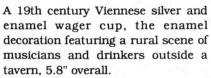

A 19th century Viennese silver and enamel wager cup, the enamel decoration featuring a rural scene of musicians and drinkers outside a tavern, 5.8" overall.
(Christie's) **$2,790**

A continental shaving set, comprising: six cut-throat razors each with steel blade and silver-mounted tortoiseshell handle, a silver-mounted tortoiseshell mirror and comb, a stone strop with lion's mask finial and a pair of scissors, contained in a silver-mounted shagreen upright casket on spreading shaped-rectangular base and with hinged domed cover, probably Portuguese, circa 1740, 11½" high. (Christie's) **$6,952**

An Edwardian child's rattle.
(Spencers) **$210**

A fine William and Mary octagonal snuffer stand and a pair of matching candle snuffers, the stand with sunken centre, scroll handle and gadrooned borders, the snuffers with scroll handles, by John Laughton, 1691, height overall 7¾", 12 ozs.

From surviving pieces John Laughton would appear to have been a most prolific maker of candlesticks from the early 1680's until his death in 1701. The earliest recorded pair of candlesticks by him are those of 1683. (Christie's) **$32,274**

A silver-mounted wood mazer, on circular foot with corded rim, the plain maple wood body applied with vertical foliage straps, the everted silver border applied with a corded rib and lower band of pierced stylized foliage, by Omar Ramsden, 1931, 8³/₄" diameter.
(Christie's)   **$23,166**

An unusual presentation punch bowl by Whiting Manufacturing Co., New York, circa 1885, with two open handles in the form of stylized dolphins, on a spot-hammered shaped circular foot; the front repoussé and chased with a face and verses, 18" long over handles, 109 ozs.
(Christie's)   **$23,100**

A Desny electroplated cocktail set, comprising a cocktail shaker of conical form with angled flange brackets and a set of six goblets, each with a conical bowl and a small conical foot connected by an angled flange, stamped *Desny, Paris, Made in France, Depose*, cocktail shaker 26cm. high.
(Spencers)   **$8,700**

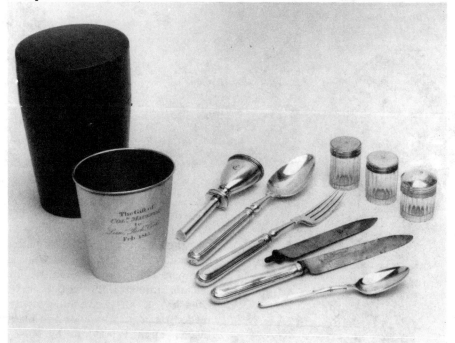

A good George III silver Campaign set in red morocco case, comprising nutmeg grater and sheathed screw, beaker, 3 condiments, three 2-piece implements and combined spoon and marrow scoop, London 1802/3. makers Eley & Fearn and William Pitts.
(Graves Son & Pilcher)   **$4,860**

A mid-Victorian unusual claret jug by George Fox formed as a wyvern, the plain baluster body chased below with close-feathered wings and similar tail divided in two parts, the upper turned-up to form the handle, the hinged head inset with ruby-gem eyes and pricked-up pointed ears, 22.5cm. high overall, 1866, 23.5ozs. This unusual jug was copied from a Viennese white porcelain chocolate pot, made circa 1745 and now in the Victoria and Albert Museum.

(Phillips) **$4,056**

A George III silver-gilt Hanoverian pattern dessert service, each engraved with the Royal crest and Garter motto, comprising: twelve spoons, by William Sumner, 1789; twelve forks, ten by William Sumner, 1789, two by Richard Crossley, 1799; twelve knives with reeded pistol grip handles and plain blades, circa 1790, four by Moses Brent contained in an 18th century velvet-lined mahogany knife-box with brass lock-plate and handles (weight without knives 28ozs).

(Christie's) **$17,325**

A pair of novelty condiments modeled as pigs, each engraved with hair, one with traces of gilding, in a fitted case, London 1912, 2¼".
(Christie's) **$1,347**

A fine pair of George III meat skewers with cast bull's head terminals probably by William Tuite 1767, 35cm. long and 32.2cm. long respectively, 11ozs.
(Phillips) **$2,805**

A George II gold-handled coral child's teething stick, chased in relief with birds, pillars, flowers and 'C'-scrolls, unmarked, circa 1750, 12.9cm. long.
(Phillips) **$2,817**

A George II pair of cast candlesticks, the canted square bases stepped and chased on each side with a raised winged cherub's head in the middle of a crescent frieze, the well wax-pans beaded and engraved on opposite sides with a crest and stylized fluting to the base of the tapering stems, 28.5cm. high.

The candlesticks are extremely rare, indeed, few extant examples by this remarkable craftsman are known or have appeared in the salerooms. Nicholas Sprimont worked only for a short period as a goldsmith, from 1742, when he registered his first mark, the year these candlesticks were made, and until 1747. It was as a maker of porcelain that Sprimont is better known; indeed, while he was working as a goldsmith, he became manager of the celebrated Chelsea Porcelain Factory, where he remained until, due to poor health, he was forced to sell in 1769. Sprimont spent his latter years in Chelsea and Richmond.

(Phillips)   **$310,000**

A pair of Victorian silver novelty bedroom candlesticks each modeled as three grotesque faces, one sleeping, one yawning and one smiling, 21cm. high, by Henry William Dee, 1878, 19½oz.

(Phillips)   **$7,700**

A fine and rare silver cake basket by Van Voorhis & Schanck, New York, circa 1791–1793, with flaring sides, a reeded bail handle, and a pierced oval foot, the brim pierced with a border decorated with bright-cut engraving and roulette-work banding, 10½" high overall, 34 ozs.

(Christie's) **$57,200**

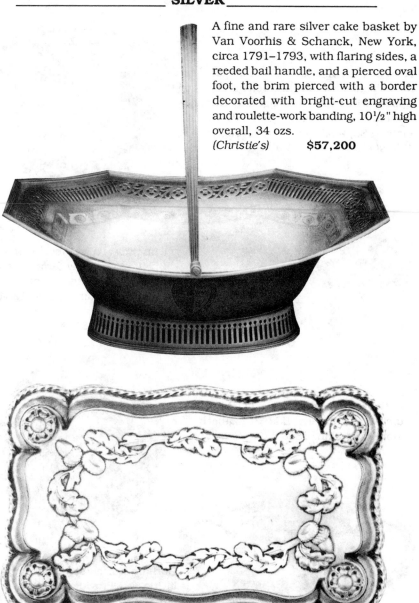

A shaped rectangular cigarette box, the interior with separate covered vesta compartment, the cover with floral boss in each corner, chased with a wreath of acorns and oak leaves, the rim of ropework design, the interior of the base with Tudor rose bosses in each corner, 1935, 11.5cm. long, gross weight 9.5ozs.

(Phillips) **$3,850**

A French circular silver chamber pot, on molded foot and with scroll handle applied with fruit and foliage and with everted molded rim, by Vetray, Paris, circa 1880, 9¹/₄" diameter, 1,126grs
(Christie's)   **$2,970**

An Edwardian novelty table bell, realistically formed as a boar, with hinged snout and tail, by William Hornby, 1904, 6" long.
(Christie's)   **$5,667**

A Georgian silver nipple shield, 2" diameter, maker: *E.M.* (Elizabeth Morley) London, 1808.
(Christie's)   **$321**

Gorham Martele sterling presentation loving cup, Providence, Rhode Island, circa 1902, the baluster body finely chased and repousse with water lilies and cat-tails, intertwined snake handles, presentation inscription to *Charles A. McCaffrey, Jr.*, dated 1919, 950 standard, date code *CMB*, 11" high, approximately 92 troy ozs.
(Skinner Inc)   **$6,500**

A highly important engraved cann engraved by Joseph Leddel, New York, 1750, cann made by Bartholomew Le Roux II, New York, before 1750, with a flaring rim and a scroll handle, on a molded circular foot, the sides engraved with six scenes from the life of Joseph, 4¹/₂" high, 9 ozs.

Joseph Leddel, a pewterer, is well-known among silver scholars as the engraver of a Philadelphia-made tankard decorated with classical scenes and a French beaker decorated with a political cartoon. The discovery of this cann, the third known piece of silver with engraving signed by Leddel, helps answer previous questions about the attribution, ownership, and iconography of this highly individual group of engraved silver.

(Christie's) **$242,000**

A George I King's Messenger's badge, by Francis Garthorne, circa 1720-23.
(Phillips) **$20,250**

Black, Starr and Frost sterling vase, New York, early 20th century, the hand raised baluster form with hammered texture, with an overall chased flowering clematis vine, engraved inscription, 14³/₄" high, approximately 44 troy ozs.
(Skinner Inc) **$2,800**

Russian troika with blue painted carved and scrolled frame, gilt detail. *(Lots Road Galleries)* **$1,890**

A painted and decorated pine sled, American, late 19th century, of typical form, with two peaked runners with wrought iron blades centering a shaped seat decorated with an oval American flag flanked by mustard and dark blue diapering, the runners inscribed *Village Romp* in gold letters, 52¼" long. *(Christie's)* **$8,250**

Snuff bottles, as opposed to the more familiar boxes, were the fashionable way of carrying one's snuff in China, where they were made by the finest craftsmen. About 2 1/2 " high, they were made of precious materials such as ivory, jade, agate, porcelain or glass. Usually they would be carved out of a solid piece of raw material (this is true also of glass examples) and the criteria of workmanship are therefore the size of the interior and the narrowness of the neck aperture. Most highly prized are porcelain examples from the late 17th and early 18th centuries, followed by those made from carved hardstone such as agate, quartz and amethyst. They were also used in Europe to some extent from the 17th century onwards.

An exceptionally rare 'Mutton Fat' jade snuff bottle, seal mark and period of Qianlong, attributed to the Peking Palace Workshops, of small size and pear shape, supported on a neatly finished, slightly flared footrim, two loop handles on the shoulders, the translucent material of a very pale brownish tone.
(Sothebys)   **$55,825**

Chalcedony agate snuff bottle, Suzhou School, mid 18th or mid 19th century.
(Christie's)   **$27,077**

An Imperial carved ivory snuff bottle, mark and period of Qianlong.
(Sotheby's)   **$67,375**

A fine Imperial green jadeite globular snuff bottle, 18th century, well hollowed, flattened at the base and slightly waisted at the short cylindrical neck, the semi-translucent rich green stone suffused with small dark green flecks, pearl stopper with coral collar and ivory spoon.
(Christie's)   **$98,717**

Famille rose European subject gilt-copper enamel snuff bottle, incised Qianlong four-character mark, the bottle 18th or 19th century.
(Christie's)   **$36,102**

A very fine large black and white jade snuff bottle, superbly carved in the manner known as Suzhou School, of ovoid form carved in high relief with a sage on a donkey, probably Zhu Geliang, a boy attendant behind clutching the branches of a prunus tree, 18th century.
(Christie's)   **$50,820**

A South Staffordshire enamel snuff-box formed as a cat on a cushion, the hinged base painted with a spray of flowers within a scrolling cartouche, circa 1765-75, 2" long.
(Christie's) **$4,958**

A South Staffordshire enamel snuff-box formed as a frog on a grassy knoll, the base painted with lovers in a landscape, with gilt-metal mount, circa 1765–75, 2" long.
(Christie's) **$6,021**

An early Victorian briar table snuff box, the hinged cover with a colored transfer of a fox hunting scene, on silver wheels, makers Rawlings & Sumner, London 1841, 10" long.
(Woolley & Wallis) **$4,450**

A rare South Staffordshire snuff-box formed as a couchant hare, on a grassy tuft, the hinged base painted with a running hare in a landscape within a scrolling cartouche, with gilt-metal mount, circa 1765–75, 3¹/₄" long
(Christie's) **$5,313**

A good and rare George III fox-head snuff box, the head realistically chased with hair and wearing a buckled collar, the unmarked flat circular cover inset with a bright-engraved gold garter inscribed *Who oop*, by Phipps & Robinson, 1795, 9.5cm. high, 5.25ozs. *(Phillips)* **$3,498**

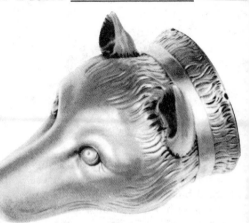

SPOONS

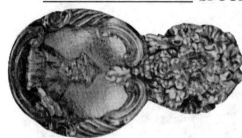

A rare George III cast caddy spoon, the oval bowl decorated in relief with a Chinese Mandarin holding a tea plant, the handle profusely decorated with flowers, by Edward Farrell, 1816. *(Phillips)* **$2,200**

A Charles II cannon-handle basting spoon, the oval body with short rat-tail and engraved with a crest within a plume cartouche, by John Ruslen, circa 1680, maker's mark only struck twice, 16" long, 5ozs. *(Christie's)* **$24,750**

A rare William IV die-stamped eagle's wing caddy spoon, the bowl chased with overlapping feathers, the handle modeled as an eagle's head in profile, by Joseph Willmore, Birmingham, 1832. *(Phillips)* **$1,408**

A good Charles I naked female figure spoon, with traces of gilding, the straight hexagonal stem surmounted by the large cast demi-figure of a woman, naked to the waist with arms folded across the breasts, with the initials *RM*, apparently a rebus for John Quycke of Barnstaple, circa 1630, the back of the bowl with the prick-dotted date and initials.

(Phillips) **$2,595**

Mixed-metal applied lap-over pierced ladle by Tiffany & Co., New York, 1880-1885. The hammered flaring handle applied with butterflies in copper and gold, the circular bowl with a ruffled edge and pierced with a geometric Japanesque design, marked, 8⁵/₈" long, gross weight 3oz.

(Christie's) **$4,400**

A rare Edward IV diamond point spoon, with deep fig-shaped bowl and tapering hexagonal stem, circa 1475, the bowl struck with the 'Arctic' leopard's head mark only, 5¹/₂" long.

A Georgian Gibson spoon, stamped *C. Gibson Inventor*, 5³/₈" long, maker C.G., London 18.

The 'Arctic' head mark is a particularly rare mark, only two examples having been recorded.

(Christie's) **$756**

(Christie's) **$33,000**

Staffordshire was without a doubt the home of the popular English pottery industry in the 19th century. Not for nothing was the area around Stoke on Trent known as 'The Potteries' and at one stage there were over four hundred factories within a ten-mile radius of the town all turning out Staffordshire pieces.

It is hardly surprizing therefore that pieces from the heyday of the Staffordshire potteries, in the mid to late 19th century, are in plentiful supply, and, although they form a rich source of collectibles, they seldom fetch really large sums. It is the earlier items, dating from, say the late 18th century up to 1820 that are really sought after, and saltglaze stoneware from 18th century Staffordshire will regularly sell for enormous sums. These are often of fine quality, well colored and with amusing subject matter and are well worth looking out for.

A Staffordshire saltglaze polychrome baluster pepperpot with pierced domed pink top, the body painted in a famille rose palette with Orientals at discussion in a continuous wooded landscape, circa 1755, 12cm. high. *(Christie's)* **$9,609**

A Staffordshire saltglaze lobed oval soup-tureen and cover and a stand, with green loop handles and finial, painted with bouquets and flower-sprays, the stand with moths, insects and flower-sprays, within gadrooned rims, the tureen terminating on four imp's mask and green paw feet, circa 1760, the tureen 30.5cm. wide. *(Christie's)* **$51,359**

A Staffordshire creamware equestrian group of Hudibras of Ralph Wood type, seated astride his brown-glazed horse and drawing his sword, in dark-brown hat and boots, yellow ruffed olive-green jacket and green breeches, on a white saddle-cloth, the horse supported by a tree-stump on green and brown rockwork, circa 1785, 30cm. high.

(Christie's) **$22,176**

A rare pair of boxing figures of Tom Cribb and Molyneaux, both with fists raised and wearing brown and yellow breeches, circa 1811, 9" high.

(Christie's) **$4,235**

A Staffordshire slipware 'cat and mouse' charger by Ralph Simpson, the cream ground decorated in dark and light-brown slip, the center with a stylized 'cat' with a human face and two triangular ears, flanked by a mouse and the 'cat's' detached tail, the well with interlocking ovolo and diamond-pattern within a border of diamonds and stylized flowerheads, inscribed *Ralph Simpson* within a rectangular ribbon cartouche, circa 1680, 47cm. diameter.

(Christie's) **$157,080**

A documentary Staffordshire slipware press-molded clock-face dish by Samuel Malkin, the cream slip ground with a molded clock dial with dark-brown slip chapters and hour hand pointing to 12, the center of the dial inscribed in raised script *Sam Malkin The Maker in burslam* flanking the raised figure 17 within a rectangular cartouche, 1712, 36cm. diameter. This dish is the only intact example recorded; another dish, from the same mold, from the Allman collection and now in the British Museum is incomplete, the lower left-hand part, including part of the inscription having been made up. There is also a fragment from another dish in existence.

These dishes are the only Malkin dishes bearing his name in full and the discovery of the Allman example attributed the whole range of *SM* marked dishes to Samuel Malkin.

(Christie's)   **$83,160**

A rare set of eleven Wilkinson Royal Staffordshire pottery character jugs modeled by Sir F. Carruthers Gould, as caricatures of King George V, Field Marshal Sir John French, Earl Haig, Lloyd George, Admiral Jellicoe, Admiral Beatty, Marshal Joffre, Lord Kitchener, Marshal Foch, President Wilson and General Botha, 25-30cm. high.

(Spencers)   **$8,415**

A lead and stained glass window designed by M.H. Baillie-Scott consisting of four large and four small rectangular panels, in green, blue and puce-colored glass with swallows before elongated tulips, within wooden frame (1897–1898), 313.6cm. wide. *(Christie's)* **$24,310**

Peonies blown in the wind, with Kakemono border, leaded glass window, by John La Farge, circa 1893-1908, 57" x 27".
(Christie's) **$242,000**

Steuben gold aurene acid cut-back plaque, the decorative amber glass disc with gold iridescent surface cut in stylized acid-cut floral design with sunburst border, 13³/₄" diameter. *(Skinner Inc)* **$4,500**

Steuben blue Aurene and intarsia decorated vase, the flared applied gold Aurene cuff-rim with medial band of white and deep blue zig-zag intarsia design above bulbous ovoid body of brilliant purple-blue, cased to opal white and randomly decorated with silvery gold Aurene leaf and vine motif, signed *Aurene* on base, 7⁵/₈" high. *(Skinner Inc)* **$7,000**

Steuben rose quartz vase, with flared rim on baluster-form body of splotched pink, crackled within and having acid cut-back sculptured pattern of blossom and leaf designs and applied frosted handles, branches and leaves in the mat-so-no-ke manner, 11¹/₂" high. *(Skinner Inc)* **$5,250**

Rare and important Gustav Stickley inlaid two-door bookcase, designed by Harvey Ellis, circa 1903–1904 with single central vertical mullion and glass panels, centered by four square fruitwood floral inlaid medallions, 55³/₄" wide. There is purportedly only one other known example.
(Skinner Inc) **$48,000**

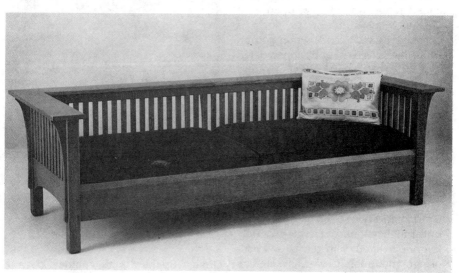

Rare L. & J.G. Stickley spindle 'Prairie' settle, circa 1912, no. 234, the broad even sided flat crest rail over spindles and seven arched corbels, two-section seat, unsigned, 86" wide. There are currently only three known examples in private collections including the Forbes collection and the Marrin collection.
(Skinner Inc) **$85,000**

The Arts and Crafts movement found one of its greatest exponents in the U.S.A. in Gustav Stickley (1857–1942). He was the eldest of six brothers and although he trained as a stone mason he became a famous furniture designer. In his youth he designed mainly chairs in the American Colonial style, but in 1898 he founded the firm of Gustav Stickley of Syracuse, New York, which specialized in the Arts & Crafts or Mission style of furniture (from the furniture supposedly housed in the old Franciscan missions of California). He also published a magazine 'The Craftsman', which popularized this new style.

Like Art Nouveau, of which this was an offshoot, the style was seen as being a return to the simple, functional style of the medieval period. Oak was the most popular wood, and construction was simple, often with obvious signs of handwork, such as exposed mortice and tenon joints. Chairbacks were usually constructed as a series of flat vertical or horizontal boards.

Interestingly five of the brothers went into the same line of business, and the relationship between them seems to have been a highly political one. George and Albert worked in Grand Rapids, Michigan from 1891, and formed the firm of Stickley Bros. Co. around 1901. Their furniture is similar to the Craftsman style, often characterized by through tenons, but it was generally inferior in quality in terms of wood, design and finish. It was marketed as Quaint Furniture. They also produced independent designs similar to English cottage furniture.

The other two brothers, Leopold and J. George, were at first employed by Gustav but left his employment to found L. & J.G. Stickley at Fayetteville, in 1900. They too based their designs on Craftsman furniture, sometimes using veneers and laminated members, and their pieces are identifiable by the name L. & J.G. Stickley in red. They were open to other influences, however, which may help to account for their survival, and made furniture designed by Frank Lloyd Wright, the Morris chair, and by 1914 were turning out reproduction furniture as well.

Gustav Stickley work cabinet, circa 1905-07, with two cabinet doors over two drawers with square wooden pulls, paneled sides, arched corbel centering lower shelf with exposed keyed tenons, signed with red decal, 36" high. *(Skinner Inc)* **$14,000**

A hammered copper chamberstick, by Gustav Stickley, circa 1913, 9¹/₄" high. *(Skinner Inc)* **$700**

When one refers to 'Stickley' it is undoubtedly Gustav who springs most readily to mind. Certainly he was the most original designer of the family, he was also the purist, and his pieces are often austere in their unadorned simplicity. His brothers were perhaps more realistic in seeing that their products also had to find a market, and they were readier to compromise in terms of putting some embellishments on the basic style. It may have been Gustav's unwillingness to compromise his ideals that led to the break with Leopold and J. George, and it may also be why, by 1915, he was bankrupt. He attempted to soldier on, selling new lines based loosely on 18th century styles, or in bright colors, but to no avail. It was left to L. & J.G. to buy him out in 1916, when the business became the Stickley Manufacturing Co. Under this name it is still active, chiefly producing American Colonial reproduction furniture in cherrywood.

Four piece wrought iron fireplace set, attributed to Gustav Stickley, circa 1905, including stand with oval base and two scrolled arms supporting tongs, brush and shovel, unsigned, 33¹/₂" high.
(Skinner Inc) **$5,500**

L. & J.G. Stickley dinner gong, Fayetteville, New York, 1912, the arched frame supporting circular bronze gong over lower shelf and shoe foot base, signed *The Work of L. & J.G. Stickley*, 34¹/₄" high.
(Skinner Inc) **$7,000**

Gustav Stickley inlaid music cabinet, designed by Harvey Ellis, circa 1904, the flat overhanging top above the flat sides centering cabinet door with two inlaid recessed panels over four lower vertical sections, lower arched skirt, signed with decal in a box, 49⁷/₈" high, 23⁵/₈" wide. *(Skinner)*   **$42,500**

The Eastwood chair was the largest production chair made by Gustav Stickley. It was first seen in the November 1901 edition of 'The Craftsman', and was still featured in Stickley's 1913 catalogue. Despite being in production for 12 years it remains one of the rarest Stickley pieces. Only three are known to be in private collections, and one, found in a garage, was part of the original furnishings of an inn on the coast of Maine. It is a particularly fine example and fetched $28,000 (£16,666) at auction.

Gustav Stickley table with twelve Grueby tiles, 1902–1904, the four flat rails framing four-inch green tiles over arched skirt and lower rectangular shelf with keyed tenons, slight splay to legs, dark finish, signed with red decal, 24" wide.

(Skinner Inc) **$20,000**

L. & J.G. Stickley mantle clock, Fayetteville, New York, circa 1910, designed by Peter Heinrich Hansen, with circular copper dial, applied squares and pendulum window, canted base, signed with Handcraft decal, 22" high.

Peter Hansen was born in Germany and emigrated to America around the turn of the century. He was employed by Gustav Stickley before moving to L. & J.G. Stickley's employment about 1909. It has been speculated that Hansen saw the work of Joseph Olbrich, Josef Hoffman, and other Secessionist designers in Germany and may have been influenced by them. This clock is similar to an example by C.F.A. Voysey of England.

(Skinner Inc) **$7,500**

A pair of 19th century red serpentine obelisks, each of square tapering form, with one face incised with hieroglyphics, on a stepped square base, 25½" high.

(Christie's) **$5,775**

An Elamite grey steatite standing male figure, the robe decorated with incised designs, a plain collar surrounds the rounded neckline where the limestone bust is affixed, 14.2cm. high, 3rd Millennium B.C.

(Phillips) **$11,270**

An Egyptian limestone figure of Thoth, the god of wisdom, arts and sciences, in the form of a baboon squatting on its haunches its tail curled round to its right foot, its hands resting on the inner sides of its knees, 15.8cm. high, late Dynastic period.

(Phillips) **$10,150**

Stools seem to have a value quite disproportionate to their size, function and aesthetic potential. Maybe it's because they are a relatively intimate piece of furniture, essentially a 'comfort' item. Perhaps, it's their size that is the attraction – one can, after all, comfortably house a dozen or more stools in the space which would be required for one sideboard or dining table. Whatever the cause, the greatest furniture makers of all periods have turned their hand to making them, and the result is that they make a first-class collectible – if you can afford them!

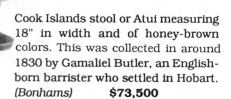

Cook Islands stool or Atui measuring 18" in width and of honey-brown colors. This was collected in around 1830 by Gamaliel Butler, an English-born barrister who settled in Hobart. *(Bonhams)* **$73,500**

A fine Empire carved mahogany, parcel-gilt and ormolu mounted 'X'-frame stool, attributable to Jacob Desmalter after designs by Percier and Fontaine, with stuffover rectangular panel seat on cornucopiae supports headed with lion masks and lotus foliate ornament united by a foliate embellished stretcher and applied with brass flowerhead and neo-Classical decoration terminating in paw feet.

Jacob Desmalter was the most fashionable cabinet maker in Paris during the First Empire of Napoleon.

He employed as many as 350 workmen in his workshops in the Rue Meslée near the Porte Saint-Denis. He, like his rivals, drew upon the designs of Charles Percier and Pierre Francois Fontaine, the official architects to the Emperor.
(Phillips) **$35,000**

A Regency mahogany and parcel-gilt x-frame stool, the dished rectangular padded seat covered in striped fawn material flanked by four leopard masks joined by baluster arm-rests, 32" wide. This stool relates closely to a design for a stool in Thomas Hope's Household Furniture and Interior Decoration, 1807.

(Christie's) **$21,175**

A George I walnut stool, the rectangular top upholstered in gros and petit point floral needlework on square cabriole legs carved with acanthus and claw-and-ball feet, 26" wide.

(Christie's) **$15,752**

A George III honey pot on stand modeled as a skep, formed as simulated bound straw bands and the cover with a honey bee finial, 1803 by Paul Storr, 10cm. high, 13.8oz.
(Lawrence Fine Art) **$17,507**

A fine pair of early Victorian claret jugs by Paul Storr, the frosted glass, faceted bodies of bulbous onion form, with waisted necks and elaborate silver-gilt fruiting vine mounts, 1838, 27cm. high.
(Phillips) **$22,490**

A George III silver-gilt wine coaster, the sides cast and pierced with bacchante, lions and trailing vines above a narrow band of acanthus foliage and with a reed and tie rim, engraved with a coat of arms, by Paul Storr, 1814, 5³/₄" diameter.
(Christie's) **$13,475**

A rare George III magnum wine funnel by Paul Storr with fluted body and frieze of shells, scrolls and anthemions, an unusually long spout and detachable rim and base with tongue border, and plain thumbpiece, 1816, 30cm. high, 13.25ozs.
(Phillips) **$21,625**

STRAW-WORK

A Regency straw-work flower picture with assorted flowerheads and leaves in a glazed black and gilt-japanned frame decorated with chinoiserie scenes, 15" x 19". *(Christie's)* **$2,502**

An Ashford in the Water black marble occasional table by Samuel Birley, the octagonal top with thumb molded edge, inlaid with a garland of roses, peonies, daisies, convolvulus, lily of the valley, daffodils and other flowers in various colored marbles, raised upon a baluster turned pillar issuing from a concave triangular platform, and on squat bun feet. 47cm. wide. The underside bearing a label inscribed *This Table Was Made From Black Marble Quarried At Ashford, Derbyshire. It Was Turned And Inlaid By Samuel Birley at Ashford About 1899. This Work is Now A Lost Art And The Black Marble Is No Longer Quarried.*
(Spencers) **$5,950**

A George III figured mahogany urn-table, the undulating crossbanded frieze with a slide, on molded cabriole legs with shell headings and pendant flowerheads, 27½" high.
(Christie's) **$37,840**

Carved 'Lotus' center table, executed by John Bradstreet, Minneapolis, circa 1905, the top with overlapping broad leaves and pods on standard made up of intertwining stems, base with overlapping organic leaves with whimsical turtle, 30" diameter.

John Bradstreet (1845-1914), was born and raised in the Salem/Boston area, a vital center for the China trade since the 18th century which probably influenced his interest in the Orient. After working for Gorham Manufacturing Co. in Providence, Rhode Island in the 1860's and 70's, Bradstreet contracted tuberculosis and moved to the drier air of Minneapolis. There he established John S. Bradstreet & Co., 'Manufacturers of Artistic and Domestic Furniture of Modern Gothic and other Designs'. He was extremely successful forming the Minnesota Society of Arts & Crafts among other organisations. He followed the work of William Morris closely and had a considerable reputation at Liberty & Co., London, where he was thought to be among the foremost Americans in his field of design. Responding to the demand for the Japanese style, popular after the Centennial Exposition in Philadelphia, Bradstreet began experimenting with 'Jin-di-sugi', the traditional Japanese practice of aging wood to raise the grain.
(Skinner Inc) **$25,000**

A fine Chippendale carved mahogany scallop-top tea table, Philadelphia, 1765-1785, the top circular with scalloped and molded edge, 29½" high.
(Christie's N. York) **$51,700**

A fine Regency calamander veneered and brass inlaid sofa table, the hinged top with an ebony border, the frieze containing two drawers and dummy drawers to the reverse, on **saber** legs headed with oval moldings united by a concave undertier, 58" x 30". *(Phillips)*   **$28,800**

A Chippendale mahogany drop-leaf table, Rhode Island, 1760–1780, the oval twin-flap top with rounded edge above an arched apron on cabriole legs with sharp knees on ball-and-claw feet, 50" wide. *(Christie's)*   **$38,500**

A Regency mahogany Carlton House desk with balustraded three-quarter gallery, 61½" wide. *(Christie's)* **$213,840**

A fine Regency satinwood games table with crossbanded rounded rectangular twin-flap top, the central reversible section inlaid with a chessboard in ebony and fruitwood and enclosing a backgammon well with pierced ivory counters, some emblematic of chess, on solid trestled ends with splayed legs and gilt claw feet, 49½" wide. *(Christie's)* **$23,625**

A rare Chippendale mahogany tilt-top tea table attributed to John Goddard, Newport, Rhode Island, 1760-1790, the circular dished top tilting on shaped cleats above a columnar pedestal, on three arched legs with channel-carved sides and ending in ball-and-claw feet, 27³/₈" high. This table has the distinctive five-toed claws found on the highest quality Newport tilt-top tables, unusual carved channels on the sides of the legs, and finely-shaped cleats.
(Christie's) **$28,600**

Rare and important Chippendale mahogany carved card table, attributed to Thomas Affleck, Philadelphia, circa 1770s, the molded hinged top of figuratively grained mahogany above a straight skirt with knees, brackets, and cabriole legs with intricate rococo carving of naturalistic foliate 'C' scrolls, cabochons and acanthus leaves, ending in hairy paw feet. The carving on this table, believed to have been made by Thomas Affleck, one of the finest Philadelphia cabinetmakers, was executed by a skilled but as yet undocumented carver familiar with the richly carved furniture that General John Cadwalader, a prominent and wealthy Philadelphian, ordered from cabinetmakers, Benjamin Randolph and Thomas Affleck.
(Skinner Inc) **$60,000**

When tea was first imported from China at the beginning of the 17th century, it was, not unnaturally, regarded as the greatest luxury. With prices at about $20 per lb, the precious commodity was carefully guarded and kept in special lockable boxes, which came to be known as caddies (from the Malay kati, meaning a measure of tea of 1¼ lb).

The first caddies were mainly of porcelain or pottery and were fairly simple in design, but as tea drinking became a major social event, involving the caddy itself being brought into the parlor for the hostess to dispense the tea herself, so they became more and more decorative and elaborate. They were made from all sorts of materials, from fine woods to gold and silver, and the greatest craftsmen of the day, such as Sheraton and Chippendale all produced caddies to match the style of their furniture. These, and others of similar quality, have joined the first rank of collectible antiques, with prices to match.

A Georgian pear tea caddy with steel key escutcheon, 6".
(Graves Son & Pilcher)   **$2,975**

A George III treen (applewood) tea caddy formed as a large apple with hinged cover and ebonized stem, 6" high.
(Christie's)   **$4,653**

A Georgian melon tea caddy with stained segmental sections and steel ring handle and key escutcheon, 4.5".
(Graves Son & Pilcher)
$3,237

A George III oval paper scroll tea caddy within giltwood borders, with the original mahogany, boxwood strung and glazed display case, 7" wide.
(Christie's) **$2,100**

A Böttger red Steinzeug hexagonal teacaddy and cover molded with alternating panels of birds in trees, issuing from terraces, covered with a lustrous black glaze in imitation of Chinese lacquer, the molded detail and ribbed panels enriched with gilt and copper lustre, circa 1715, 12.5cm. high.
(Christie's) **$42,214**

A George III mulberry-wood tea-caddy by Thomas Sharp 'made' from the Mulberry Tree in Stratford-upon-Avon, the rectangular stepped top carved with Mulberry fruit and leaves and mounted with a brass handle, the front and back carved with Shakespeare's spear on a shield flanked by acanthus, the left-hand side with a coat-of-arms of the Rylands and the motto *Not the Last*, and bearing a brass plaque inscribed Shakespeare's Wood, stamped *T. Sharp* twice, 10¼" wide.

The brass plaque inscribed *Shakespeare's Wood* attached to the caddy authenticates it as having come from the highly prized and much venerated mulberry tree, which according to Sir Hugh Clopton (d. 1751) of New Place, Stratford-upon-Avon, had been planted in his garden in 1609 by the dramatist William Shakespeare (d.1616). The tree was felled in 1756, and much of the timber was acquired for souvenirs by the silversmith and clockmaker Thomas Sharp (d. 1799) for sale at his 'Mulberry Tree' shop in Stratford. Although the caddy bears Sharp's name, it is possible that it was actually sculpted by his employee the specialist carver George Cooper, whose name appears on a related box at the Victoria and Albert Museum and bears the date 1759.

(Christie's) **$5,800**

An exceptionally fine and rare George III satinwood and scrolled paper tea caddy, of hexagonal form, decorated with filigree effect panels of flower heads, leaves, scrolls and ovals, the sides set with stamped white paper classical figures laid on pink ground within crimped paper outlines, the whole retaining its original bright colors and gilt edges, the hinged cover with brass loop handle, 16.5cm. wide.

(Spencers) **$4,287**

A Shelley 'Intarsio' teapot in the form of a caricature of Austin Chamberlain, Rd. No. 363131.
(William H. Brown Fine Art) **$563**

A Bayreuth fayence hausmalerei famille rose baluster teapot and cover with dragon-head spout, strap handle and seated lion finial painted in the manner of Adam Friedrich von Löwenfinck, in the Delft doré style with indianische Blumen issuing from rocks with fences and terraces, circa 1740, 18.5cm. wide.
(Christie's) **$11,082**

A Meissen teapot and cover modeled as a seated rooster (Hahnenkanne) by J.J. Kändler, the flat cover with a seated dog finial, the rooster with its legs tucked under and his neck outstretched, crossed swords marks, circa 1735, 19.5cm. wide. They mainly have seated rabbit finials, the dog finial would appear to be considerably rarer. *(Christie's)* **$7,036**

Royal Doulton Old Charley teapot, D 6017, produced in 1939, 7" high.
(Abridge)   **$1,360**

A Chelsea acanthus-leaf-molded teapot and cover with bamboo molded handle, the crisply molded overlapping leaves painted in a bright palette with scattered flowers and insects, the cover with two flowers, a caterpillar and a cricket and with oakleaf and acorn finial, incised triangle mark, circa 1745–49, 12cm. high.
(Christie's)   **$38,962**

A Meissen (Augustus Rex) baluster teapot and cover, painted in the manner of J.G. Höroldt with Orientals taking tea and at discussion on terraces and by plants within Böttgerluster, gilt, puce and iron-red Laub-und Bandelwerk cartouches, blue AR mark, circa 1728, 11.5cm. high.
(Christie's) **$39,039**

An exceptionally rare and important Bottger stoneware teapot and cover after a model by Irminger, circa 1710–15.
(Phillips) **$60,750**

The most widely accepted account of how the Teddy bear got its name is the one which tells how, while on a hunting trip in 1902, President Theodore 'Teddy' Roosevelt could not bring himself to shoot a bear cub which he had in his sights. It was, after all, conveniently tethered to a post by some well meaning aide. Such fore 'bear'ance on the part of the notable hunter captured the attention of the popular press, and the incident was recreated in a cartoon of the day. It certainly did no harm to the Presidential image, and Roosevelt adopted the image of a cuddly little bear as his own. When his daughter married in 1906, the wedding breakfast tables were decorated with tiny bears made by the Steiff toy company.

It was thus that the greatest name in bear-making came onto the stage. Margarete Steiff, a crippled German toy maker, had been making toy bears since about 1900, but it was the new craze for cuddly plush bears that was to make her fortune. The style of her early models is perhaps not the most appealing to modern taste, for she designed them with humped backs, long muzzles, elongated arms and legs and long bodies. They were stuffed with wood shavings and covered in plush, and most had a growler. All Steiff bears made before 1910 are very valuable, and if the growler still works the price rockets.

Margarete had the good commercial sense to distinguish her bears by a button on their left ear, and while some of these may have been lost in the loving attentions they have received over the years, it is still usually possible to tell a genuine Steiff bear from its general style and shape.

Around 1914, the style began to change however, the hump disappeared, the muzzle shrank, and the bears adopted altogether a more human form, which made them even more appealing. After 1920, the stuffing changed to kapok.

Steiff bears now regularly fetch four figures at auction but two successive records have been set quite recently.

The first was by Alfonzo, a red plush bear with a most romantic history. He was owned by Xenia Georgievna, a second cousin of Czar Nicholas II. Red plush is extremely rare, and it is possible that Alfonzo was made as a special commission for the Princess. In any case, he was with her when she came to spend a holiday at Buckingham Palace in the summer of 1914. She was stranded in London by the outbreak of war and was never to return to her homeland. In view of all this, it is perhaps hardly surprising that Alfonzo should have fetched $19,600 when auctioned by Christie's.

Even more amazing however is the new record fetched by Sothebys, when they auctioned a dual-plush Steiff teddy bear, dating from circa 1920. The bear had originally come from Ireland, and had been in the same family for some considerable time. Dual-plush is also very rare but hardly enough to justify the final hammer price of $96,000. The bear was bought by the Chairman of a US toy company on behalf of a private friend, and it seems to have been simply a case of two bidders having turned up at the same auction with instructions to 'Bag that bear'.

Gold plush teddy bear purse, the teddy bear with brown eyes, black stitched snout, his back in the form of a purse with handle, having jointed body, 10" long.
(Hobbs & Chambers) **$650**

A dual-plush Steiff teddy bear, German, circa 1920, which sold at Sotheby's for a record price of $96,000.

The bear was bought by Jack Wilson, Chairman of The House of Nisbit, teddy bear manufacturers, on behalf of a private friend in the U.S.A.

A very rare short red plush teddy bear, called Alfonzo, with button eyes, excelsior stuffing and felt pads dressed as a Russian, having belonged to Xenia Georgievna, Princess of Russia and second cousin to Tsar Nicholas II. Xenia was stranded in England following a summer holiday at Buckingham Palace when war broke out in 1914, 13" high with Steiff button (voice box inoperative, front paws recovered in chamois leather), 1906–1909.

(Christie's) **$19,600**

A fine Steiff black mohair plush teddy bear with wide apart rounded ears, black boot button eyes mounted on red felt discs, cut stitched snout, on an excelsior filled body with swivel joints, hump back and elongated felt pads, 19", button in ear marked *Steiff*, circa 1912.

A similar example may be referred to in the 'History of the Teddy Bear and his Friends, Button in Ear' by Jurgen and Marianne Cieslik, where it is stated that 494 of this type, serial no. 5335 were produced, for the English market and available in five sizes ranging from 14" to 19".

(Phillips) **$15,500**

The origins of the telephone are somewhat controversial. It is Alexander Graham Bell who is usually given the credit for its invention, though an American, one Elisha Grey, actually filed a patent on a similar device on the same day as Bell. Unfortunately, in terms of international time, he did so a few hours later, so lost his claim in an ensuing Supreme Court action.

Going back to basics, however, it was in fact neither of these gentlemen who put the first rudimentary telephone together, but Professor Philip Reis of Friedrichsdorf in Germany. For the microphone, he hollowed out the bung of a beer barrel, which he then covered with a German sausage skin to make a diaphragm. He attached to this a strip of platinum which vibrated with the diaphragm to form a make and break electrical circuit. Then he took a knitting needle, surrounded with a coil of wire which he attached to a violin to act as a sound box. This, incredibly, reproduced the sound received by the bung covered with sausage skin. The first telephone had been created!

Most early telephones found today are of the Ericsson type and originate from Scandinavia, Germany and England. Apart from their functional value, they were obviously conceived as decorative objects in their own right, with polished walnut and mahogany stands and intricate metal fittings.

An English Stanley hand telephone from 1880, fetched $650 when auctioned recently by Auction Team Koeln in Cologne, while, at the same sale, a decorative early Norwegian wall telephone with finely molded backplate and imitation wood, tin covered writing surface, did even better, to sell for $1,722.

A highly decorative L.M. Ericsson & Co. desk telephone, circa 1910. *(Auction Team Koeln)* **$1,092**

A Praezisions telephone, the first model by Siemens & Halske after Bell's patent, with wooden earpiece and leather covered stem, circa 1880. *(Auction Team Koeln)* **$2,629**

Norwegian wall telephone with decorative cast iron back plate by Aktieselskabet Elektrisk Bureau Kristiania, Oslo, circa 1890. *(Auction Team Koeln)* **$1,722**

A 19th century French terracotta bust of Rouget de L'Isle, by David d'Angers, the sitter looking slightly to dexter with hair en queue, signed and dated *David 1835*, 45.5cm. high.

Claude-Joseph Rouget de L'Isle (1760-1836) poet and musician, composed both the lyrics and music of the Marseillaise in a single night. He was arrested in 1793, released only after the fall of Robespierre, and died in obscurity at Choisy-le-Roi.
(Christie's) **$13,282**

A Victorian terracotta garden gnome wearing a pointed red hat and green shorts, 27" high.
(Heathcote Ball) **$300**

A pair of terracotta garden ornaments in the form of seated grayhounds, each wearing a studded collar and on oval bases, the dog looking to his right, the bitch to her left, 33" high, 19th century.
(Bearne's) **$7,144**

Textiles are a vast subject, and one which provides a fascinating insight into the life and culture of past ages. In buying old textiles, you really are buying a piece of history, whether it be a child's sampler, a piece of oriental silk, a Flemish tapestry, a patchwork coverlet or an embroidered cushion cover. None are likely to have been mass-produced by machine, so you are investing in hours, perhaps months, in the life of someone from that bygone age.

More functional items, too, are rapidly becoming collectible, such as curtains designed by, say, William Morris. There is even a thriving market in second-hand items by modern interior designers, with a set of eight-year old curtains in apricot silk recently fetching $4,000 at auction. Hardly as emotive, perhaps, as your early 19th century New England sampler, but an interesting reflection nonetheless on the collectible potential of textiles as a whole.

A fine and important kanat of fine cotton, printed and painted with bold lilies with perching birds, late 17th, early 18th century, Mughal, 52" x 84". *(Christie's)*   **$53,900**

President Chester A. Arthur's parade flag, red wool field of several sections, American, circa 1883, 69" x 45". *(Skinner Inc)*   **$1,400**

An embroidered purse worked with silver gilt thread with a large stylized plant with flowers on coiling stems on either side, lined with yellow silk, trimmed with tassels, 4" square, 17th century.
(Christie's)   **$1,732**

A Brussels silk and wool garden tapestry, late 16th century, based on the courtship of Vertumnus and Pomona. Vertumnus, clad as a warrior, faces Pomona, who is pruning a small fruit tree on a marble terrace with animals and birds, the caryatid figures supporting architectural colonnades with fruit and flowers and a structure in the background surrounded by a navy blue scrolling vine and rosette border, 11ft. 1" x 12ft. 8".
(Christie's)   **$74,800**

A rare silk-on-silk embroidered coat of arms, Massachusetts, mid-18th century. Diamond-shaped, centering an eagle worked in silver threads supported by a leafy branch above an elaborately designed yellow, gold, and green armored helmet and silver and gold breastplate over a shield featuring a finely detailed grayhound with gold and silver threads on a silver diamond-stitched ground surrounded by red, gold, russet, and green leafy mantling above a silver and gold pendant banner on a black silk ground, 24½" x 24½".

In the mid-18th century fashionable Americans began to assume coats of arms by commissioning artisans who achieved their results by combining various elements of coats of arms shown in books of English heraldry. Many of these affluent Americans sent their daughters to schools where among other skills, they learned to work their family's coat of arms in needlework. Boston area schools frequently relied upon their designs created by the Gore family of Massachusetts.
(Christie's)   **$28,600**

A fine and rare pictorial needlework single pocketbook, probably Rhode Island, third quarter 18th century, worked in wool tent stitch, the front depicting scattered flowers on an olive ground, the back inscribed *MW* above a scene depicting a brick house flanked by two hunters with their prey, 5" high. Pocketbooks worked entirely in tent stitch are exceedingly rare, the small, time-consuming stitch allowing the intricate design shown in this example.

(Christie's N. York) **$18,700**

A Jacobean embroidered and applied needlework picture, depicting a gentleman, a lady playing the lute, a lion, a deer, and other animals, birds, snails, insects, flowers, trees, buildings and a fountain surmounted by a figure of Cupid, within a silver thread border, 20" x 23³/₄".

(Geering & Colyer) **$5,775**

One of a pair of Jacobite embroidered hangings dated 1719.
(Phillips) **$66,500**

A magnificent and rare Coptic tapestry panel with a bust of a female, in classical pose with head turned to the right in three-quarter profile, wearing wreath made up of four lotus pods in her hair, pendant earrings comprising gold mounted blue square with drop pearl, and necklace with pendant, her left breast and shoulder bare and right shoulder draped, 9.5" x 9", late 4th/ early 5th century.

This remarkable tapestry panel was most probably made as a pair. They rank amongst the finest tapestries of this type, of which there are but a small number in public or private collections, and are in a superb state of preservation. The subjects are not easy to identify but are most probably deities rather than portraits of individuals owing to the ritual nudity of the figures. The illusionistic modeling of the figures particularly of their faces, is of the highest quality, whilst their outlined dark eyes foreshadow the 'goggles' of later Coptic portraits.

(Christie's) **$56,000**

A souvenir concert program for
The Beatles/Mary Wells tour, 1964,
signed on the cover by each member of
the group and inscribed *love Paul
McCartney xxx*.
(Christie's) **$2,500**

A rare 'Beatles' dress of cotton printed
with pink and white polka dots, and
facial portraits of the four Beatles,
signed by Brian Epstein, John Lennon,
Paul McCartney, George Harrison,
Ringo Starr and Cynthia Lennon in
blue and green ink, and inscribed *To
Rosemary* in the latter's hand, worn
by one of the usherettes at the world
prèmiere of The Beatles film 'A Hard
Day's Night', July 6th, 1964, and
autographed on the evening whilst
the usherette was wearing the dress.
(Christie's) **$4,662**

Paul McEatney
STAR CLUB
Grosse Freiheit 39
Hamburg Altona

Dear Anne,

Ta very much for your letter. Yours was the first one I got.

The club where we're playing is good but not as good as Liverpool. The boss is good but will still be glad to get back. — I think we'll be making some records soon, and we'll get them released in Liverpool as soon as possible.

The clubs here are open till 4 in the morning but we don't go to them — they're too expensive, about 7/- for a beer or Coca-cola.

The farewell show went down great — I don't know about the people having to be turned away, but it was packed out. Anyway, thank again for the letter, Ta-ta for now.

Love, Paul

'An early autograph letter to a fan' signed from *Paul McCartney, Star Club, Grosse Frethirt 39, Hamburg Atlana*, thanking Anne? for her letter *'...Yours was the first one I got. The club where we're playing is good but not as good as Liverpool...I think we'll be making some records soon, and we'll get them released in Liverpool as soon as possible...'*

The opening paragraph of the letter suggests that Paul McCartney is replying to the first fan letter he received in Germany during the Beatles' visit in 1962 and their engagement at the Star Club in Hamburg, from April 13th - May 31st. *(Christie's)* **$5,379**

Chelsea porcelain thimble with wavy rim and brightly painted with birds and a conifer branch within gold line bands and inscribed *Souvenez vous de moy*.
(Bearne's) **$3,850**

A Meissen porcelain gold-mounted thimble-case, painted with four rural scenes of ladies and gentlemen in landscapes, the gold mount chased with interlaced ribbons, with gold suspension loop, containing a two-color gold thimble, circa 1770, 2" high.
(Christie's) **$1,369**

Meissen thimble decorated in Schwarzlot and gold by I. Preissler.
(Sothebys) **$7,800**

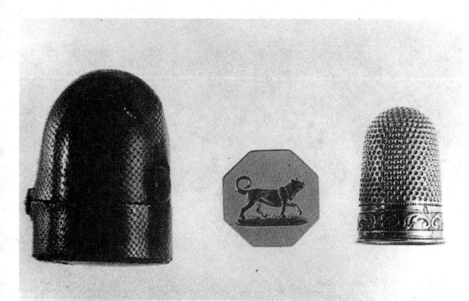

An Empire combined thimble, seal and scent-bottle, the thimble chased with scrolls and paterae, the miniature glass scent-bottle facet-cut, the base formed as a seal in gold engraved with a hound, Paris, 1798–1809, in original shagreen case, 1" high.
(Christie's) **$3,325**

Louis Comfort Tiffany (1848–1933) was the son of the founder of Tiffany & Co., the New York jewelers. Having studied painting in Paris, he started work as an interior designer in the 1870's and in 1879 established the firm which by 1900 had become Tiffany Studios.

From 1880 he designed furniture which often reflected oriental and near-eastern influences, but his overriding interest was in glass, and, in particular, in reproducing the appearance of ancient glass. In 1880, after years of experimentation, he patented an iridescent technique which came to be marketed as Favrile and which was produced in a wide range of colors. In his designs, Tiffany avoided surface decoration, believing that ornamentation should be integrated into the body of the glass. He also avoided cutting and molding, preferring fluid, organic forms.

The company made vases, paperweights and later, pottery and jewelry (Tiffany became Art Director of Tiffany & Co. in 1902) but the item most closely associated with his name is the Tiffany lamp. After 1900 a special section was established to produce bronze objects incorporating Favrile glass, and a typical Tiffany lamp will have a cast bronze stem in the form of a stylized plant with a shade of multicolored opaque Favrile glass set in a bronze mounting.

Tiffany withdrew from the studios in 1919, but the firm continued until 1936.

A centerpiece bowl by Tiffany & Co., New York, 1883-1891, the sides decorated with a frieze of elephants in relief against an etched ground of foliage, on four chrysanthemum-clad ball feet, the gilt interior decorated with etched stylized foliage in the center and sides, marked, 11" diameter, 52 ozs. The drawing of the design for this bowl, dated 1883, is in the Tiffany Archives.
(Christie's)   **$16,500**

A mixed-metal salver by Tiffany & Co., New York, circa 1880, of circular form with a raised rim, on four stylized ball feet, the spot-hammered surface with inlaid patinated copper blossoms on a silver branch applied with an insect, and inlaid with a wasp in gold, marked, 12" diameter, gross weight 28oz.
(Christie's) **$13,200**

A patinated mixed-metal caster by Tiffany & Co., New York, 1879-1883, with a long cylindrical neck and a pierced circular cap, on four stylized bracket feet, the surface decorated with shaped panels of patinated copper and inlaid gold, against an etched foliate ground, marked, with French control marks, 5" high, gross weight 4 ozs 10 dwt. This caster was undoubtedly designed by Edward C. Moore, who is known for his adaptation of Japanese metal-coloring techniques. Moore's works in this style were acclaimed by the French critics at the Paris Exposition of 1878. A number of small exquisitely-crafted and colorful pieces by Moore in the Japanese taste, like this piece, bear French import control marks, indicating their continued popularity at Tiffany's store in Paris.
(Christie's) **$24,200**

An important and rare Tiffany Studios leaded glass table lamp, the shallow domed shade edged with the bodies of bats, their overlapping wings in leaded glass of nocturnal hues, the bronze base with further bats in relief against some iridescent glass mosaic, 48cm. high.

(Phillips) **$105,600**

A fine Tiffany red Favrile glass 'Tel El Almarna' vase.
(William Doyle) **$16,500**

Tiffany bronze and glass lily pad table lamp with pansy shade, the four-light standard above extraordinary blue-green striated Favrile glass 'pumpkin' raised upon bronze pond lily pad platform with two pond lily buds, signed *Tiffany Studios New York*. The sixteen inch shade of green-white shaded mottled panels above and below broad irregular floral belt with repeating clusters of brightly colored pansy blossoms, buds, stems and leaves, signed *Tiffany Studios*, 21" high, shade diameter 16".

(Skinner Inc) **$40,000**

A rare parcel-gilt chamberstick by Tiffany & Company, New York, circa 1880, with vasiform candlecup applied with a beetle and fitted with a flaring circular nozzle, the cast handle formed as a dragonfly perched on the dish and supporting a conical snuffer, the surface spot-hammered and chased with swirling channels, 3³/₄" high, 11 ozs. *(Christie's)* **$16,500**

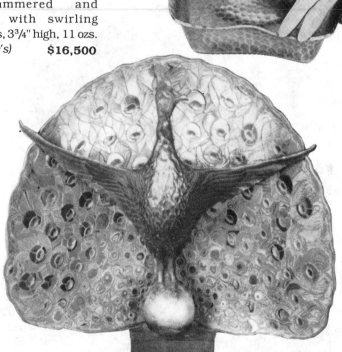

Tiffany bronzed metal and mosaic glass Favrile peacock, the conventionalised full figure bird standing before an arched and curved mosaic depiction of feather plumage assembled from Favrile glass segments (tesserae) arranged in naturalistic progression with peacock-eyes and feather fronds created by the iridescent swirls and striations, 31" high. Louis Comfort Tiffany was fascinated – almost to the point of obsession – by the peacock's brilliant crested head, green and blue plumage and long iridescent tail feathers spread like a fan. According to his friend and mentor, Sigfreid Bing, Tiffany spent an entire year attempting to capture in glass the beauty of the peacock in nature. *(Skinner Inc)* **$48,000**

Tiffany leaded glass lamp shade on Grueby pottery base, early 20th century, with dome shaped shade in acorn pattern in colors of green variegated slag glass on shaped bronze arms and standard, acorn inial pulls. The squat bulbous pottery base with molded broad leaf decoration, dark matte green glaze, impressed *Grueby Pottery USA Boston*, artist initialed *A.L.* for Annie Lingley (1899-1910).

(Skinner Inc) **$20,000**

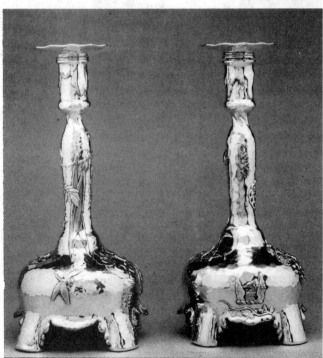

A fine and rare pair of mixed-metal candlesticks by Tiffany & Co., New York, circa 1880, each with a domed circular base on four shaped feet, with a removable serpentine nozzle, the surface spot-hammered, pierced and applied with animals, insects, foliage, clouds and other ornament in the Japanese taste, 11 1/4" high, gross weight 35 ozs.

(Christie's) **$49,500**

A fine and rare pair of Japanesque mixed metal candlesticks by Tiffany & Co. of New York, circa 1878, of hollow-ware silver construction and decorated with butterflies and flowers in mixed metals and Mokume work and incised trailing vines, 7.25" high, 16ozs. gross. *(Boardman)* **$42,000**

An Exposition Navajo vase set with stones by Tiffany & Co., New York, finished April 11, 1900 for the Exposition Universelle, Paris, 1900, and the Pan-American Exposition, Buffalo, 1901. The corn-cob handles set with baroque pearls flanked by stylized cornstalk leaves of amazonite, the shoulder set with a band of alternating diamond-shaped amazonite and oval-shaped opals set against band of black oxidation between gilt die-rolled borders, 6$^{1}/_{2}$" high, 9$^{3}/_{4}$" wide, gross weight 89oz. For the Paris Exposition, Tiffany & Co., endeavored to create silver objects which demonstrated the beauty of native American design and materials. This vase, based on an American Indian form and using American semi-precious stones, well represents Tiffany's intention. *(Christie's)* **$44,000**

George Tinworth (1866-1913) was the illiterate son of a Walworth wheelwright who became an artistic genius with a world famous reputation. He studied sculpture at Lambeth School of Art and was one of the first students to work for Henry Doulton who quickly recognized his talents. He produced many terracotta panels with religious themes as well as humorous figures of people and animals and incised and painted vases and jugs.

A tea party with pale green mice seated on brown chairs, the hollow oval base inscribed *Tea-Time Scandal*, circa 1885, 3¹/₂" high.
(Abridge)   **$1,760**

An umbrella stand modeled naturalistically with a brown glazed kangaroo holding a dark brown ring, incised *Doulton Lambeth*, circa 1885, 38³/₄" high.
(Abridge)   **$6,400**

It was Wednesday, April 10, 1912, the day the Titanic sailed on its first and final voyage. While hundreds aboard the ship were occupied with the celebrations of embarkation, one little girl's attention was concentrated on an incident which, in the light of history, now appears as an ominous start to the liner's fatal maiden voyage.

The new view on the Titanic's sailing comes from one of its youngest passengers, Eileen Lenox-Conyngham, then aged 9 or 10, whose letter written from the ship has just come to light at Phillips in London.

"The Titanic," wrote Eileen in a childish hand, "is the biggest ship in the world there is a swimming bath a gymnation Turkish baths in it the ship started about 12.15 then we had a long delay because this ship broke the ropes of another ship the Oceanic at (as) it went flotting about and knocked into this ship but they got it all right after a bit ..."

The Titanic, in leaving the quayside at Southampton, had created a swell that affected two other liners moored side by side, the Oceanic and the American ship New York. It was the latter that was the cause of a scare. Its mooring ropes broke with a loud crack and the vessel drifted dangerously near – to within four feet – of the Titanic. A tug prevented collision in the nick of time.

Little Eileen obviously confused the Oceanic and the New York. Her impression that the Titanic was in collision could have arisen from the dramatic noise of breaking ropes, the giant liner's shuddering halt and the fact that in the course of its drifting the New York bumped yet another liner, the Teutonic.

Eileen's three-page letter is under the printed heading, 'On board R.M.S. Titanic', bearing the pennant logo of the White Star Line.

Fortunately for Eileen and her brother, they were traveling in the Titanic (with their parents) only as far as Queenstown in Ireland where the ill-fated liner put in the next day for mail and to pick up more passengers.

Eileen's letter ("Dear Lusia") was written to her governess, Lusia Stirling. It sold for $2,700 at Phillips.

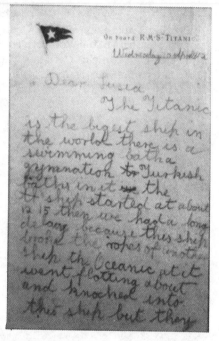

The fate of the 'Titanic' has fired the imagination of each succeeding generation, and interest in what seems likely to become one of the greatest legendary tragedies of our times continues unabating. The recent seabed pictures of her hulk have only served to increase this fascination, which is reflected in the prices paid for almost any object connected in some way with the great liner.

'White Star Triple-Screw R.M.S. Olympic and Titanic 45,000 tons each, The Largest Steamers in the World', a color postcard from R. Phillips to Mr Wm. Squires, 4 Northfield Cottages, Ilfracombe, Devonshire, postmarked Queenstown 5.45pm 11 April.
(Onslows)   **$3,260**

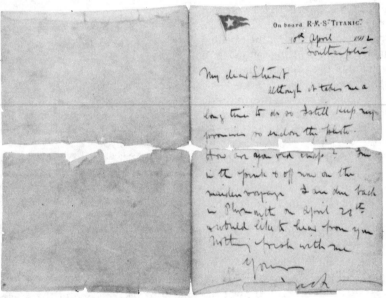

On board R.M.S. Titanic, an autographed letter on official writing paper with embossed company burgee, signed *Jack 10th April 1912 Southampton My dear Stuart Although it takes me a long time to do so I still keep my promises so enclose the photo. How are you old chap? I'm in the pink and off now on the maiden voyage. I am back in Plymouth on April 26th and would like to hear from you. Nothing fresh with me yours Jack.*
(Onslows)   **$2,975**

№657
WHITE STAR LINE.

R.M.S. "TITANIC."

This ticket entitles bearer to use of Turkish
or Electric Bath on one occasion.

Paid 4/- or 1 Dollar.

White Star Line RMS Titanic Turkish bath ticket No 657, 5cm. x 8cm., together with letter of provenance.
(Onslows) **$1,575**

S.S. Titanic, the cast brass nameplate from Lifeboat No. 12, 322mm. long x 39mm. wide.
(Onslows) **$9,129**

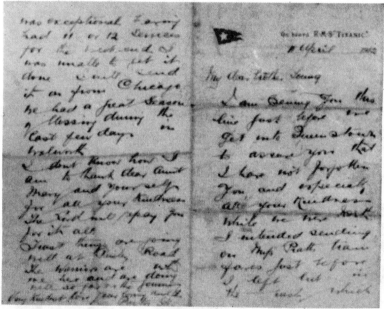

On board R.M.S. 'Titanic', an autographed letter on official writing paper signed by Pastor John Harper, 11th April 1912.

My Dear Brother Young, I am penning you this line just before we get into Queenstown to assure you that I have not forgotten you and especially all your kindness while we were North. I intended sending on Mrs Pratt's train fares just before I left but in the rush which was exceptional having had 11 or 12 services for the week-end I was unable to get it done. I will send it on from Chicago. We had a great season of blessing during the last few days in Walworth. I don't know how I am to thank dear Aunt Mary and yourself for all your kindness the Lord will repay you for it all. Trust things are going well at Paisley Road. The warriors are with me here and are doing well so far on the journey. Very kindest love your loving auld Pastor J.H.
(Onslows) **$6,200**

The name 'Toby' has long associations with conviviality and it was used by Shakespeare in his Toby Belch and by Laurence Sterne in his character Uncle Toby in 'Tristram Shandy'. Today it has come to signify a jug made like a seated male figure in a tricorn hat with a pipe or mug of beer on his knee. This is particularly due to the creations of Doulton who took up and developed the long history of the Toby jug and made it beloved by a vast collecting public.

From 1815 when John Doulton first set up his business, the firm made Toby jugs but the earliest examples were only brown salt glazed as they had been for centuries. In 1925 however, colored Toby jugs were added to the range by Harry Simeon and their potential was immediately recognized by Charles J. Noke who made their colors even more vivid and developed them into one of the company's best selling lines.

One of the distinguishing marks of the Toby jug is that one corner of his tricorn hat is always used as a pourer for the beverage he carries.

A Wilkinson Ltd., 'Winston Churchill' Toby jug, designed by Clarice Cliff, circa 1940, 12" high.
(Sothebys) **$1,971**

Charlie Chaplin Toby jug, produced 1918, 11" high.
(Abridge) **$6,000**

George Robey Toby jug, produced 1925, 10½" high.
(Abridge) **$5,600**

A fine Toleware covered cream pitcher, probably New England, mid 19th century, the hinged lid with yellow star and leaf border above sides decorated with a townscape over a yellow and black feathered inner border, 5¼" high.
(Christie's N. York) **$4,950**

A fine green Toleware coffee pot, New England, mid 19th century, decorated on obverse and reverse with large red, yellow and blue flowers with yellow leaves and surrounded on top and bottom with yellow leaf borders on a dark green ground, 11" high.
(Christie's N. York) **$3,960**

A black Toleware apple dish, probably Connecticut, mid 19th century, the brim with gilt rolled edge and red cherries and green leaves on a white ground above yellow feathered decoration on a black ground, 11⅞" diameter.
(Christie's N. York) **$880**

A 19th century Toleware bottle carrier, the two co-joined cylindrical canisters with a central carrying handle, the blue ground heightened in gilt with fruiting vine and painted with reserves of Italianate landscapes, 13" wide.
(Christie's) **$1,000**

TOLEWARE

A red and gilt tole coal-scuttle and cover, of sarcophagus shape with domed lid, scrolling decoration and a coat-of-arms, with lion-mask and ring handles on claw feet, detachable liner, re-decorated, 16" wide.
(Christie's)   **$3,465**

THOMAS TOMPION

The 'Sussex Tompion' is a highly important and rare grande sonnerie striking ebony bracket clock, dating from 1676–80. It was long thought to be one of a series of three by Tompion with two-train 'grande' sonnerie movements and square dials of similar layout, the other two being the Tulip and Castlemaine clocks. The Sussex clock was thought to be the earliest of the three. In the early 1980's however, a fourth clock was documented, in which the strike selection, pendulum regulation and locking are effected at the back of the movement through a falseplate, whereas in the other three these functions have all been brought forward to the dial. The Sussex clock is thus seen as one of the earliest examples of a repeating clock and a verge escapement with spring suspension and rise-and-fall regulation. It sold for $566,720 at Christie's.

Thomas Tompion (1639-1713) was born in Northill, Beds. and moved to London in 1671, where he became a brother of the Clockmakers' Company by redemption. In 1674 he met Dr Robert Hooke, who brought him to the attention of King Charles II, after which he received many royal commissions. In 1703 he was Master of the Clockmakers, and when he died he was buried in Westminster Abbey.

The previously undocumented boxwood Tompion night clock is the most significant Tompion discovery of the last 50 years. Dating from 1678–80, it is a product of Tompion's first great flush of achievement and is the finest piece of his yet known from that period. It is a highly complex and unique boxwood and ebony parquetry miniature longcase day and night clock of month duration, with ting-tang quarter hour strike, Roman notation hour strike, tic-tac escapement and a brief sounding 'alarm'. At 6ft 1" it is the smallest longcase clock yet known by Tompion, and no previous night clock by him is known.

The clock belonged by repute to one Sir James Douglas, a 'Scotch West Indian' of mixed parentage, who was a fur trader, a member of the Hudson Bay Company and subsequently Governor of Vancouver and then British Columbia. After his death in 1877 it passed down through his family until bought by a Canadian collector.

The case is of unusually heavy construction, and the rectangular movement is also unusually massive. The purpose of the 'alarm' sounding seven blows briefly on the fifth bell is unclear. Perhaps it served as a reminder in the morning to snuff out the night lights. The boxwood Tompion night clock sold for $1,416,800 at Christie's.

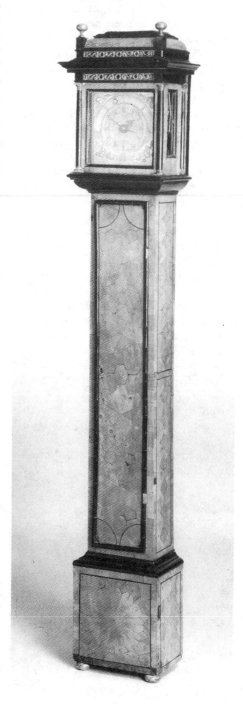

Old toys form a unique insight into a bygone age when there were no such things as television to keep children amused. Dolls from the 16th and 17th centuries, however, were intended as playthings not for children, but for society ladies, who dressed and undressed them, and carried them around with them in the same way as a little girl might do today, often in pairs, one with day wear and the other with night attire. They command very high prices when they come onto the market.

Similarly, the ingenious automatons of the 18th century were intended as an adult diversion, and it was not until the later 19th century that toymaking for children became a real industry. The toymakers of that time displayed wonderful genius with optical and mechanical devices such as zoetropes, kaleidoscopes, stereoscopes and so on, all of which had a legacy of adult appeal. Then, from Germany came a host of mechanical tinplate toys. And anyone wondering why Noah's Arks should have proved so popular has only to reflect that, in these God-fearing days, it was often the only plaything allowed to a child on a Sunday.

A rare early Donald Duck puppet made from plaster, the earliest known example in puppet form, made by Munzberg, Germany in 1937, 17cm. high.
(Auction Team Koeln)   **$3,200**

A Steiff fox, plush covered, button in ear, circa 1912.
(Woolley & Wallis)   **$717**

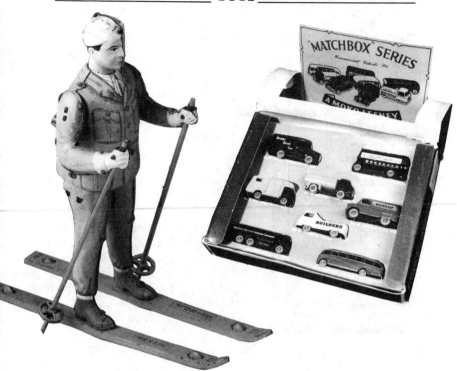

'Skirolf', a clockwork tinplate figure, by E.P. Lehmann, No. 781, the standing figure with skis and poles and dressed in blue stenciled suit and white hat, when operated the figure pushes himself along with the poles, 18.7cm. high.
(Lawrence Fine Art) **$2,150**

A Matchbox commercial vehicle set, in mint condition but box worn.
(G.E. Sworder) **$385**

English butcher's shop, mid 19th century, 26½" high.
(Christie's) **$8,344**

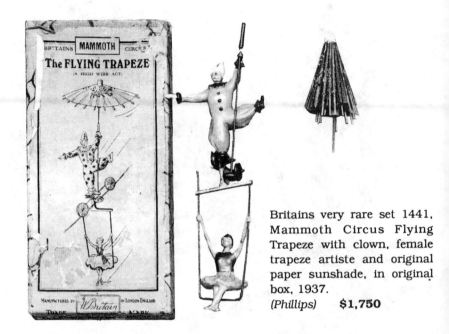

Britains very rare set 1441, Mammoth Circus Flying Trapeze with clown, female trapeze artiste and original paper sunshade, in original box, 1937.
(Phillips) **$1,750**

Anyone who has not lived alone in a tent at the North Pole for the last sixty-odd years must surely be familiar with that most beloved cartoon creation Mickey Mouse. Fewer, perhaps, are aware of how close he came to being called Mortimer. For this was the name that had been decided for him by his creator Walt Disney, and the story goes that it was Mrs Disney who called her husband back as he prepared to drive off to the studios on that fateful morning to ask "Why don't you call him Mickey?"

Since then Mickey and his near contemporary Donald Duck have adorned everything from money banks to teaspoons, from clocks to car mascots, and it is early images of them, in whatever form, which now attract the biggest sums.

A tin plate toy in the form of a Mickey Mouse organ grinder with Minnie dancing on top, circa 1930, 8" high.
(G.E. Sworder) **$2,310**

No 24 set of motor cars, comprising an ambulance, limousine, town sedan, vogue saloon, super streamlined saloon, sportsman's coupe, sports tourer 4 seater, sports tourer 2 seater, boxed.
(Phillips) **$8,850**

Hide covered rocking horse, attributed to Whitney Reed Corporation, Leominster, Massachusetts, 19th century, covered with dapple-brown hide, horsehair tail and mane, glass eyes, tooled leather saddle and tack, rockers painted green-gray with black flourishes and pinstriping, 43" high. *(Skinner Inc)* **$4,800**

One of the earliest patents for a cast iron mechanical novelty bank was taken out by J. Hall on 21 December 1869 for his Excelsior Bank. Most 19th century examples are in fact American, and made of tin. They sell for between $200 and $750 depending on rarity. Occasionally, however, a hitherto unknown example comes onto the market like this one featuring a girl skipping, which sold for $16,000.

French cookie tin, lithographed tin plate, circa 1920, 78.5cm. long.
(Christie's) **$5,020**

A painted wooden Noah's Ark, decorated with columns and a printed paper
frieze, with sliding side containing over two hundred animals and eight
figures, including moles, grasshoppers, rabbits, flies, monkeys, camels,
dogs, cats and anteaters, 27" wide, Sonneberg, 19th century.
(Christie's) **$11,550**

A painted wooden doll's house, of five bays and four stories, opening to reveal ten rooms with hall, staircase and landings, interior doors, bathroom fittings, four side windows and contemporary wall and floor papers,50" wide. *(Christie's)* **$17,380**

A painted wooden toy Butcher's Shop, with transfer decoration, marbleized slabs, two original tables, plaster joints, carcases, butcher and customers, 20" wide, stamped *C.H. Schutzmarke* on base for Christian Hacker, circa 1895. *(Christie's)* **$10,000**

Dinky pre-war 28d delivery van Oxo 1st type. *(Christie's)* **$2,695**

Britains rare miniature motor car no. 1399, two-seater coupe, brown and tan finish, white rubber tyres, in original box, 1936.
(Phillips) **$4,550**

Pre-war No 68 set camouflaged aeroplanes, comprising an Armstrong Whitworth Whitley bomber, Frobisher liner, 3 Hawker Hurricane fighters, 3 Vickers Supermarine Spitfire fighters, Armstrong Whitworth Ensign liner, 2 Bristol Blenheim bombers and a Fairey Battle bomber, boxed.
(Phillips) **$11,500**

Rare Dinky 920 Guy Warrior Heinz van, in original box.
(Christie's) **$5,390**

Many kinds of posters are collectible, but it is travel posters which seem to fetch the largest sums. Perhaps it is because they speak to us of far-away, exotic places, or call forth our nostalgia for a more gracious and leisurely age, now gone. What is interesting is that some of the leading artists of the day did not scorn to turn their talents to creating them. Take, for example, Laura Knight's design for the Yorkshire coast, which sold for $10,200, or A.R. Thomson's wonderful 'Take me by the Flying Scotsman' which must surely call to the long buried 'I want to be an engine driver' small boy in all of us and which will now fetch $8,500. These are fantastic sums for a piece of paper which was originally intended to grace the wall of a railway platform for a few months before being plastered over with a new design.

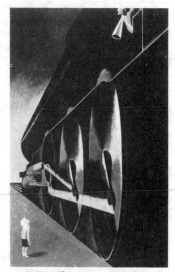

A.R. Thomson poster design 'Take me by the Flying Scotsman', signed, gouache, 27" x 17". *(Onslows)* **$8,500**

London and North Eastern Railway poster, 'You always dine well on the L.N.E.R., *(Onslows)* **$1,925**

'Cunard Line Europe-America' poster by Kenneth D. Shoesmith.
(Onslows)   **$4,704**

'East Coast by L.N.E.R.', by Tom Purvis, printed by Baynard Press, quad royal, 40" x 50".
(Onslows)   **$8,750**

Lacquerware tea tray, Japan, early 19th century, the oval tray inlaid with mother-of-pearl stringing and floral sprigs centering oval reserve with gilt American spreadwing eagle with shield at breast grasping arrows and foliage with talons and a bannerole in its beak inscribed *E. Pluribus Unum*, the gallery pierced with hand holes, 42" wide.*(Skinner Inc)* **$24,000**

A rectangular lacquer tray with concave border and indented corners decorated in ivory and lacquer high relief with the eight chief rakan in a bamboo grove, around a crystal tama on a lotus base standing on an ivory table, the border with panels containing aoimon, kikumon, dragons, scrolling tendrils and other designs, signed *Harui*, late 19th century, 73.6cm. x 54.9cm. *(Christie's)* **$42,350**

A good early 18th century lignum vitae Wassail bowl and cover, the multiple turned body on short stem and circular foot, the domed lid surmounted by a melon fluted knop, 38cm. high.
(Phillips) **$10,710**

A fine Lignum wassail, the base with three brass taps and molded circular plinth, 18th century, 20" high.
(Christie's) **$2,656**

One of a pair of Regency brass-bound mahogany coasters with brass liners, 5" high.
(Christie's) **$2,300**

It was as far back as 1714 that an Englishman, Henry Mill, first took out a patent for 'An Artificial Machine or Method for the Impression or Transcribing of Letters Singly or Progressively one after another, as in writing, whereby all Writing whatever may be Engrossed in Paper or Parchment so Neat and Exact as not to be distinguished from Print'. His design never went into production however, and it was not until nearly 130 years later, in 1843, that the American Charles Thurber in turn patented his idea of a mechanical typewriter. From then on the concept really caught the imagination of inventors and there were numerous attempts to produce readable copy. None were successful however until, in 1867, the first practical typewriter was invented by three Americans, Sholes, Glidden and Soule. Their machine worked on a shift key mechanism, which forms the basis of modern machines today.

There are plenty of early typewriters still to be found, mainly because of the enormous output of early manufacturers to cope with the immediate demand. In the 1870's alone, the companies of Remington, Oliver, Smith, Underwood and Yost sold over 50,000 models.

They are often fascinating in their eccentric design. The Lambert 2908 had a circular dial, like that of a telephone, in the center, and a Hammond model had piano type keys.

German machines by companies such as Edelmann are rarer as is the Gühl and Harbeck Kosmopolit typewriter with gilt and black finish and in a walnut case, for despite having a cracked fiber type-sector, an example was sold by Christie's for $16,830. Even more amazing was the price paid for the very rare American Morris machine dating from 1885, of which only four are known to exist. When one of these came up for sale at Auction Team Koeln in Cologne, it fetched a staggering DM37,950 ($22,950).

A rare 'The Pocket Typewriter, Swan Arcade, Bradford', with name and characters on circular white enamel dial, 10cm. long, circa 1887. *(Phillips)* **$1,936**

'Sampo', 1894, Sweden's first typewriter, only six known worldwide, a scarce and highly desired collectors' item. *(Auction Team Koeln)* **$12,200**

A Kosmopolit typewriter by Guhl & Harbeck, with fiber type-sector, gilt and black finish and walnut case. *(Christie's S. Ken)* **$16,632**

By Nathaniel Mills, a good large Victorian vinaigrette, the rectangular cover raised in relief with a view of Westminster Abbey from the back, the base engine-turned, Birmingham, 1845.

(Phillips) **$3,200**

A pear-shaped silver-gilt-mounted agate vinaigrette, comprised of twenty-five panels of vari- colored hardstone, the silver-gilt mount engraved with scrolls and foliage and with ball finial, probably Scottish, 19th century, 3" high.

(Christie's) **$4,276**

A very rare early Victorian silver-gilt cat vinaigrette, the oblong body engraved with peacocks and foliate scrolls, the cover applied with a cat, curled up and set with a 'blister pearl', by James Beebe, 1837.

(Phillips) **$4,550**

A mahogany octagonal waste-paper basket with sides pierced with Chinese fretwork and handles, on bracket feet, 13³/4" high.
(Christie's) **$1,972**

One of a pair of Edwardian satinwood wastepaper baskets painted with ribbons and roses, each with brass liner and caned tapering body on molded foot, 14" diameter.
(Christie's) **$3,896**

Gustav Stickley slat-sided wastebasket, circa 1905, no. 94, signed, 14" high.
(Skinner Inc) **$2,500**

It was the First World War that saw the development of the wristwatch, the concept being eminently suitable for fighting men in uniform.

Probably the most sought after watch is the Rolex Oyster, first produced in 1927 and worn as a sign of affluence ever since. The Oyster was the first weather and climate proof watch and is renowned for its workmanship and reliability. Curiously, a lady's Rolex Oyster will sell for only half as much as a man's, and ladies' watches are generally priced lower right across the board.

Women's watches however became, in the 30s and 40s, an art form in their own right and were produced studded with diamonds and other precious stones. In particular Art Deco examples by good makers such as Patek Philippe can be very valuable.

It was in fact a man's watch by Patek Philippe which made a British record price recently when sold at Sotheby's. This was the Patek Philippe no. 198103 platinum moonphase calendar wristwatch dating from 1935 with fully damascened nickel movement (ebauche by Victorin Piguet). The official description lists it as having compensation balance, blued steel spiral spring and regulator, silvered dial with baton numerals surrounded by outer calendar ring, aperture for the moon phases beneath 12, subsidiary seconds hand at 6 and apertures in the center for the day and the month, in a platinum Calatrava case.

Interestingly, however, Patek Philippe's records show that the watch was not always so popular. Originally in a tonneau case, it remained unsold at their Paris branch, was recased in platinum at the request of the eventual purchaser and sold on 4 December 1935 for Sfr 1135.

The simple moonphase calendar wristwatch was produced by Patek Philippe in a limited quantity, and records show that they were manufactured in gold and platinum. To date, it would appear that there are only three platinum models in existence.

It was bought with a telephone bid from a far eastern bidder for $523,600, and the owner was recorded as being 'amazed', having thought it was only worth a few thousand!

An unusual plated open-face keyless pocket watch advertising Guiness Beer, the white dial with Arabic numerals, subsidiary seconds with automaton toucan, the Guiness motif pictured to the center, 50mm. diameter.
(Christie's) **$500**

A nephrite silver, gold, coral and enamel watch-set paperknife, the 9" nephrite blade headed by bowed rectangular silver handle with gadroon coral mounts and winder and champlevé enamel decoration, the conforming rectangular Deco dial signed *Cartier France*, 13" long.
(Christie's) **$14,602**

A fine gold hunter-cased grande sonnerie clockwatch with split second chronograph and perpetual calendar, Swiss, retailed by Sir John Bennett, Ltd., London. The keyless gilt three quarter plate lever movement with going and striking trains wound alternately by crown, release lever for striking on band, with selection switches for strike/silent, grande/petite sonnerie under bezel, chronograph train under dial, activated by button on band, white enamel dial with roman chapters, within a heavy 18K gold case, 60mm. diameter.
(Christie's N. York) **$66,000**

A rare early 17th century finely engraved silver pendant watch in the form of a cross, the case decorated all over with scenes depicting the life of Christ, the front showing the angel foretelling the birth of Christ, the silver dial plate showing the resurrection, now with later enamel dial, the shaped movement with eight amphora shaped pillars, signed *Benoit Giraud A Paris*, 64mm. x 42mm.
(Phillips)   **$13,520**

A gold and enamel minute-repeating hunting cased watch with concealed erotic automaton, circa 1890, diameter 2¹/₈".
(Sotheby's)   **$17,600**

An extremely rare American locomotive and tender copper weathervane, circa 1882, the locomotive reproduced in fine detail is mounted on track with two ball finials at tracks end, and attached ball counterweight, in fine original condition with verdigris surface, 17" high, 61" long, 8" deep. *(Skinner Inc)* **$185,000**

A fine and rare molded and gilt copper weathervane, American, 19th century, modeled in the form of a centaur with bow and arrow, retaining traces of original gilding, 32" high, 40" long. *(Christie's N. York)* **$71,500**

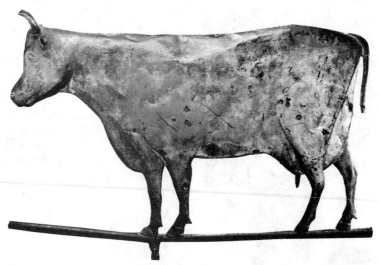

A large molded and gilt copper cow weathervane, American, late 19th century. The standing cow with horns rising above copper ears and large molded eyes, the tail cylindrical, retaining traces of original gilding, 22½" high x 36" long.
(Christie's)   **$3,850**

Rare fire hose wagon weathervane by L.W. Cushing & Co., Waltham, Massachusetts, last quarter 19th century. The full-bodied figure of a copper horse pulling a copper and iron hose wagon having painted spring box and star ornaments on hose reel, driven by a full-bodied polychrome copper and zinc figure of fireman. 25" high, 53" long.
(Skinner Inc)   **$55,000**

A rare carved and painted pine weathervane in the form of a spotted hen, New England, 1850-1860. Realistically carved, the standing figure of a hen constructed in five sections, the surface painted with a gray-blue ground with black spots, standing on a metal arrow base, 16½" high, 22¼" long.
(Christie's) **$24,200**

A cast molded and gilt pig weathervane, American, 19th century, the standing pig with applied ears and cast zinc curlique tail on a base (two bullet holes, traces of original gilding), 16" high, 26" long.
(Christie's) **$8,800**

An extremely rare and important molded copper and zinc horse-and-rider weathervane, J. Howard and Company, West Bridgewater, Massachusetts, circa 1860.

The elegant full-bodied rearing horse with molded cast zinc forequarters embellished with incised eyes and nostrils, and the forelock of cut and twisted copper, the shaped sheet copper ears above crinkle-cut and molded mane over molded body with crinkle-molded tail above molded copper prancing forelegs and bent rear legs; the mounted rider seated upright in top hat with flat brim wearing a long coat with rows of repoussé buttons holding a tapering crop upright in one hand, the rider's legs in twisted copper stirrups with star spurs holding twisted copper reins, the left hindquarter stamped Made by J. Howard & Co., W. Bridgewater, Mass., 76¹/₂" high, 36¹/₂" wide.

In 1860 a large red barn was built on Blackie Farm in Chelmsford, Massachusetts. In addition to cows and chickens, the Blackies raised teams of prize-winning horses and so it seemed appropriate to select a horse-and-rider weathervane for the cupola on the barn.

Jonathan Howard was one of 19th century America's leading commercial weathervane manufacturers. His company flourished between 1850-1868, when it was purchased by Horatio L. Washburn.

(Christie's) **$104,500**

Webb cameo glass animal portrait vase in rare topaz colour layered with white opal glass, cameo cut and carved, with finely detailed landscape scene of two alert deer, a doe and a buck with pine bough border, signed *G Woodall* below the scene and *Thomas Webb & Sons* banner mark on base, 8" high.
(Skinner Inc)   **$19,000**

Webb cameo Paris Exhibition vase, executed by George Woodall and the Woodall Team, with flared elongated neck above platformed rounded oval of brilliant turquoise blue glass, overlaid in white and then lustrous red, cameo carved by hand over the entire surface with scrolling interconnecting foliate devices centering conventionalized floral medallions at front and back, tripartite borders in minutest detail above and below, marked on base *Thomas Webb & Sons Gem Cameo Paris Exhibition 1889 Tiffany & Co.*, 19¹/₂" high.
(Skinner Inc)   **$42,000**

Webb Gem cameo tri-color plaque, the topaz-brown dished plate overlaid with white and yellow, meticulously cameo cut and carved with repeating stylized floral and geometric elements and border designs, around a central carved medallion, marked *Thomas Webb & Sons / Gem Cameo*, 9¼" diameter.
(Skinner Inc) **$19,000**

Webb Gem cameo vase by George Woodall, with raised cuffed rim on pedestaled ovoid body of topaz-brown layered in white, cameo cut and hand carved with a realistic desert scene of two giraffes by palm trees, signed at lower right *G Woodall* and marked *Thomas Webb & Sons / Gem Cameo*, 7" high.
(Skinner Inc) **$22,500**

Webb cameo tri-color plaque, the brilliant turquoise blue dished plate layered with white and red, intricately cameo cut and hand carved in mirror repeating floral and scrolling designs surrounding stylized peacocks with tassel, scallop and linear border, marked *Thomas Webb & Sons Gem Cameo*, 9¼" diameter.
(Skinner Inc) **$18,000**

Robert Heron bought the Gallatown Pottery in Kirkcaldy, Fife in 1883. He renamed it after the nearby Wemyss Castle, home of the Grosvenor family, who did much to popularize his products with their upper class friends in London. Initially it was very much a family affair. Heron's sister was a talented amateur artist, painting wildlife and flowers, and she had a considerable influence on the factory's style of decoration, as did her friend Lady Grosvenor.

The most important factor in the factory's early success was undoubtedly the engagement of a young Bohemian, Karel Nekola, as Art Director. It was Nekola who was responsible for the distinctive Wemyss decorative style, and he taught local decorators and his own two sons to paint the factory's wares with such designs as pink cabbage roses with dark green foliage.

None of the factory's output was signed, but it is possible to identify different artists by their style. The factory made everything from buttons to garden seats, but it is perhaps for its highly characteristic pigs and cats that it is best remembered.

Thomas Goode & Co., the Mayfair china shop, became the sole outlet for Wemyss ware in London, and also sent up special orders for individual customers.

Nekola retired from the factory because of ill-health in 1910, and he worked from home until his death in 1915. In 1916 Edwin Sandland took over as Art Director. He continued such popular lines as character jugs and pieces painted with mottoes, and also introduced new decorative styles, such as chrysanthemums painted on a black ground.

Meanwhile, Wemyss was declining in popularity. In an effort to stem the tide, Sandlands starting importing porcelain tea services from Stoke for his artists to decorate with roses. To no avail. Goode cancelled their order, and Sandland died in 1928. Just two years later, the factory closed.

There is, however, a short codicil to the tale. The Wemyss molds were bought by the Bovey Pottery in Devon, which employed Nekola's youngest son Joseph, and they continued for some time to decorate pieces in the Wemyss style. In the late 1930's a Czech called Jan Plichta took over as sole proprietor until the factory went out of business in the early 40's.

Wemyss is certainly back in fashion today, it achieved a new record at Christie's Glasgow, when a black and white striped Wemyss cat sold for $14,960.

A large and early Wemyss model of a pig, decorated with shamrocks, 44cm. long.
(Phillips) **$5,900**

A Wemyss pottery toilet set with rose pattern and green border decoration comprising bowl, ewer, toilet bucket and cover with cane handle, and a matching soap dish and cover, impressed and painted mark.
(Andrew Hartley) **$6,300**

A Wemyss pig, the seated pig decorated overall with pink roses, 17" long, marked *Wemyss Made in England.*
(Michael Newman) **$5,075**

A most remarkable Whieldon teapot in the form of a bear, its head forming the cover, 15cm., circa 1750.
(Phillips)   **$82,500**

A Whieldon tortoise-shell coffee pot and cover of baluster shape with domed cover, circa 1760.
(Phillips)   **$8,010**

1789 A.C. Meukow & Cic, Grande
Champagne Cognac.
(Christie's) **$15,384**

1811 Château d'Yquem.
(Christie's) **$30,525**

Half-bottle 1784 Château Margau.
(Christie's) **$31,680**

A 'Façon de Venise' silver-mounted gambling glass ('drinkuit'), the bowl engraved in diamond-point with the inscription *Ick bringt u mijn lief* (I offer you my love), within borders of waved line and dot ornament above a band of lattimo threads, the silver mount surmounted by a pierced globe enclosing a dice and applied with a diagonal band inscribed *Bybe cum gavdio vinvm tvvm Eclesiastes IX cap.* (Drink thy wine with a merry heart, Ecclesiastes 9, 7), the glass Antwerp, last quarter of the 16th century, the mount 17th century, 17cm. high.

The earliest diamond-engraved example of a footless glass, but with a round funnel bowl, dates from 1570 (Museum Kunsthandwerk, Frankfurt/M) and is decorated with a bird, floral arabesques and an inscription in thin-stroke Roman capitals without hatching. An identical glass, but surmounted by a silver mill, is engraved by the same hand with arabesques and a text in similar letters. A third glass of the same type (damaged), excavated in 's-Hertogenbosch in 1978, is engraved with warriors, trees and some text in small Roman characters.

The earliest example of the type of bold hatched Roman lettering, as found on the present gambling-glass, dates from 1577 and was in use, especially on the so-called Verzelini vessels, until the early years of the 17th century.

(Christie's)   **$122,500**

A plychrome enameled armorial opaque-twist wine-glass attributed to William Beilby, the funnel bowl enameled in yellow heightened in iron-red, black and white and gilt with a coat-of-arms and with trailing foliage, the reverse with a branch of fruiting-vine pendant from the rim, on a double-series stem and conical foot, circa 1765, 15.5cm. high.
(Christie's) $18,045

A stipple engraved goblet on a 19th century replacement parcel gilt lower section, by Frans Greenwood, circa 1744, 24.3cm. high overall.
(Christie's) $43,416

A two- color opaque-twist wine glass, the cobalt-blue ogee bowl supported on a clear stem with swelling waist knop filled with spiral threads, terminating on a cobalt-blue conical foot, circa 1765, 16.5cm. high. Although wine-glasses of this type combining green and clear glass are known, this glass would appear to be the only recorded example in blue.
(Christie's) $24,310

A cylinder-knopped baluster goblet, the flared funnel bowl with a solid lower part enclosing a tear, supported on a cushion knop above a collar and cylinder section enclosing a large tear terminating in a double-basal knop, on a folded conical foot, circa 1715, 17cm. high.
(Christie's) **$7,106**

The 'Breadalbane II' amen glass, of drawn-trumpet shape, the stem enclosing an elongated tear and supported on a conical foot, the bowl engraved in diamond-point with a crown above the Royal cipher of King James VIII, the letters *JR* direct and reverse and with the figure *8* worked into the monogram at the base, below the word *AMEN*, flanked by two verses of the Jacobite anthem, 1745-50, 17cm. high.
(Christie's) **$50,592**

A Hall-in-Tyrol 'Facon de Venise' large goblet, the flared funnel bowl lightly molded with an allover 'beech-nut' pattern, supported on a hollow compressed knop molded with vertical ribs and with traces of gilt enrichment, the high conical foot with folded rim, perhaps workshop of Sebastian Höchstelter, 16th century.
(Christie's) **$31,845**

Royal Worcester lobed jar and cover with long horned cattle in highland setting signed *John Stinton*, date code for 1912, 7.5" high.
(Phillips Manchester) **$3,500**

A 'Worcester yellow-ground armorial baluster mug with grooved loop handle, the impaled arms within a lozenge flanked by puce scrolls and loose colored bouquets and scattered flowers and a moth, beneath an iron-red scrolling foliage border reserved with gilt flowerheads, circa 1770, 12cm. high.
(Christie's) **$13,282**

A highly important and unrecorded Worcester wine cistern probably modeled after a silver original, the lobed oval vessel with flared rim and raised on spreading foot, heavily embossed with rococo scroll cartouches surrounded with modeled flowers, shell and gadroon bands and large stiff leaves, the handles formed as Bacchic half-figures, one male, one female, 62cm. overall width, circa 1754-56. Vessels of related shape occur in English silver from the 1740s, and figurehead handles such as these occur on a number of silver vessels.
(Phillips) **$51,000**

A Worcester plate from the Duke of Gloucester service, the center luxuriantly painted with a pear, a peach, strawberries and redcurrants, a ladybird and a moth, the border with five colored moths within blue and gilt scroll cartouches, gold crescent mark, circa 1775, 22.5cm. diameter. Seventy pieces from this service from the collection of H.R.H., the Duke of Cambridge were sold in June 1904.
(Christie's) **$23,595**

A late Victorian Royal Worcester porcelain vase and cover painted by C.H.C. Baldwyn.
(Spencers) **$7,875**

A Worcester yellow-ground shaped oval honeycomb-molded dish, the center painted with three butterflies and a ladybird, the border molded in low relief with arched panels painted with trailing flowers reserved on a yellow honeycomb-molded ground, circa 1765, 30cm. wide.
(Christie's) **$18,287**

A fine Royal Worcester porcelain jardinere painted by Harry Stinton. *(Spencers)* **$6,475**

Pair of Worcester vases and covers signed and painted by *Harry Stinton*, date mark for 1911, marked in puce, 11.5" high.
(Phillips Manchester) **$6,125**